Upgrading to Windows™ 3.1

QUE DEVELOPMENT GROUP

que

Upgrading to Windows 3.1

Library of Congress Catalog: 92-70877

ISBN: 0-88022-965-9

95 94 93 92 4 3

Interpretation of the printing code: the rightmost double-digit number is the year of the book's printing; the rightmost single-digit number, the number of the book's printing. For example, a printing code of 92-1 shows that the first printing of the book occurred in 1992.

Screen reproductions in this book were created with Collage Plus from Inner Media, Inc., Hollis, NH.

Upgrading to Windows 3.1 is based on Windows Version 3.1.

Publisher: Lloyd J. Short

Acquisitions Manager: Rick Ranucci

Product Development Manager: Thomas H. Bennett

Managing Editor: Paul Boger

Book Designer: Scott Cook

Production Team: Claudia Bell, Keith Davenport, Denny Hager, Audra Hershman, Betty Kish, Bob LaRoche, Laurie Lee, Caroline Roop, John Sleeva, Kevin Spear, Allan Wimmer, Phil Worthington, Christine Young

CREDITS

Product Director
Timothy S. Stanley

Production Editor
Cindy Morrow

Editor
Jeannine Freudenberger

Technical Editor
Anthony Rairden

Acquisitions Editors
Chris Katsaropoulos
Tim Ryan

Composed in *Cheltenham* and *MCPdigital*
by Que Corporation

TRADEMARK ACKNOWLEDGMENTS

Que Corporation has made every effort to supply trademark information about company names, products, and services mentioned in this book. Trademarks indicated below were derived from various sources. Que Corporation cannot attest to the accuracy of this information.

Adobe Type Manager is a trademark of Adobe Systems, Inc.

AT&T is a registered trademark of AT&T.

Cardfile is a trademark of Digital Research, Inc.

CompuServe is a registered trademark of H&R Block, Inc.

Facelift for Windows is a trademark of Bitstream, Inc.

Fastback is a registered trademark of Fifth Generation Software.

Hewlett-Packard is a registered trademark of Hewlett-Packard Company.

Microsoft, Microsoft Excel, Microsoft Word for Windows, MS-DOS, and Windows are registered trademarks of Microsoft Corporation.

SideKick is a registered trademark of Borland International, Inc.

Tandy is a registered trademark of Radio Shack.

Trademarks of other products in this book are held by the companies producing them.

CONTENTS AT A GLANCE

TABLE OF CONTENTS

1

CHAPTER

An Overview of Windows 3.1

Upgrading to Windows 3.1 will be pure pleasure for any Windows user who loves the Windows icon- and menu-based graphical user interface (GUI), but loses patience when the hourglass mouse pointer monopolizes the screen. (The hourglass appears when you must wait for Windows to complete an operation behind the scenes.) Windows 3.1 is so much faster than previous versions of Windows that the once-common hourglass is now scarce. In fact, you might be startled the first few times a previously slow-loading Windows program slams on-screen immediately after you double-click its icon or darts off-screen when you click Exit.

The first change you will probably notice in Windows 3.1 is Program Manager's multiline icon titles, which are just one of many ways in which the Windows graphical user interface (GUI) has been enhanced. File Manager has been redesigned from the ground up to be much faster and more useful. Figure 1.1 shows File Manager's new default startup screen, which positions a directory tree alongside a file list in the current subdirectory. In addition, TrueType scalable fonts provide high-quality WYSIWYG (What-You-See-Is-What-You-Get) documents in most Windows programs.

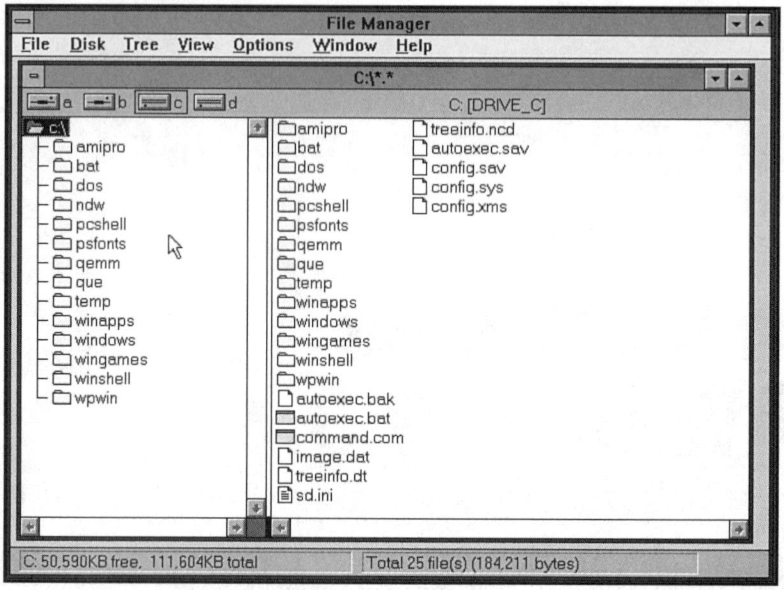

Fig. 1.1.

File Manager's new default startup screen.

This chapter provides a brief overview of the new capabilities of Windows 3.1. It also introduces many of these capabilities so that you can use them immediately. This chapter mentions the following:

- Major speed improvements in Windows 3.1
- Program Manager enhancements, including icon changes and the new StartUp Group, which automatically launches your choice of programs each time you boot Windows
- Additional changes in the Windows GUI, including redesigned dialog boxes that are easy to use and similar in appearance
- The new File Manager's performance and speed improvements, including expanded "drag and drop" file copying, moving, and printing
- TrueType fonts, which produce high-quality WYSIWYG documents in Windows programs
- Full use of the mouse in windowed DOS applications
- Faster job handling, which enables you to use your computer quickly while printing continues in the background
- An on-line tutorial for new Windows users
- Better context-sensitive help, particularly in dialog boxes

- Improved multitasking of DOS programs
- Improvements in SMARTDrive, the Windows disk cache
- A built-in screen saver to protect your monitor from screen burn-in and to password-protect your work from prying eyes
- Object Linking and Embedding (OLE), a powerful means of hot-linking data between Windows programs so that linked data changed in one document is also changed in linked documents
- Object Packaging, another new way to use hot-linked data
- New utilities and drivers that provide support for multimedia, enabling Windows to interface with CD-ROM drives and sound boards, as well as provide compatibility with other innovative hardware and software
- Improvements in serial port handling, which is important if you use a modem, a serial printer or plotter, a mouse, scanners, or other devices that use the serial ports
- Automatic reconnection with printers and network drives

CAUTION: Windows 3.1 offers two operating modes: Standard and 386 Enhanced. If you used Real mode to run pre-Windows 3.0 applications under Windows 3.0, you need to upgrade these programs. Otherwise, you risk data loss and other problems.

Windows 3.1's Speedier Performance

Windows 3.1 is much faster than its predecessor. Programs now load and terminate more quickly, although the speed improvements are not limited to these tasks. Saving documents is nearly instantaneous in most Windows programs—even with lengthy data files. Windows' new method of updating graphical elements and on-screen data means that scrolling documents is as smooth and quick in Windows programs as in your favorite DOS applications. The new Print Manager handles print jobs so much faster that you can use the computer almost immediately after sending a file to the printer. Printing continues in the background while you work.

One important reason for the increased speed of Windows 3.1 is the redesigned SMARTDrive, a disk cache that markedly improves Windows speed. SMARTDrive uses the following two strategies to make Windows 3.1 speedier:

- Like the version of SMARTDrive included with Windows 3.0, the new SMARTDrive reads information from disk—before an active program actually needs it—and holds it in your system's RAM. When a program tries to access the information from your hard drive, SMARTDrive instead supplies the information from RAM, which is much faster memory.
- The new SMARTDrive increases performance even more by caching writes, which means that SMARTDrive temporarily holds in memory data to be written to the hard drive. SMARTDrive then writes this data to the drive when system resources are less in demand.

Although SMARTDrive is responsible for much of Windows 3.1's increased speed, it does not account for all of it. Even when SMARTDrive is not loaded, Windows 3.1 is faster than previous versions of Windows. This increased speed is an important consideration for those who, because of compatibility problems, limited memory, or other reasons, were not able to use SMARTDrive with Windows 3.0 and might not be able to use it with Windows 3.1.

Increased Power in Program Manager

Many of the more noticeable changes in Windows 3.1 are modifications to the graphical user interface. Nearly every element of Windows 3.1 includes new touches and features that make the application simpler, more efficient, and more powerful. Because Program Manager's main role is acting as the Windows command center, changes made in Program Manager will affect most Window's 3.1 users.

This section covers the following enhancements to Program Manager:

- The new StartUp Group, which enables you to launch programs automatically each time you boot Windows
- New methods for handling icons
- Techniques for modifying the look of Windows 3.1, including changing the typeface and type size of icon titles, using new color

schemes and extra icons, inserting bit-mapped graphics files as a "wallpaper" background, and switching from VGA to Super VGA or from 16 colors to 256 colors

- Other important changes to Program Manager

Understanding the New StartUp Group

The StartUp Group is another of Windows 3.1's powerful new features. If you place the icon of a program into StartUp Group, that program loads automatically each time you boot Windows. The only limitation to the number of programs you can add to the StartUp Group is the resources available on your system. Figure 1.2 shows File Manager added to the StartUp Group, along with the Windows Clock utility.

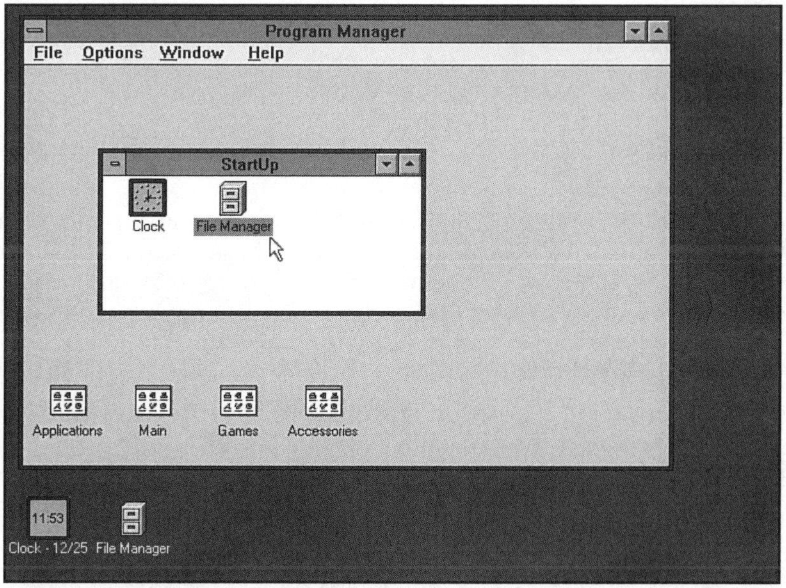

Fig. 1.2.

Clock and File Manager icons in the StartUp Group.

Changes to the Icons

When you open the Windows 3.1 Program Manger, you might immediately notice that the title for each icon can now be two or more lines long. This change makes describing the contents or purpose of each file easier. Figure 1.3 shows a set of 12 spreadsheet files installed as icons in a Program Group. The group's multiline icon titles provide details about the spreadsheet files.

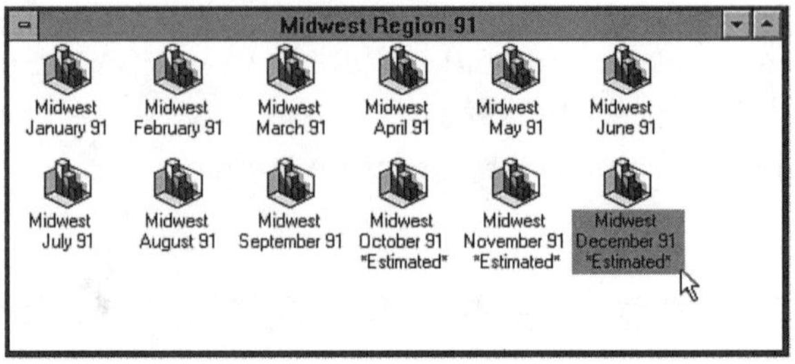

Fig. 1.3.

Multiline icon titles detail file contents.

The appearance of icons is also different in the Windows 3.1 Program Manager. The icon that appears when you minimize a DOS application also appears in its program group; you no longer see the dreary, gray DOS icon that you saw when you minimized a DOS program in Windows 3.0.

You now can change the typeface and font size of the icon title lines by editing the WIN.INI file.

Should you want to change the icons themselves, Windows 3.1 includes nearly 150 extra icons that you can use. Two Windows files, PROGMAN.EXE and MORICONS.DLL, contain the bulk of these extra icons.

Windows 3.1 makes changing to an icon in a program group much easier. You can scroll a list of available files to find a file that contains an icon, and then preview the icon before installing it into a program group. Figure 1.4 shows the preview window from the Change Icon dialog box. This window displays some of the more than 40 icons embedded in the Program Manager executable file, PROGMAN.EXE.

Finally, you can save the position of icons within program groups, as well as the size and position of each Program Group window, each time you exit Windows.

Drag and Drop File Copying and Moving

File Manager's redesign makes drag and drop file copying, or moving, a useful part of Windows 3.1 Using drag and drop to copy a file is much faster and simpler than trying to remember and correctly type the proper DOS syntax for copying the file. The performance improvement is even more dramatic when moving a file. DOS contains no single command for moving a file; in DOS you must first copy the file, and then delete the source file. Using drag and drop, the same operation requires a simple mouse movement.

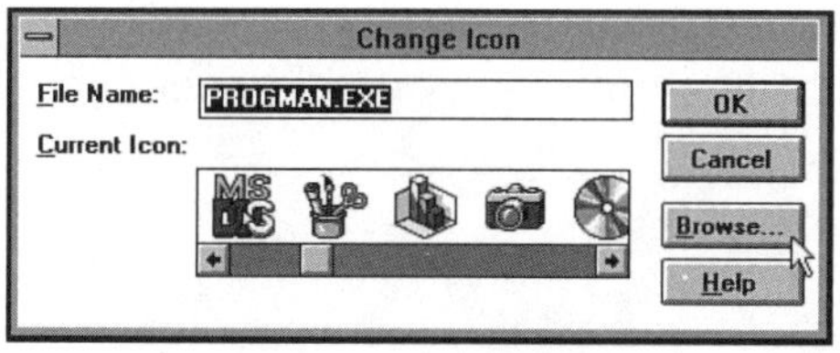

Fig. 1.4.

The Change Icon dialog box displays icons embedded in PROGMAN.EXE.

Figure 1.5 illustrates what you see on-screen when using drag and drop. Notice the mouse pointer on top of the document icon in the file list window for the D drive. That icon indicates that a drag and drop operation is underway.

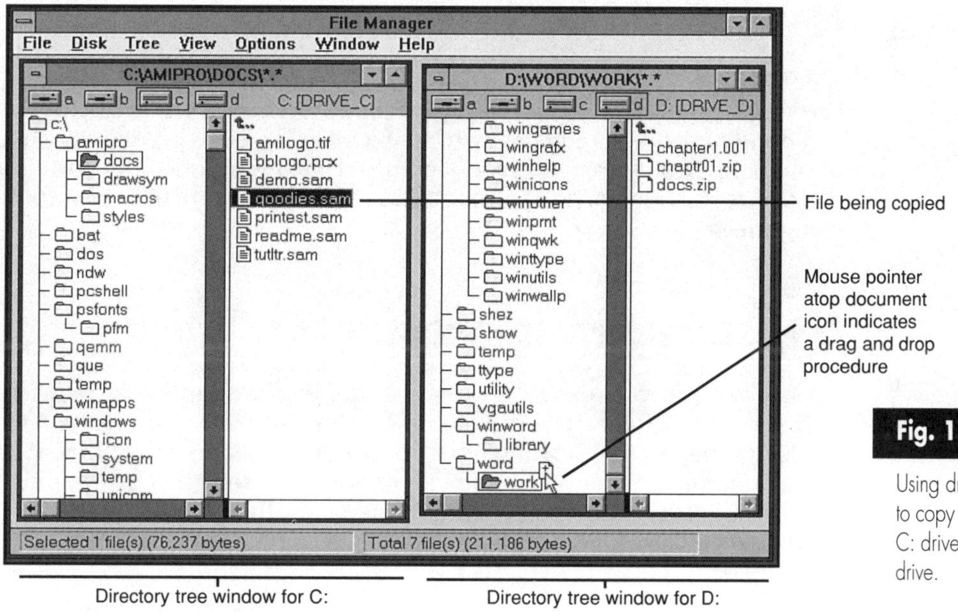

Fig. 1.5.

Using drag and drop to copy a file from the C: drive to the D: drive.

More Color Schemes

Windows 3.1 offers numerous additional color schemes that enable you to customize the Windows desktop. Available color schemes include color configurations for the LCD screens on laptop computers, as well as several desktop computers. These schemes include Tweed, a business-like color combination, and Valentine, a hot pink color scheme. You can choose one of the new default color schemes, or use one of the basic schemes as a starting place to create your own set of Windows colors. You can change Windows colors in Control Panel. For more information, see Chapter 3.

More Wallpaper Files

Windows 3.1 also includes many new wallpaper files. You can use these bit-mapped graphics files to decorate your Windows desktop, the normally blank screen behind Program Manager.

New Screen Saver

Windows 3.1 includes a screen saver to protect your monitor from screen burn-in and to password-protect your work from prying eyes. You can configure the screen saver to blank your screen, or you can use one of the animated graphic screens included with Windows 3.1. You then must enter a password to unblank the screen. For information about using the screen saver, see Chapter 3.

Mouse Improvements for LCD Video

Windows 3.1 also offers a new feature that enables laptop users with LCD screens to follow the mouse on-screen. Mouse Trails shows a trail of mouse pointers to indicate where your mouse has been and how it has traveled across the screen. You can enable Mouse Trails by opening the Windows Control Panel, choosing Mouse, and then choosing the Mouse Trails check box.

Switching Video Modes Within Windows

You might have a Super VGA monitor but occasionally run Windows in VGA mode, or you might sometimes switch from 256-color mode to 16-color mode. Windows 3.1 now enables you to make these changes from within Windows, rather than having to exit Windows and run the Setup program from DOS. To get to this dialog box, choose Windows Setup from Program Manager's Main group, and then choose Change System Settings from the Options menu. Figure 1.6 shows the Change System Settings dialog box.

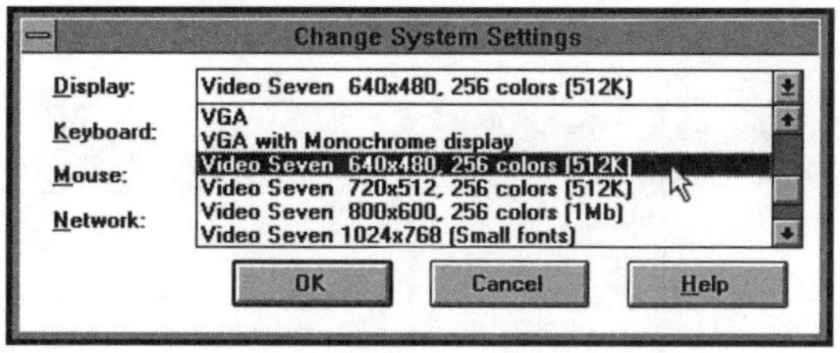

Fig. 1.6.

The Change System Settings dialog box.

Launching a Program as an Icon

You now can launch a program so that it is minimized as an icon, rather than displayed in a window or full screen. To do so, you must enable Program Manager's new Run Minimized option.

File Manager Works Harder

Windows 3.1's File Manager has been completely redesigned. It now should instantly win over many who continued to use Norton Commander or PC Tools Shell to manage files under Windows 3.0.

File Manager's primary window is now split into a graphical directory tree on the left and a display of files in the current directory on the right. (This configuration is the feature that made many Windows users stay with their favorite DOS shells after switching to Windows.) This design enables you to browse your system's subdirectories and files easily, without opening separate windows for each subdirectory.

Drives, network paths, and directory tree windows are more clearly labeled in the new File Manager. The status line displays more information about available disk space. Enhanced network support makes connecting to and disconnecting from network drives easier.

The new File Manager also lets you open directory tree windows on more than one drive at a time. This feature makes drag and drop useful for those who need to copy files from a hard disk to a floppy disk, or from a local drive to a network drive. Figure 1.7 shows File Manager with directory tree windows displaying drives C and D.

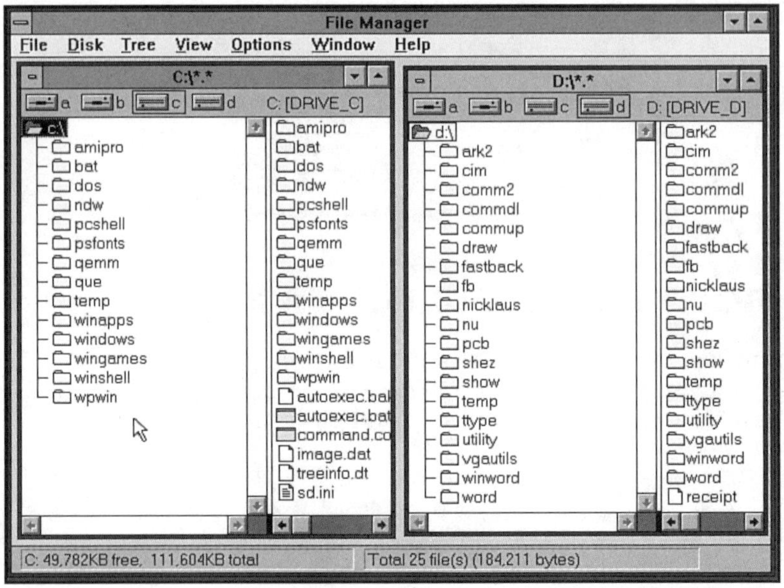

Fig. 1.7.

File Manager can open directory trees on more than one drive.

TIP The font and type size used to display most File Manager elements can be changed from File Manager's Options menu. For more information, see Chapter 5.

Understanding the File Manager Screen

File Manager's default screen is split into two parts: the directory list, with file folder icons that represent subdirectories of the root drive, and the file list window. In the directory list, the current subdirectory is represented by an open file folder, and the subdirectory name is highlighted. You can view the entire directory tree (all subdirectories on the drive) by choosing Expand all from the Tree menu. Figure 1.8 shows an expanded graphical directory tree.

The file list window shows the files contained in the current directory, as well as the subdirectories beneath the current directory. As in the directory list window, subdirectories are represented by file folder icons. Notice that the icons for executable files (*.COM, *.EXE, *.BAT, and *.PIF) are different from the icons for data files. You can launch programs directly from File Manager by double-clicking the icons that represent *.COM, *.EXE, *.BAT, and *.PIF files.

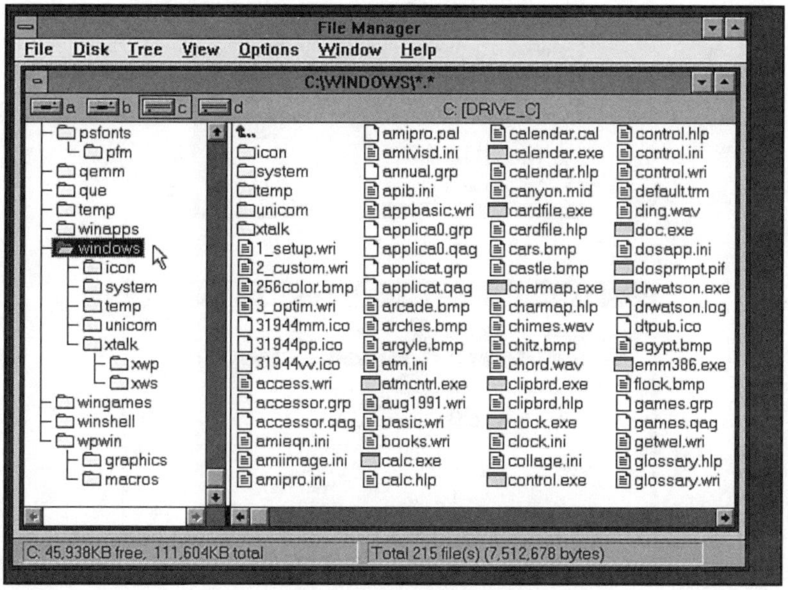

Fig. 1.8.

File Manager's expanded graphical directory tree.

Using File Manager for DOS Tasks

File Manager is quite efficient for common DOS tasks, such as deleting, copying, and moving files; changing file attributes; and deleting or creating subdirectories. File Manager also searches for files; copies, labels, and formats diskettes; and includes a new Quick Format command. Quick Format reformats previously formatted floppy disks more quickly than the normal Format command. Figure 1.9 shows File Manager's Format Disk dialog box with the Quick Format option selected.

Changing the Font in File Manager

You can change the typeface and font size used to display most File Manager elements. The File Manager's Options menu, which allows you to make these changes, also lets you choose the case (upper- or lowercase) of subdirectory and file names and choose whether to display the status bar, which provides information on available disk space. Figure 1.10 shows the Font dialog box, where you choose the font you want to use in File Manager.

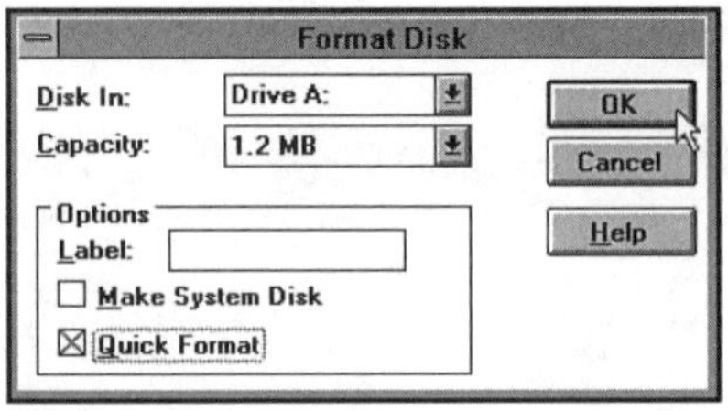

Fig. 1.9.

File Manager's Format Disk dialog box with Quick Format selected.

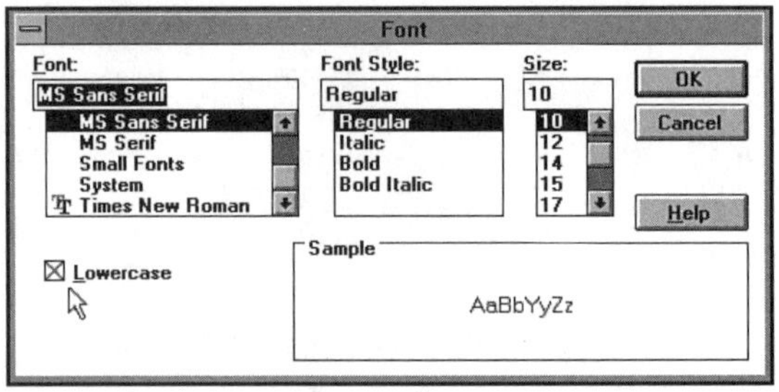

Fig. 1.10.

File Manager's Font dialog box.

Loading File Manager Automatically upon Startup

Windows 3.1 enables you to launch File Manager automatically each time you boot Windows. You then can double-click the File Manager icon to restore File Manger, and then instantly format a diskette or move a file. You no longer have to load File Manager or shell to DOS each time you need to accomplish a file-maintenance task.

Additional Performance Enhancements

Raw speed isn't the only performance improvement in Windows 3.1. Windows now requires less memory. On machines with limited system resources, such as a 386 running in 386 Enhanced Mode with less than 4M of RAM, this improvement can mean the difference between being able to multitask programs and having to run them exclusively.

Windows 3.1 also includes a suite of important new capabilities to run and display DOS programs.

Full Mouse Support in Windowed DOS Applications

Windows 3.1 now offers full use of the mouse in windowed DOS programs. Figure 1.11 illustrates using the mouse in a windowed DOS program to save a document.

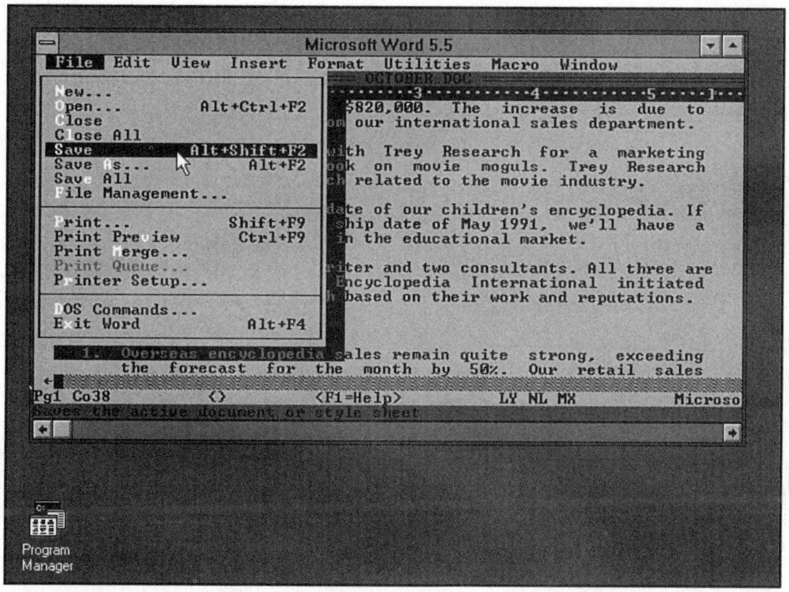

Fig. 1.11.

Using the mouse in a windowed DOS program.

Changing the Font Used in Windowed DOS Programs

Windows 3.1 also enables you to choose the screen font that displays in windowed DOS programs. This feature will be especially useful if you had trouble reading the typeface Windows 3.0 used in windowed DOS applications. You can choose a large, easy-to-read typeface. The Fonts Selection dialog box, which is located in the Control menu of each DOS program, enables you to choose the screen font for a windowed DOS program (see fig. 1.12).

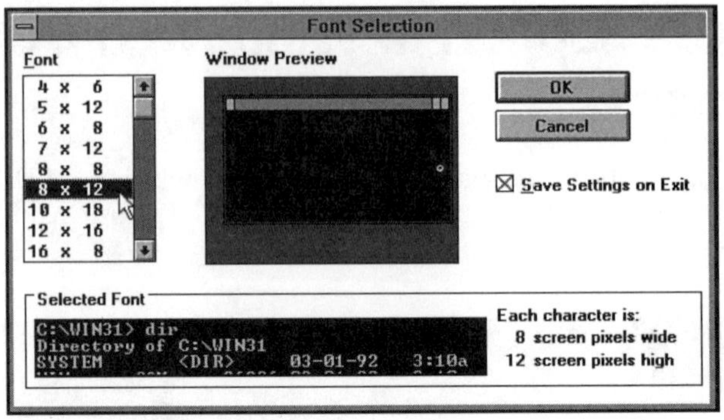

Fig. 1.12.

The Font Selection dialog box.

NOTE Windows 3.1 determines the size of the window that appears for DOS applications by the size of the screen font used to display the program. If you want to reduce the size of a program window, choose a smaller screen font for the program.

Setup Configures More DOS Applications

The Windows 3.1 Setup program searches for DOS programs installed on your system. When it finds a DOS program it is designed to recognize, Setup creates a program information file (PIF) that will optimize the program under Windows. In addition, Windows 3.1 includes several icons for the DOS programs that Setup is designed to recognize; when Setup configures one of these programs to run under Windows, it automatically installs the proper icon in the Applications group.

Improvements in Virtual Memory

Another reason for improved performance is that Windows is now better at using virtual memory, a process in which Windows uses available hard drive space as if it were RAM (random-access memory). You now can run more DOS applications in the background and move between those programs quickly and smoothly. Depending on the amount of space available on your hard drive, Windows can run more programs than the physical resources of your system would allow.

In creating virtual memory, Windows uses two swapping schemes. If you have enough available hard drive space, you can create a permanent swapfile for exclusive use by Windows. This scheme gives Windows the fastest possible access to the hard drive and allows it to multitask DOS programs much more quickly and smoothly. The major drawback of this swapping method is that Windows reserves permanent swapfile space, even when you are not running Windows. If you have a limited hard drive space and do not want to allocate any of it permanently to Windows, Windows can create temporary swapfiles.

Swapfile Utility Integrated into Control Panel

The utility used to create a permanent swapfile now is an integrated part of Windows Control Panel. You can create or modify the size of an existing swapfile by opening Control Panel and choosing the 386 Enhanced setting. Then choose the Virtual Memory command button. The Virtual Memory dialog box opens (see fig. 1.13). For more information about creating a permanent swapfile, see Chapter 3.

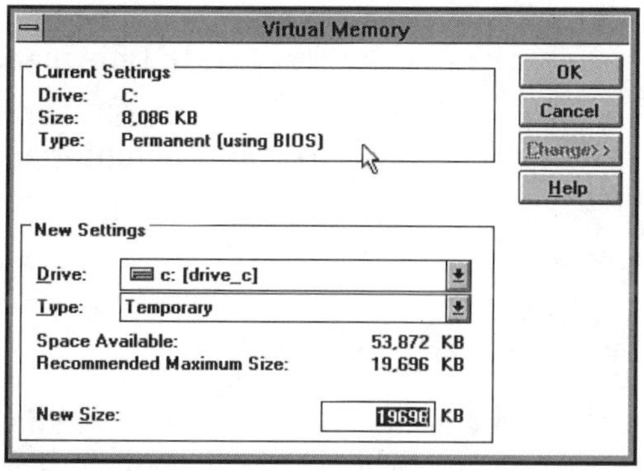

Fig. 1.13.

The Virtual Memory dialog box.

Improvements in Printing and Printer Configuration

Print-job handling is much faster in Windows 3.1, curing a major headache for many Windows 3.0 users. In Windows 3.0, a print job could tie up your system for lengthy periods while you waited for Print Manager to spool a print job to disk. The Windows 3.1 Print Manager, however, returns your system to you within moments—even when you are printing multiple documents. The performance enhancement is due to the new Print Manager, as well as improved Windows printer drivers. Installing new printers and connecting to network printers is now easier and smoother. You can perform both tasks from Print Manager and Control Panel.

Another important printing enhancement is that you can print many files without opening the program in which they were created. With the Print Manager running, use File Manager to drag and drop onto the Print Manager window the icon for a document to print. Print Manager launches the program that created the file and prints the document.

You can add new printers from within Windows by opening Control Panel and choosing the Printers icon. For more information on adding printers to Windows, see Chapter 3.

TrueType Fonts for WYSIWYG Documents

The new TrueType scalable typefaces included with Windows 3.1 enable you to see on-screen exactly how fonts will print on your dot-matrix or laser printer. With TrueType fonts, you get high-quality documents without purchasing special cartridges or a separate type manager.

Windows 3.1's TrueType fonts include Arial, Courier New, Symbol, and Times New Roman. They are copied to your computer automatically by the Windows Setup program.

Character Map Utility

The Character Map is a new utility that works hand-in-hand with TrueType fonts, as well as any other fonts supported by Windows. The Character Map inserts special characters not found on most keyboards into documents; for example, the © character, or characters from the Greek alphabet, such as α or β.

Most fonts available in Windows contain special character sets. Using the Character Map utility, you can view these special character sets and insert them into a document quickly and easily. Although you can insert more than one character at a time, they all must be from the same font. Figure 1.14 shows the Character Map dialog box and its display of special characters. Positioning the mouse pointer on a character and holding down the left mouse button enlarges the character.

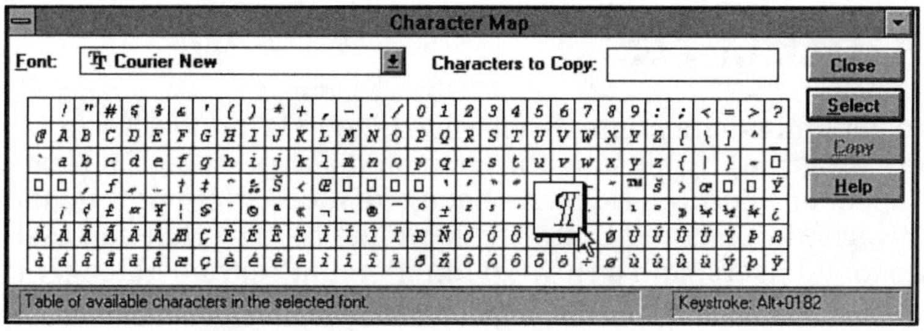

Fig. 1.14.

The Character Map dialog box.

Uniform Dialog Boxes

Many Windows dialog boxes now are easier to navigate because they look more similar. After you learn to choose options in one of these new dialog boxes, you will probably feel more comfortable with the next. These uniform dialog boxes appear throughout Windows, but you probably will notice them immediately in Windows Write and the utilities that come with Windows. The Open, Save As, Print, and Browse commands open the new dialog boxes. Figure 1.15 shows the Open dialog box from the Calendar.

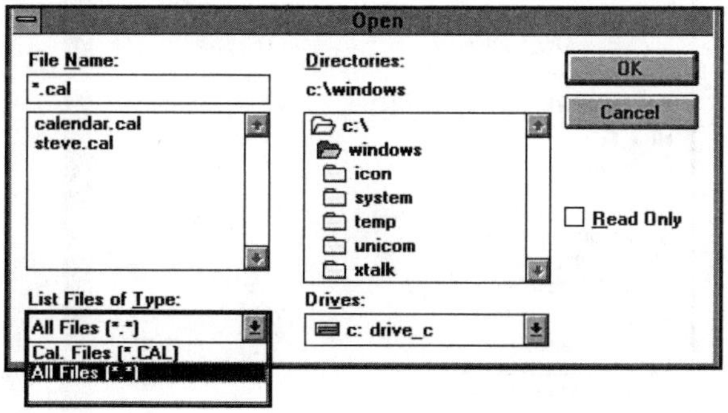

Fig. 1.15.

The Open dialog box from the Calendar accessory.

Many of the redesigned dialog boxes, particularly those that require you to make choices about Windows' configuration, now offer immediate, context-sensitive help. The others offer help from their Help menu choices. For additional information about Windows 3.1's expanded help, see the section "Getting Help in Dialog Boxes" later in this chapter.

Enhanced Help

You can get immediate context-sensitive help in Windows 3.1 (and in any Windows program) by clicking the Help menu or pressing F1. Nearly every aspect of Windows Help has been enhanced. Help now includes newly designed Command buttons, an on-line tutorial that can assist even seasoned users, and a How-To function in Program Manager Help that explains the basics of operating Windows.

Each main help topic is broken into subtopics (see fig. 1.16). These subtopics are underlined, and they appear in a different color than the main topics—usually green. These subtopics are called Jump Text because clicking the colored, underlined text takes you to detailed help on that subject. In the Contents screen, for example, clicking the Program Manager Keys subtopic displays a screen that details using the keyboard in Windows. Some underlined words within a help explanation are also underlined with dots. Clicking one of these words provides a quick pop-up explanation of the term.

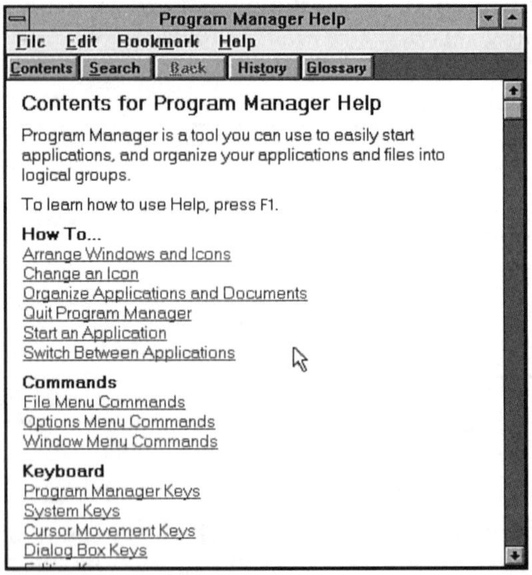

Fig. 1.16.

Program Manager help is broken down into topics.

Windows now offers context-sensitive help in many places where it was not previously available, particularly in dialog boxes where choices can be confusing. You will now find help for dialog boxes in Windows Setup, Program Manager, File Manager, Print Manager, PIF Editor, and Control Panel.

New Command Buttons

Windows Help now features new Command buttons. A new History button, for example, lets you revisit any of the last 40 Help topics you viewed in the current Windows session. A Contents button returns you immediately to Help's table of contents. Help buttons appear along the top of the Help window and enable you to move through Help easily. If a button's function is currently unavailable, the button is dimmed.

To choose a Help button, click the button or type the underlined letter on the button.

Table 1.1 describes the Help buttons you might see when using Windows. Some Windows programs might have Help buttons not described in the table. The browse buttons (<< and >>) appear only if a program's Help offers a browse function.

Table 1.1 Available Help Buttons

Button	Function
Contents	Displays available Help topics for Program Manager or the program you are using.
Search	Lists the Help keywords for Program Manager or the program you are using. By choosing or typing a keyword, you can find and go to a specific Help topic.
Back	Redisplays the last topic you viewed. Clicking the button more than once moves you back one topic at a time in reverse order of how you viewed the topics.
History	Lists the last 40 topics you viewed during the current Windows session, with the most recent topic listed first. To return to any topic on the list, double-click it.
<<	Displays the previous topic in a series of related topics. When you reach the first topic in the series, the button dims.
>>	Displays the next topic in a series of related topics. When you reach the last topic in the series, the button dims.

Getting Help in Dialog Boxes

Windows now offers context-sensitive help about many dialog boxes, particularly where the number of choices can be confusing. When Help is available in a dialog box, you see a Help command button. Click the button to view the help information. Figure 1.17 shows the help on the Cursor Blink Rate selection in Control Panel's Desktop Item.

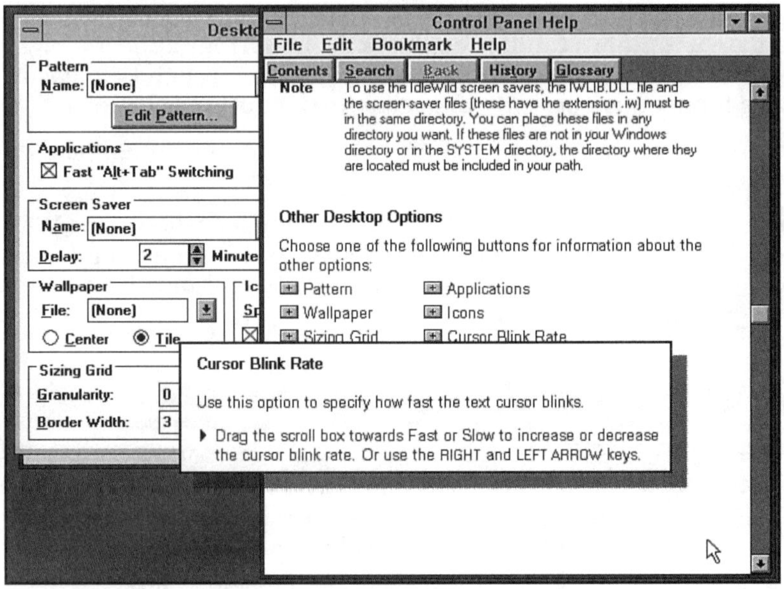

Fig. 1.17.

Help for Control Panel's Desktop Cursor Blink Rate dialog box.

New On-Line Tutorial

Windows 3.1 includes an on-line tutorial that takes you through several short lessons on running Windows so that you can practice working with a mouse and performing basic Windows tasks. To run the Tutorial, you must have a mouse, and your system must have an EGA or VGA monitor.

You can run the Tutorial when you first install Windows using Setup, or any time afterward. To run the Tutorial after you have set up Windows, choose Windows Tutorial from the Help menu.

New Multimedia Utilities

Windows 3.1 includes support for an advanced form of technology integration called multimedia. The term loosely describes a computer controlling external hardware devices so that the output can include sound, animation, video, and other nontraditional means of conveying information.

Multimedia technology enables your computer to use data from devices like CD-ROM drives, video-disc players, music synthesizers, or sound boards, and devices that are compatible with the Musical Instrumental Digital Interface (MIDI). CD-ROM drives and MIDI interfaces are not new to computing, but Windows integrates them with other multimedia hardware and provides a good platform for multimedia.

Two of Windows' new utilities, the Media Player and the Sound Recorder, let you take advantage of Windows' multimedia support.

The Media Player

The Media Player controls hardware-like music synthesizers, CD-ROM drives, video-disc players, animation files, sound boards, and MIDI sequencer files (see fig. 1.18).

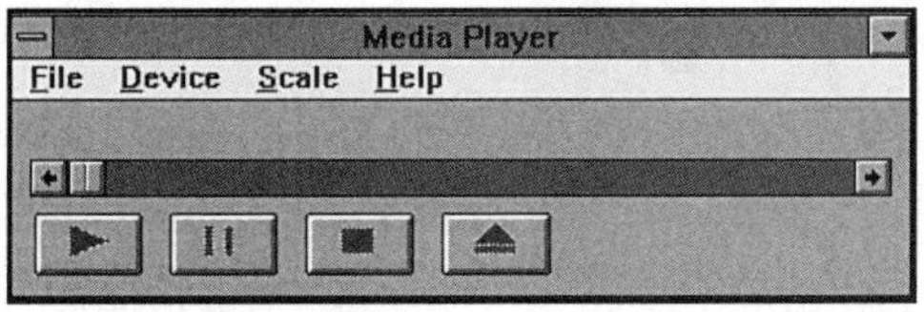

Fig. 1.18.

The new Media Player multimedia utility.

The Sound Recorder

You can use Sound Recorder to play, record, and edit sound files that use the *.WAV (WAVE) format (see fig. 1.19). You can configure the Sound Recorder for your sound board or MIDI device, and then assign these sounds to system or application events, such as starting or quitting Windows. You also can use the sounds in other applications that support Object Linking and Embedding (OLE), which is discussed in the section "Object Linking and Embedding" later in this chapter.

Fig. 1.19.

The Sound Recorder multimedia utility.

Object Linking and Embedding

Object linking and embedding (OLE) is a powerful new capability that enables you to transfer and share information. OLE lets you create a drawing, sound file, or other element using an application such as Paintbrush or Sound Recorder. You then link that element to as many documents as you want, provided that the Windows program in which you created the data and the one in which you want to link the data support OLE. Programs that support OLE include Windows 3.1's Write, Paintbrush, Cardfile, and Sound Recorder; Excel 3.0; Word for Windows 2.0; and Ami Pro 2.0.

Linking Information Using Object Packager

Object Packager, a new Windows utility, offers another way to embed or link objects. Instead of linking the element, as you do when using OLE, you embed an icon that represents the element. This icon is called a *package*. When you double-click the package, the element appears in the application used to create it. If the element is a sound or animation file, it plays.

Suppose, for example, that you write a report that refers to an earlier document on the same topic. You want the earlier report to be available to those who are interested. The information in the earlier document will be easily available if you embed it as a package in your report. Anyone interested in the earlier document can double-click the icon. Figure 1.20 shows Object Packager linking an object within a document so that you can double-click the icon to view the object.

Fewer Unrecoverable Application Errors

Those who were frustrated by the undefined Windows system crashes known as UAEs (Unrecoverable Application Errors) will find Windows 3.1 much more stable. Windows runs on top of MS-DOS, but other programs also run inside Windows. Partly because of this layering of programs within programs, Windows is prone to problems if any of the programs it is running happen to function incorrectly.

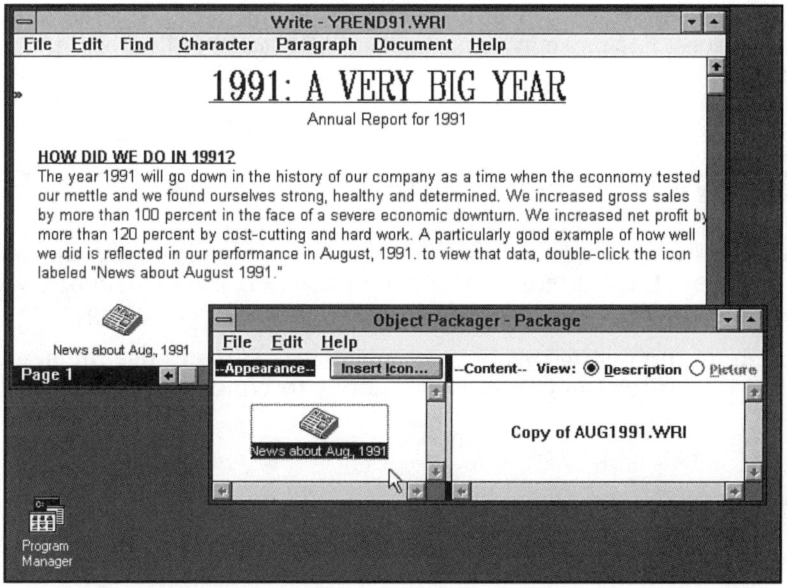

Fig. 1.20.

Object Packager used to link an object as an icon.

Since the release of Windows 3.0, Microsoft has spent enormous energy isolating the causes of UAEs. The company even asked thousands of Windows 3.0 users to run a diagnostic program called Dr. Watson and send the results to Microsoft's Windows development team. The result is that Windows 3.1 is much more stable.

NOTE When a UAE occurs in Windows 3.1, Windows offers much more detailed information on the problem than did Version 3.0. You then can adjust your configuration, if necessary, or alert the software manufacturer of the problem.

Improvements in Serial Port Handling

Windows 3.1 enables you to use serial ports that previously were not recognized by Windows. It also lets you use COM ports 1 and 3 simultaneously and use COM ports 2 and 4 simultaneously.

This change can be important to someone who has more than one or two devices that use the computer's serial port. These devices include a mouse, serial printers or plotters, modems, fax cards, scanners, and other devices. For more information on COM port configuration, see Chapter 3.

Summary

In this chapter, you learned the highlights of many of the enhancements to Windows 3.1, including greater speed and performance, changes in Program Manager, and the completely redesigned File Manager.

Throughout the rest of this book, you will learn how to use the new and enhanced features to upgrade successfully to Windows 3.1.

CHAPTER 2

Installing Windows 3.1

This chapter leads you through the process of using the Windows Setup program to upgrade to Windows 3.1. If you do not already have a copy of Windows 3.0 installed on your computer, you still can follow most of the installation instructions to install Windows 3.1.

The Windows Setup program is designed to make upgrading to Windows 3.1 as simple as possible. If you use Express Setup, the mode intended for most users, you need only replace the diskette in your floppy drive when Setup needs the next disk, type your name so that it can be written to your installed files for display each time you boot Windows, and then provide basic information about your printer. Setup does the rest. If you are an experienced computer user, you can choose Custom Setup, which gives you much more control over how Windows is installed and the modifications made to your system. Figure 2.1 illustrates the Windows Setup window in which you initialize your Windows diskettes.

This chapter focuses on strategies for upgrading to Windows 3.1. This chapter presents ideas for preparation that will make the upgrade go as smoothly as possible. You also find a hands-on guide to running Windows 3.1's Setup in two modes: Express Setup and Custom Setup. In this chapter, you learn the following:

- System requirements for Windows 3.1
- Upgrading strategies to consider before running Setup
- What information you need about your system hardware and software before running Setup

- How to prepare your system for Setup, including your AUTOEXEC.BAT and CONFIG.SYS files
- How to use DOS 5.0's EMM386.EXE and other memory managers
- Differences between Express Setup, which is designed to be as fast and easy as possible, and Custom Setup, which gives you greater control over the Windows installation
- Instructions for running Setup
- Instructions for configuring and using SMARTDrive
- Troubleshooting ideas—what to do if Windows 3.1 doesn't install properly or will not run after it is set up
- Windows utilities you can live without if disk space is at a premium

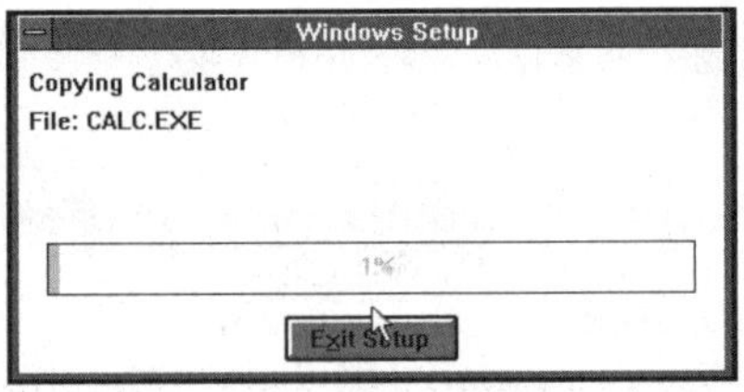

Fig. 2.1.

The Windows Setup window, where you initialize your Windows files.

TIP If you have optimized Windows 3.0 by making changes to WIN.INI and SYSTEM.INI, use Windows Write to print WININI.WRI and SYSINI.WRI from the Windows subdirectory after you run Windows 3.1's Setup. Those files detail WIN.INI and SYSTEM.INI options that are new in Windows 3.1.

System Requirements for Windows 3.1

The system requirements for Windows 3.1 depend on how you plan to use it. One of Windows' more powerful features is that it can run more than one program at a time. You can work in one program (the foreground application) while other programs continue to run and do their work in the background. This process is called *multitasking*. Using this capability, you can write a report in a word processor in the foreground, for example, while a spreadsheet program recalculates a worksheet in the background.

Windows' multitasking capabilities, or operating modes, are different depending on the hardware configuration of your system. This section lists first the basic requirements for running Windows. Then you learn the system requirements of Windows' operating modes. Here are the minimum requirements for Windows 3.1:

- DOS 3.1 to 5.0
- A personal computer with the Intel 80286, 80386, or 80486 processor
- A floppy disk drive
- A display adapter supported by Windows
- A printer supported by Windows, if you want to print
- For a 386 system, 5M to 6M of available hard drive space to upgrade, up to 10.5M for a new installation
- For a 286 system, 5M to 6M of available hard drive space to upgrade, up to 9M for a new installation
- A mouse supported by Windows. Although not an absolute requirement, a mouse is highly recommended so that you can take full advantage of Windows' icon- and menu-based graphical user interface.
- A Hayes, MultiTech, or TrailBlazer (or Hayes-compatible) modem if you want to use Terminal, which is the Windows telecommunications program

Here are the Windows operating modes and their system requirements in addition to the minimum requirements just listed:

- *386 Enhanced mode* is required to run multiple DOS programs or to run DOS programs at the same time you are running Windows programs. System requirements are a computer with the Intel 80386 or higher processor and 2M or more of RAM (640K of conventional memory and 1024K of extended memory).
- *Standard mode* enables you to multitask programs written specifically for Windows rather than DOS. You can run DOS programs in Standard mode; but when a DOS program is in the foreground, the operation of other programs is suspended, and the operation of DOS programs is suspended when a Windows program is in the foreground. System requirements are a computer with the Intel 80286 or higher processor and 1M or more of RAM (640K of conventional memory and 256K of extended memory).

Protecting Your Data and Programs

Windows 3.1's Setup makes necessary modifications to your Windows 3.0 configuration and upgrades all system files and drivers that have been modified in Windows 3.1. Setup also makes necessary changes to the two text files that determine the Windows start-up configuration—WIN.INI and SYSTEM.INI—although most changes you have made to these files are preserved. Setup preserves the choices you made in Windows 3.0 for your computer, monitor, mouse, keyboard and keyboard layout, language, network, and other drivers. Setup also preserves font changes, groups you have created, colors, and other desktop options.

Because of the thoroughness and ease of the way Setup handles upgrading to Windows 3.1, many Windows users will give little thought to protecting their Windows 3.0 configurations. These users might simply unpack their Windows 3.1 disks, insert the first disk into their floppy disk drive, change to that drive, type *SETUP*, and install the new Windows files over the old files. On the other hand, users who have optimized their Windows 3.0 installation through a long process of trial and error might try to protect their configurations by installing Windows 3.1 in a different subdirectory from Windows 3.0, perhaps C:\WIN31. Both installation strategies have their shortcomings.

Installing the new Windows files over the old ones without first saving your Windows 3.0 configuration is a dangerous approach for anyone who uses Windows every day. You should be sure to consider the possibility that Setup might not run flawlessly on your system or that Windows 3.1 might not run after installation. In such a case, you would need to go back to your Windows 3.0 configuration for a short time while you worked through the problems.

Protecting your Windows 3.0 configuration by installing Windows 3.1 in a different subdirectory isn't a good choice either because Setup will not be capable of integrating the new features and capabilities of Windows 3.1 with the changes you made in Windows 3.0. If you choose this alternative, be sure to remove the Windows 3.0 subdirectory from your path after setting up Windows 3.1. Some components of Windows 3.0 cause serious conflicts if used with Windows 3.1.

> **CAUTION:** Microsoft urges you to make a backup of your entire system before running Setup. If you disregard this suggestion, you run the risk of damaging not only your Windows setup but also the other software and data installed on your system.

Probably the best upgrade strategy, even if you have a recent full backup of your system, is to make a separate backup of your Windows 3.0 configuration, and then run Windows 3.1 Setup to upgrade your existing version of Windows. This procedure enables Setup to install all of Windows 3.1's new features and integrate the changes you have made, but still preserve the Windows 3.0 configuration in case something goes wrong. Be sure to back up both Windows subdirectories: C:\WINDOWS and C:\WINDOWS\SYSTEM (if Windows is installed on a drive other than C, substitute the proper drive letter).

Be sure that you make a backup of your complete system before running the Windows Setup program. A full backup of your system ensures that if running Setup damages the programs and data on your system, you will not lose data. If you have a full backup and want to do a quick backup of your Windows 3.0 configuration, use one of the following methods:

- Use a backup program like FASTBACK to do a backup of C:\WINDOWS and C:\WINDOWS\SYSTEM. If Windows 3.1 doesn't run properly, you can quickly restore those two subdirectories.
- Use PKZIP or another compression utility to archive all the files in the subdirectories C:\WINDOWS and C:\WINDOWS\SYSTEM. If Windows 3.1 doesn't run properly, you can quickly unzip these archives into the proper subdirectories and return to your original Windows 3.0 setup.

Gathering Information

No matter which Setup mode you choose, the program prompts you for some specific information. Your setup operation will be smooth and easy if you have all the information at your fingertips before you start the actual setup.

Information for Express Setup

If you use Express Setup, you have to supply very little information. You type your name so that it can be written to your Windows disks, and you provide basic information about your printer. Setup does the rest.

Information for Custom Setup

Using Custom Setup requires you to know a great deal about your computer. If you plan to run Custom Setup, you should prepare this information in advance so that your upgrade to Windows 3.1 will go as quickly and smoothly as possible. You need to know the following information about your system if you run Custom Setup:

- The subdirectory where you want to install Windows files
- The type of computer you are using
- The display type, the screen resolution, the number of colors you want to use, and, with some video cards, the amount of video RAM on your card
- The brand and type of mouse you are using, if you are using one
- Your keyboard type
- The language you want Windows to use
- Your network, if any
- Your printer brand and model number and printer port, if any
- Applications you will run in Windows that are already installed on your system

Setup Changes to AUTOEXEC.BAT and CONFIG.SYS

Unless you choose Custom Setup and override the defaults, Setup automatically makes certain changes to your CONFIG.SYS and AUTOEXEC.BAT files. These changes are necessary to run Windows 3.1. If you choose Custom Setup, you are given the option of making these changes before Setup makes them or making them yourself later. Setup makes the following changes to your AUTOEXEC.BAT file:

- Adds to your path the directory where you install Windows, if required.
- Adds a command line for the Windows disk cache, SMARTDRV.EXE, if appropriate for your system configuration.
- Creates a TEMP subdirectory, C:\WINDOWS\TEMP, that Windows will use to store its temporary files. If you already have an environment variable pointing to another subdirectory, Windows will use that subdirectory.
- Adds an environment variable that directs temporary files to this TEMP directory (if you do not already have a *temp* variable). This environment variable reads `SET TEMP=C:\WINDOWS\TEMP`.

Setup makes the following changes to your CONFIG.SYS file:

- Adds the line `DEVICE=HIMEM.SYS` to enable the driver used by Windows to access high memory on your system.
- Adds the line `DEVICE=SMARTDRIVE.EXE /double_buffer`, if needed. This line enables a special buffering scheme for SMARTDrive; this scheme might be needed on machines whose BIOS is more than three years old.
- Updates EMM386.EXE, if you are using it with DOS 5.0 to load device drivers high or to emulate expanded memory.
- Updates RAMDRIVE.SYS, if it is in use.
- Updates your Microsoft or Hewlett-Packard mouse driver.
- Deletes any known incompatible drivers.
- Adds or updates your EGA.SYS driver. You need this driver if you are using an EGA display or a Mouse Systems mouse.
- Adds the appropriate parameter to the `386MAX` line, if it is present.

Preparing Your System for Setup

Because the Windows Setup program must detect a great deal of information about your computer, its available memory, its operating system, and other details about your configuration, you might need to prepare your system for running the Windows 3.1 Setup program. The best course of action for most people is to allow Setup to work with the least complex system configuration possible. Remove as many device drivers and terminate-and-stay-resident (TSR) programs as possible from memory before you run Setup. This step might seem unnecessary, but some TSRs and device drivers that are compatible with Windows 3.1 can cause problems with Setup, particularly drivers not supplied with DOS. Allowing Setup to run on a system booted from “plain vanilla” CONFIG.SYS and AUTOEXEC.BAT files will help it better optimize Windows for your system (see fig. 2.2). It also will avoid Setup problems that can include lockups and various other difficulties common to software conflicts.

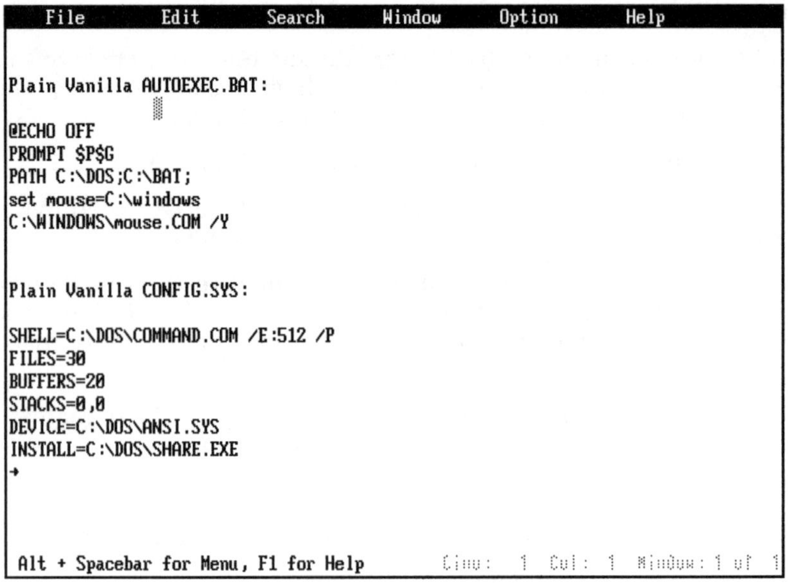

Fig. 2.2.

"Plain vanilla" CONFIG.SYS and AUTOEXEC.BAT files.

The modifications you might need to make to CONFIG.SYS and AUTOEXEC.BAT depend on your current setup. You should, for example, remove references to Windows 3.0’s SMARTDRV.SYS from CONFIG.SYS and reboot the system before running Setup. Do not, however, remove the line in AUTOEXEC.BAT or CONFIG.SYS that loads MOUSE.COM, MOUSE.SYS, or RAMDRIVE.SYS (if it is used). You also should not remove any device driver needed by your hard drive-partitioning software or controller. Generally, such device drivers are loaded first in CONFIG.SYS. For more information on drivers needed by your hard drive, see your system or disk-partitioning software documentation.

After you decide which device drivers and TSRs to remove, use a plain text editor to edit your CONFIG.SYS and AUTOEXEC.BAT files. You can use a plain ASCII editor like Qedit or Windows Notepad. Do not use a word processor unless it can save files without inserting document formatting codes. A word processor's formatting codes will make CONFIG.SYS and AUTOEXEC.BAT useless and could cause system lock-ups when you boot.

When editing your CONFIG.SYS and AUTOEXEC.BAT files, you might either remove the line that loads an unwanted device driver or TSR or disable the line by placing the letters *REM* (for *remark*) in front of it. The REM entry might result in a harmless error message when you reboot your machine, but you can disregard the message. Later, editing CONFIG.SYS and AUTOEXEC.BAT to load the device drivers and TSRs you are removing will be a simple matter.

Some users might decide they prefer to run the Windows setup program without first removing nonessential device drivers and TSRs. If you choose this option and experience problems during Setup, immediately check your CONFIG.SYS and AUTOEXEC.BAT files. You might need to edit these files.

Before you modify your AUTOEXEC.BAT and CONFIG.SYS files, make backup copies. When editing these files, use an ASCII text editor like Windows Notepad so that formatting codes are not inserted.

While you are editing CONFIG.SYS, remove the line that loads the Windows 3.0 version of SMARTDrive (DEVICE=SMARTDRV.SYS). Windows 3.1 comes with a new version of SMARTDrive (SMARTDRV.EXE), which Setup installs in AUTOEXEC.BAT. Problems can result if both versions of SMARTDrive are inadvertently loaded at the same time.

After you have installed Windows 3.1, you can edit your new AUTOEXEC.BAT and CONFIG.SYS files to add the device drivers you removed in preparation for Setup. You should add these drivers one at a time, rebooting your machine and loading Windows each time, to ensure that the drivers do not conflict with Windows.

Loading DOS 5 Device Drivers High

If you are using DOS 5.0 to load device drivers and TSRs into high memory, Windows 3.1 forces you to make minor modifications to your CONFIG.SYS and AUTOEXEC.BAT files. Windows 3.1 includes a new version of SMARTDrive, SMARTDRV.EXE, which is loaded in AUTOEXEC.BAT rather than CONFIG.SYS, where Windows 3.0 SMARTDRV.SYS was loaded. Windows 3.1 also has a new version of RAMDRIVE.SYS, which might not load into the same upper memory region as the old version, so you might need to change the order in which device drivers are loaded to accommodate this new driver.

Although you will need to make these changes in your DOS 5.0 configuration, Setup preserves the DEVICEHIGH= and LOADHIGH (LH) settings in your CONFIG.SYS and AUTOEXEC.BAT files and the order in which device drivers are loaded. Setup saves these items because the order in which these drivers are loaded is crucial in optimizing the use of the upper-memory area. For additional help on reconfiguring DOS 5.0 to work with the new SMARTDrive and RAMDrive, consult your DOS 5.0 manual or Que's *Using MS-DOS 5.*

Using Alternative Memory Managers

Windows 3.1 is designed to work with Windows 3.0-compatible memory managers like QEMM386 and 386MAX. Setup recognizes many of those memory managers. In some cases, such as with 386MAX, it might make minor changes in the memory managers' configurations so that the memory managers work better with Windows. If you are using one of these memory managers, before running Setup you should make a backup of your AUTOEXEC.BAT and CONFIG.SYS files and then remove the CONFIG.SYS line that loads SMARTDRV.SYS.

If you experience a system lockup or other problem during Setup, you might need to remove device drivers from your setup. If this step is necessary on your system, remove from your CONFIG.SYS and AUTOEXEC.BAT files the commands used by your memory manager to load device drivers high. If removing device driver command lines doesn't solve the problem, remove the memory manager itself and boot with "plain vanilla" CONFIG.SYS and AUTOEXEC.BAT files. After Windows 3.1 is properly installed, you can edit your CONFIG.SYS and AUTOEXEC.BAT files to include the driver for your memory manager as well as your TSRs and device drivers.

Because of the new versions of SMARTDrive and RAMDrive, QEMM, 386MAX, and other memory managers will need to recalculate the high memory regions into which they load device drivers. Therefore, after

you have run Setup (and edited CONFIG.SYS and AUTOEXEC.BAT to include your drivers and TSRs, if required), you should run QEMM's Optimize, 386MAX's Maximize, or the optimization program included with your memory manager.

NOTE Before running Setup, be sure to turn off any automatic message service, such as a network pop-up or printing notification, that prints directly to your screen. These programs are incompatible with Setup.

Choosing Express Setup or Custom Setup

For most people, Windows 3.1 Setup will be greatly simplified because of the Express Setup option, which automatically detects the hardware and software you are running and configures Windows for your system. Those who want to oversee the upgrade process more closely should choose the Custom Setup option. Figure 2.3 shows the Setup screen, which is where you choose Express Setup or Custom Setup.

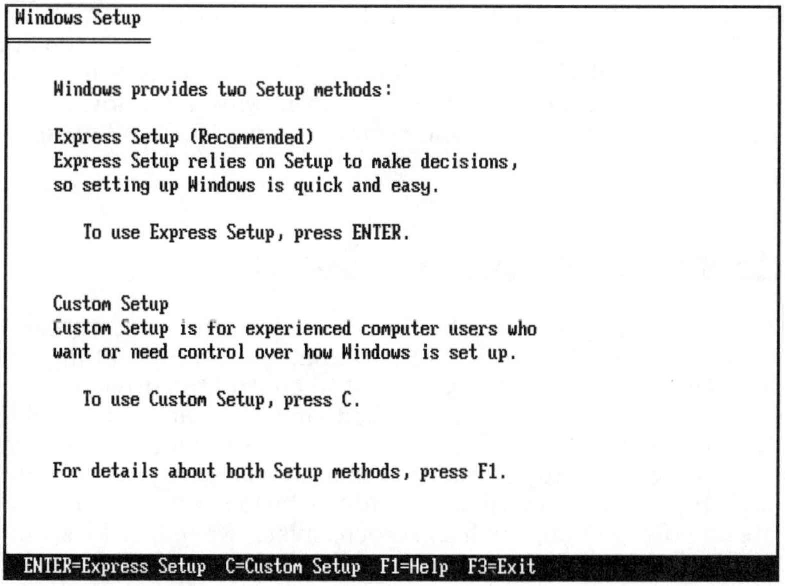
Windows Setup
Windows provides two Setup methods:
Express Setup (Recommended)
Express Setup relies on Setup to make decisions,
so setting up Windows is quick and easy.
To use Express Setup, press ENTER.
Custom Setup
Custom Setup is for experienced computer users who
want or need control over how Windows is set up.
To use Custom Setup, press C.
For details about both Setup methods, press F1.
ENTER=Express Setup C=Custom Setup F1=Help F3=Exit

Fig. 2.3.
The Setup screen where you choose Express Setup or Custom Setup.

TIP Setup notifies you if it detects system device drivers, TSRs, or other system features that are incompatible with Setup or Windows; if Setup detects such an incompatibility, it typically also tells you how to resolve it.

Understanding Express Setup

If you are upgrading to Windows 3.1, Express Setup prompts you for confirmation of the subdirectory where your old version of Windows is installed. If you are doing a new installation, Express Setup chooses the C:\WINDOWS subdirectory for you. Express Setup asks for your name so that it can be written to your Windows files, for the brand and model number of your printer, and for the printer port to which the printer is connected. Express Setup automatically installs all Windows utilities, like Notepad and Calendar; all wallpaper files; and the screen savers. Express Setup copies the README files to your Windows subdirectory and modifies your AUTOEXEC.BAT and CONFIG.SYS files.

Although Express Setup is simple, you might want to use Custom Setup, instead. For example, if you have a Super VGA display and want to run Windows in 800-by-600-by-16-color mode, you should run Custom Setup. Express Setup is likely to detect your display as a simple VGA (640-by-480-by-16 colors). You can, however, use Express Setup and then later reconfigure your video display or change other important Windows settings. To change settings later, run Setup from within Windows; or from DOS, change to the Windows subdirectory, type *SETUP*, and press the Enter key.

Understanding Custom Setup

Custom Setup is for experienced computer users who want a great deal of control over their Windows configuration. Use Custom Setup if you want special printer options, if you want to control the drive or subdirectory where Windows is installed, or if you want to control the modifying of your CONFIG.SYS and AUTOEXEC.BAT files. You also might want to use Custom Setup if you have limited space on your hard drive. Custom Setup enables you to choose not to install certain Windows components on your system, such as screen savers, wallpaper files, accessories like Notepad and Calendar, and the README files. As mentioned in the previous section, you might want to use Custom Setup if your system has a Super VGA display.

Custom Setup prompts for whether to install Windows utilities, like Notepad and Calendar; the screen savers, which are new in Windows 3.1; the wallpaper files; and the README files. You should have Setup copy the README files to your system. They include important last-minute information about Windows, and they include the files WININI.WRI and SYSINI.WRI. You will need to consult WININI.WRI and SYSINI.WRI before you make certain modifications, such as changing the font size and typeface of Windows icon titles or configuring your COM ports so that you can use COM 1 and COM 3 at the same time. WININI.WRI and SYSINI.WRI are written in the format used by Windows Write.

Running Setup

Running Setup should take between 30 and 60 minutes, depending on whether you use Express Setup, which is the fastest, or Custom Setup. If you have taken the precautions suggested in the preceding sections of this chapter, you can be reasonably sure that upgrading to Windows 3.1 will be a simple and relatively smooth process. If something does go wrong during Setup, consult "Troubleshooting Ideas" later in this chapter for help. This section provides hands-on instructions for running Setup in both Express mode and Custom mode.

TIP

If you choose Express Setup and Setup does not find a previous version of Windows on your system, Setup will not prompt you for confirmation of the drive and subdirectory to install Windows. By default, Setup copies files to the C:\WINDOWS subdirectory.

You may use the following switches when starting Setup:

- /A copies all files from the Windows setup disks to a directory on the network server and sets the read-only attribute of each file to On. Use these files to set up Windows on each workstation of a network.
- /B sets up Windows to use a black-and-white (monochrome) display.
- /H: *filename.ext* specifies a settings file so that Windows can be set up automatically. *Filename.ext* is the name of the settings file.
- /I tells Setup that you will manually specify the hardware you are using and that Setup should not try to detect the hardware on your system.

- /N sets up Windows to a wokstation attached to a network. Use this switch with Setup after you have used the /A switch. Only those files that are necessary to run Windows on a workstation are copied from the network. Each workstation shares the Windows files on the server
- /O: *filename.ext* specifies that Setup should use a custom SETUP.INF file; *filename.ext* is the name of the file.
- /S: *path* specifies the path where the Windows Setup files are located.
- /T displays on-screen which open programs should be closed before you use Setup.

Express Setup

Unless you need a great deal of control over the Setup process, you should run Setup in Express mode. This method is the easiest way to upgrade to Windows 3.1. You can stop Setup and exit at any time by pressing F3. If you do not complete the Setup procedure, however, you will need to begin again with Disk 1.

To run Express Setup, follow these steps:

1. Insert Windows Disk #1 into your floppy disk drive.
2. At the DOS prompt, change to that floppy drive by typing its letter and a colon and pressing the Enter key. (On most systems, you type *A:* or *B:* and then press Enter.)
3. Type *SETUP* and press Enter.

   The first Setup screen explains how to run Setup in Express mode and in Custom mode (again see fig. 2.3).
4. Press Enter to choose Express mode.

   Setup searches your drive for your previous installation of Windows. If Setup finds a previous version, Setup asks you to confirm the drive and subdirectory where Windows is installed (see fig. 2.4).
5. If the path displayed is incorrect or you want to install Windows 3.1 in another location, use the Backspace key to erase the path information. Type the correct path information, and press Enter.

   Setup begins the process of upgrading to Windows 3.1. Setup prompts you for the rest of the Windows installation disks, one at a time, as Setup copies files to your system.

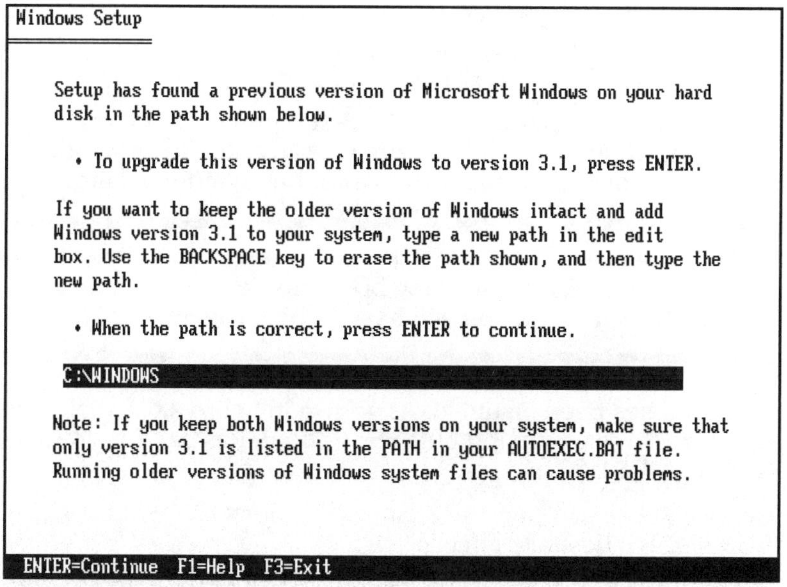

Windows Setup
Setup has found a previous version of Microsoft Windows on your hard disk in the path shown below.
• To upgrade this version of Windows to version 3.1, press ENTER.
If you want to keep the older version of Windows intact and add Windows version 3.1 to your system, type a new path in the edit box. Use the BACKSPACE key to erase the path shown, and then type the new path.
• When the path is correct, press ENTER to continue.
C:\WINDOWS
Note: If you keep both Windows versions on your system, make sure that only version 3.1 is listed in the PATH in your AUTOEXEC.BAT file. Running older versions of Windows system files can cause problems.
ENTER=Continue F1=Help F3=Exit

Fig. 2.4.

Setup prompts for confirmation of Windows location.

6. When prompted, insert the requested disk and press Enter.

   About halfway through the install process, the character-based screens give way to a graphical display run by the parts of Windows that have already been installed. After this point, you make selections in Windows dialog boxes by using the mouse or the arrow and Enter keys. Figure 2.5 illustrates the graphical display in Setup after it switches to the Windows files that have been installed.

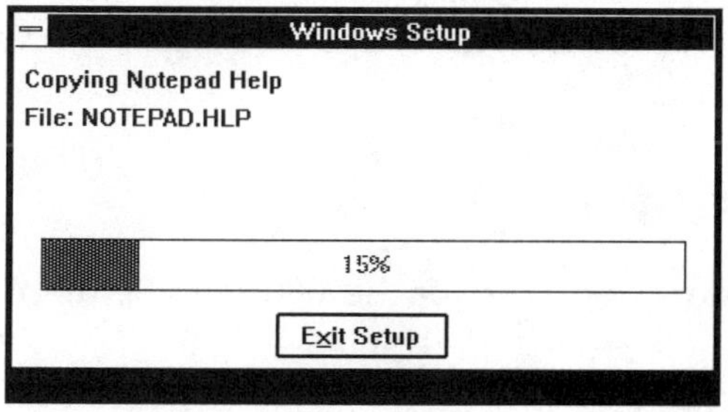

Fig. 2.5.

Setup switches to a graphical display.

If you are upgrading to Windows 3.1, Setup detects the printer already installed in Windows and quickly updates the printer driver. If you want to add, or change, a printer, you must use the printers option in Windows Control Panel.

A Windows Setup dialog box prompts you to run the on-line Tutorial. This dialog box contains four command buttons: Run Tutorial, Skip Tutorial, Help, and Exit Setup.

7. Choose Skip Tutorial to finish the Setup process. You can skip the tutorial now because you can run it at any time from Windows by choosing Program Manager Help and then Windows Tutorial.

CAUTION: Because the Setup process is not yet complete, do not choose Exit Setup from the dialog box. This selection abandons the work done thus far, and you will have to begin again with disk 1.

Windows has been installed. As shown in figure 2.6, a dialog box presents three command buttons: Reboot, Restart Windows, and Return to MS-DOS.

8. Choose Reboot so that the changes to your AUTOEXEC.BAT and CONFIG.SYS files take effect.
9. Type *WIN* at the DOS prompt and press the Enter key to launch Windows.

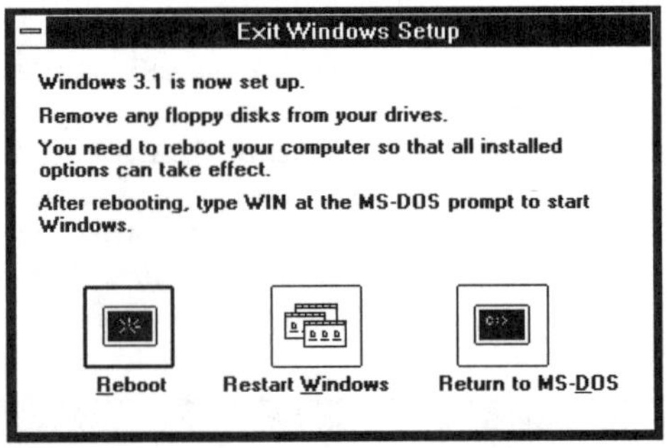

Fig. 2.6.

A dialog box prompts you to Reboot, Restart Windows, or Return to MS-DOS.

Custom Setup

You might need more control over the Windows Setup program than the Express Setup mode offers. Suppose, for example, that you want to choose the directory where the Windows files are installed or you want to choose which Windows components are installed. You then should choose Custom Setup. Custom Setup also lets you select special printer options and decide whether the README files (WININI.WRI and SYSINI.WRI and other documentation), Windows wallpaper files, screen-saver files and other Windows components are copied to your Windows subdirectory.

T I P

Even if you are short on disk space, you should allow Setup to copy the README files (WININI.WRI, SYSINI.WRI, and other files) to your hard drive. After you install Windows 3.1, browse these files, which are written in the format used by Windows Write. The files contain a plethora of information about how to optimize Windows for the way you want to use it. Later, when you want to improve a specific area of performance in Windows 3.1, these README files will tell you exactly how to do so.

To run Custom Setup, follow these steps:

1. Insert the Windows Disk #1 diskette into your floppy disk drive.
2. At the DOS prompt, change to that floppy drive by typing its letter and a colon and pressing the Enter key. (On most systems, you type *A:* or *B:* and then press Enter.)
3. Type *SETUP* and press Enter.
4. Press C to run Setup in Custom mode.

   Setup searches your drive for your previous installation of Windows. If Setup finds a previous version, Setup prompts you to confirm the drive and subdirectory where you want Windows installed.
5. If the subdirectory is incorrect, use the Backspace key to erase the path information, and then enter the subdirectory where you want Windows installed. Press Enter. If Setup does not find a previous version of Windows, you are prompted to enter the drive and subdirectory where you want Windows installed. Type the correct path information and press Enter.

   Setup analyzes your system hardware and displays the screen shown in figure 2.7, with entries for the following elements of your configuration:

   Computer type

   Display

   Mouse type

   Keyboard type

   Keyboard layout and nationality

   Language you want Windows to run in

   Network (if any)

```
Windows Setup
═════════════

   Setup has determined that your system includes the following hardware
   and software components. If your computer or network appears on the
   Hardware Compatibility List with an asterisk, press F1 for Help.

       Computer:        MS-DOS System
       Display:         VGA
       Mouse:           Microsoft, or IBM PS/2
       Keyboard:        Enhanced 101 or 102 key US and Non US keyboards
       Keyboard Layout: US
       Language:        English (American)
       Network:         No Network Installed

       No Changes:      The above list matches my computer.

   If all the items in the list are correct, press ENTER to indicate
   "No Changes." If you want to change any item in the list, press the
   UP or DOWN ARROW key to move the highlight to the item you want to
   change. Then press ENTER to see alternatives for that item.

 ENTER=Continue  F1=Help  F3=Exit
```

Fig. 2.7.

Setup's analysis of system configuration.

6. If an item on the list does not match your system configuration, use the arrow keys to scroll to the item and press Enter. Windows displays a list box like the one shown in figure 2.8, which displays options for that setting. Choose the proper entry for your system, and then press Enter.

```
Windows Setup
═════════════

   You have asked to change the type of Display to be installed.

     • To select a Display from the following list

       1) Press the UP or DOWN ARROW key to move the highlight to the
          item.
       2) Press ENTER.

     • To return to the System Information screen without changing your
       Display type, press ESC.

    8514/a
    8514/a (Small fonts)
    COMPAQ Advanced VGA 640x480 256 colors
    Compaq Portable Plasma
    EGA
    Hercules Monochrome

   (To see more of the list, press the (↓) arrow key)
 ENTER=Continue  F1=Help  F3=Exit  ESC=Cancel
```

Fig. 2.8.

Choosing system configuration options.

7. Continue this procedure until all the entries are correct. Press Enter to proceed with the installation.

   Setup now proceeds with the Windows installation, prompting you for disk changes as needed.

   About halfway through the install process, the character-based screens give way to a Windows graphical display. After this point, you can make Setup selections in Windows dialog boxes by using the mouse or the arrow and Enter keys.

   A Windows Setup dialog box offers you the opportunity to run the on-line tutorial at this time. This dialog box has four command buttons: Run Tutorial, Skip Tutorial, Help, and Exit Setup.

8. Choose Skip Tutorial. Do not choose Exit Setup because the Setup process is not yet complete; this selection abandons the work done thus far. If you choose to skip the tutorial, Setup continues installing Windows, and you can run the tutorial any time you want by clicking Program Manager's Help menu option or pressing the F1 key.

   A dialog box appears in which you must type your name and an optional company name that will be entered into your installed Windows files. This information will appear when you boot up and when you select the About option from Program Manager's Help.

   The dialog box in figure 2.9 illustrates the next Setup dialog box. This dialog box is important because it is where you choose the level of control you want over the rest of the installation process.

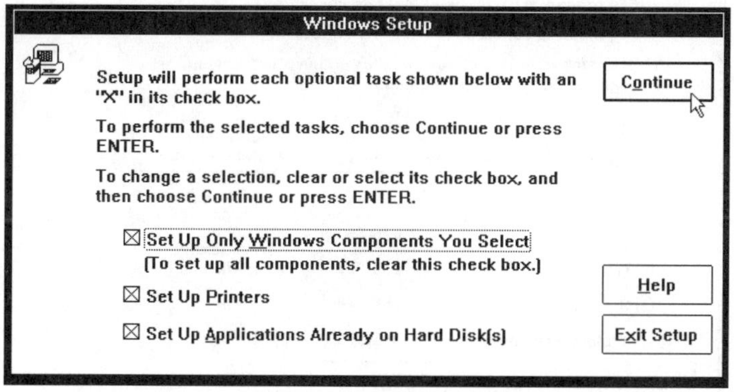

Fig. 2.9.

Choosing installation options in Setup.

Each check box concerns a general element of Windows installation, including which Windows components are installed, various options available for your printer, and the installation in Windows of programs already installed on your hard drive. You need to choose which general parts of Setup you want to control. If you do not select a particular category, Setup uses the defaults for that part of the installation process.

Setup later returns to any option chosen here and lets you make specific choices concerning each category. Setup does not return to these options immediately, however, so be prepared to answer other questions about your configuration. For example, virtual memory and printers are dealt with after you choose which Windows components to install but before you are given a choice of installing the programs Windows has found on disk.

9. Choose the parts of the Setup process you want to control by selecting the appropriate check box. If you do not want to control a particular part of the Setup process, clear its check box. After you select the parts of Setup you want to control, choose the Continue button.

   If you selected Set Up Only Windows Components You Select, the dialog box in figure 2.10 appears. This dialog box enables you to select Windows files you want installed on your system. You can choose to install all the files in a particular grouping, or you can use the Files button beside each group to open another dialog box in which you can choose specifically which files in each category will be installed.

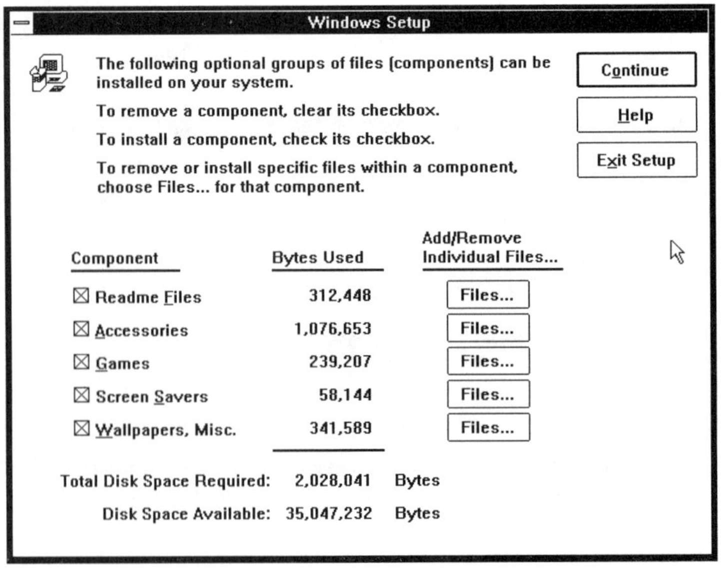

Fig. 2.10.

Choosing Windows components to install.

Beside the listing for each component group is a display of the amount of hard drive space required for installing that component group. At the bottom of the dialog box, Setup displays the total disk space required for the components currently selected and the amount of hard drive space available.

10. If you want to install an entire group of components, select its check box. If you want none of the files in a particular component group installed, clear its check box. If you want to choose specific files from each component group, select its Files button. When you are satisfied with your choices, choose the Continue button. Windows will copy the selected files to your system.

    Next, if you are installing Windows on a computer with an 80386 processor, Setup presents the Virtual Memory dialog box shown in figure 2.11. This dialog box enables you to set up a permanent swapfile. Windows uses this swapfile to create virtual memory, a process in which available hard drive space is used as if it were RAM. Setup detects the amount of RAM on your system, and available hard drive space and suggests a possible size for a permanent swapfile.

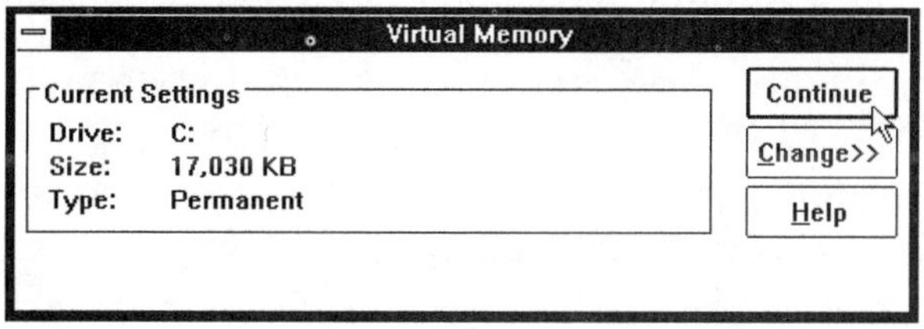

Fig. 2.11.

The Virtual Memory dialog box.

    If you are upgrading to Windows 3.1, Setup will detect the size of the permanent swapfile used by Windows 3.0, if you used one. If you did not use a permanent swapfile, or if you are doing a fresh install of Windows 3.1, Setup analyzes your system RAM and hard drive space and proposes a permanent swapfile. Setup can be a real hard drive hog when it comes to swapfile size, however. On a drive with 40M of free space, for example, Setup might propose a permanent swapfile that takes 20M.

11. To accept the permanent swapfile size proposed by Setup, choose the Continue button. To change the size of the swapfile, select Change; when the dialog box appears, type the amount of hard drive space you want used for a permanent swapfile. If you do not want any of your hard drive space used for a permanent swapfile, this dialog box lets you create a temporary swapfile (whose space is available for other programs when Windows is not running). You also can disable swapping altogether.

TIP Do not disable swapping unless you have extremely limited free space on your hard drive. Windows uses swapping to enhance the performance of Windows and DOS programs, and to multitask a larger number of programs than your system resources alone would allow.

When you finish with the Virtual Memory dialog box, a dialog box appears to prompt that your CONFIG.SYS and AUTOEXEC.BAT files must be updated for Windows to run properly. This dialog box enables you to choose to have Setup automatically make these changes, to review the changes before they are made, or to make the changes later. If you choose to review the changes before they are made, Setup produces a dialog box with two windows, one that shows your original files and another that shows Setup's proposed revision. Scrolling through either window scrolls the other so that you can compare the two versions. You can edit the proposed version.

If you choose to have Setup automatically modify CONFIG.SYS or AUTOEXEC.BAT or make changes after your review, Setup saves your old files with the extension OLD. If you prefer to make the changes later, this dialog box offers to save the proposed changes in your root directory in files named CONFIG.WIN and AUTOEXEC.WIN.

12. Choose whether you want Setup to modify your CONFIG.SYS and AUTOEXEC.BAT files automatically, to allow you to review the proposed changes, or to make the changes later. Then choose the Continue button.

Next, Setup produces the Printers dialog box shown in figure 2.12. If you are upgrading to Windows 3.1, Setup displays the installed printer or printers in the Default Printer and Installed Printers windows. Setup quickly updates your printer drivers. If you want to add or change a printer, you use this dialog box to choose from the more than 260 dot-matrix, laser, and other printers.

The command buttons in this dialog box also allow you to change virtually any part of your printer's configuration. Before you can use these command buttons, you must highlight the printer you want to configure. Here are the command buttons and their functions:

- **C**onnect enables you to choose your printer port.
- **S**etup enables you to choose the printer's resolution and set portrait or landscape mode.

- Remove enables you to uninstall a printer previously installed in Windows 3.0.
- Add enables you to choose a new printer to be used in Windows.
- Help provides help on printer configuration.
- Install copies drivers for the selected printer.

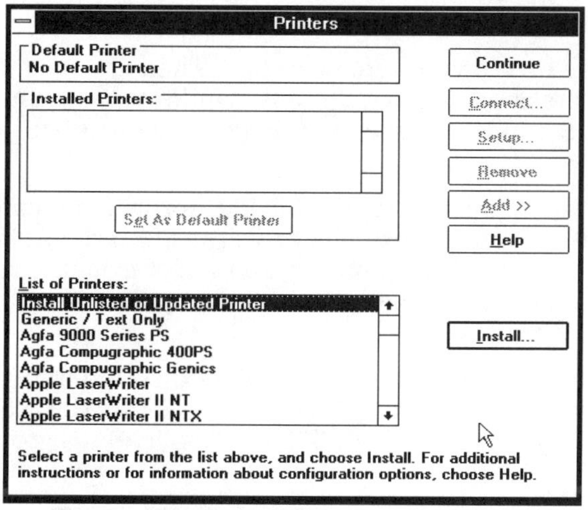

Fig. 2.12.

Setup Printers configuration dialog box.

13. If Setup detects an installed printer, it will be listed in the Installed Printers window. If you want to update your printer driver without changing or adding printers, select the Continue button. Setup will copy the new driver to your system, prompting you for the Windows installation disks that contain the drivers for your printer. If you want to change or add a printer, choose from the printers list, and then choose the Install button. Setup will prompt you for the Windows installation disks that contain the drivers for your new printer.
14. Insert the proper diskette into the floppy disk drive and press Enter or click OK.
15. Depending on your printer, you might need to configure your printer further for Windows. If additional configuration is required, or available, the Setup button will not be dimmed. You make choices for your printer in the dialog box that appears. The choices available in this dialog box vary from printer to printer. If you need help with the selections offered, choose the dialog box's Help button.

16. Choose the Connect button and select the printer port you will use to connect your printer.

    When you have completed printer configuration, select the Continue button to proceed with Setup.

    Setup updates your default program groups—Main, Accessories, and Games—and then builds the StartUp group. A dialog box appears and prompts you for which of your system drives should be searched for programs that will be installed in your Applications group (see fig. 2.13).

17. Choose the drives you want searched. Then choose OK. Setup searches the chosen drives for any Windows program and for DOS programs Setup is designed to recognize and configure for use in Windows.

    Setup might encounter executable files for which it cannot decide which of the applications in its drive the files are for. In such a case, it will pause and prompt you to select from it guesses of the correct application. It then displays the application that you specified in the dialog box.

    A dialog box appears and displays Windows and DOS programs Setup has found on your system (see fig. 2.14). The dialog box also prompts for the ones to install in the Applications group.

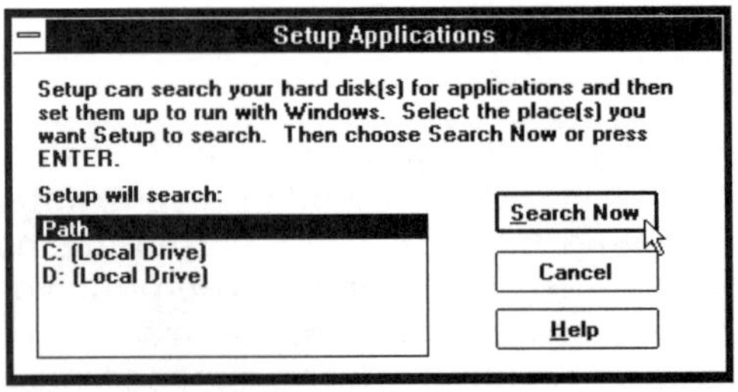

Fig. 2.13.

Dialog box prompts for which drives to search for programs Setup can install in the Applications group.

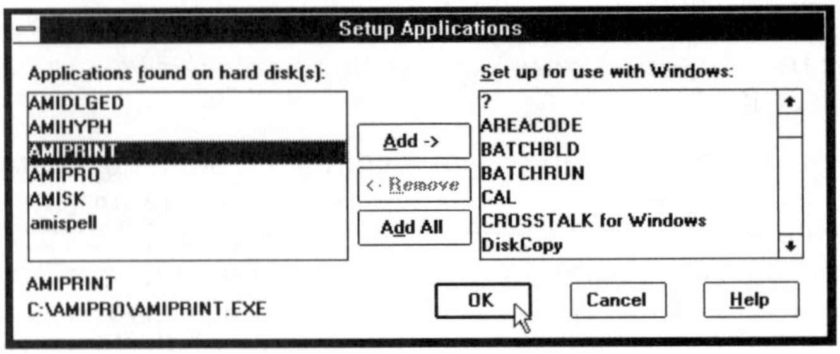

Fig. 2.14.

Choosing programs to be installed in the Applications group.

18. Choose the programs one at a time or choose Add All to create an Applications group containing all the programs Setup has found. Setup is designed to install many, but not all, DOS programs that might be installed on your system.

    Windows has been installed. A dialog box prompts you to Reboot, Restart Windows, or Return to MS-DOS.

19. Reboot your system so that changes to your AUTOEXEC.BAT and CONFIG.SYS files can take effect.

Using SMARTDrive with Windows 3.1

As mentioned in Chapter 1, an important reason for the improved speed of Windows 3.1 is the new version of SMARTDrive, a disk cache that markedly improves the speed of Windows. This section covers only the basics of using SMARTDrive.

SMARTDrive uses two strategies for speeding your system. SMARTDrive reads information from disk before an active program actually needs the data and holds it in extended memory. When a program tries to access the information from your hard drive, SMARTDrive supplies the data from the much faster memory. SMARTDrive also increases performance by caching writes, which means that SMARTDrive temporarily holds in memory data that is to be written to the hard drive. SMARTDrive writes this data to the drive when system resources are in less demand.

You should use SMARTDrive if your system has at least 2M of memory. Setup copies the SMARTDrive file (SMARTDRV.EXE) to your Windows subdirectory and adds its command line to your AUTOEXEC.BAT file. If for some reason Setup did not include the SMARTDrive command line in your AUTOEXEC.BAT file, use an ASCII editor like Windows Notepad to add the following to your AUTOEXEC.BAT on a line by itself:

```
C:\WINDOWS\SMARTDRV
```

No single setting for SMARTDrive is best for every system, so you might want to try several settings to see how they affect your system. In general, the larger SMARTDrive's cache, the less often SMARTDrive needs to read information from the disk and therefore the faster your system's performance.

In determining cache size, SMARTDrive uses two parameters, or sets of numbers on the command line. These numbers determine the size of the cache created by SMARTDrive. These parameters set the initial cache size and the Windows cache size. Because you have more extended memory available when Windows is not running, you can configure SMARTDrive to create a large cache before you load Windows, and then to shrink the cache when Windows is loaded and more of your extended memory is needed for programs to run. An example of the SMARTDrive command line, which includes the use of these parameters, is

```
C:\WINDOWS\SMARTDRV 1024 512
```

With this command line, the size of the cache before Windows is loaded is 1024K of extended memory. The size of the cache while Windows is running is 512K of extended memory.

If SMARTDrive is installed without any command line parameters, as in the first example, SMARTDrive uses default values for the disk cache SMARTDrive creates. These defaults depend on your system's memory configuration. Table 2.1 shows the default values for initial cache size and Windows cache size based on the amount of extended memory on your computer.

Table 2.1 Default Cache Sizes

Extended Memory	Initial Cache Size	Windows Cache Size
Up to 1M	All extended memory	Zero (no caching)
Up to 2M	1M	256K
Up to 4M	1M	512K
Up to 6M	2M	1M
6M or more	2M	2M

There is one need for caution with SMARTDrive: Before you turn off your computer, you should make sure that all cached information has been written to the hard disk. If you turn off your computer's power before SMARTDrive writes cached information to disk, data loss results. To make sure that all data is written to disk, type *SMARTDRV /C* at the DOS prompt. After the drive light on your hard drive goes off, you can safely turn off your computer.

NOTE You need a few updated network files, which are available from Novell, to run Windows 3.1 on Novell Netware. These updated files include the following:

IPX.OBJ
IPXODI.COM
LSL.COM
NETX.COM
TBMI2.COM

Starting Windows 3.1

As Setup finishes installing Windows 3.1, you are prompted to restart Windows, return to the DOS prompt, or reboot your system. You should return to the DOS prompt and reboot your computer. After your system has rebooted, type *WIN* at the DOS prompt and press Enter to launch Windows. Windows starts in the highest mode supported by your system. (Windows operating modes are summarized in the section on the system requirements of Windows.)

You can enter a command line parameter that overrides the automatic mode selection and determines the Windows starting mode. If you have a computer with an 80386 processor and 4M of RAM, for example, your system normally starts in 386 Enhanced mode. But you might want to start your system in Standard mode because Windows runs slightly faster in Standard mode. You cannot start Windows in a higher operating mode than your hardware supports. In other words, you cannot start Windows in 386 Enhanced mode on a computer with an 80286 processor. Here are the command line parameters used to start Windows in specific modes:

- *WIN /S* starts Windows in Standard mode on a 286 or 386 machine.
- *WIN /3* starts Windows in 386 Enhanced mode on a 386 or higher machine with 2M or more of RAM (640K of conventional memory and 1024K of extended memory).

You can find out which operating mode your computer is running in by opening the Help menu and choosing About Program Manager.

TIP

Using the WIN /3 command line, you can force a computer with a 386 processor but less than 2M of RAM to start in 386 Enhanced mode, but this mode is not the most efficient one for Windows on this type system.

Troubleshooting Ideas

The Setup program is designed to make upgrading to Windows 3.1 as simple as possible. Because Setup does such a good job of detecting a system's configuration, most users will have no problems. If you do experience trouble, you can try to work through the problem on your own, with the help of the following tips, or call Microsoft technical support.

Problems Running Setup

Certain hardware and software combinations can cause problems with Setup. If Setup hangs or aborts on your machine, here are some possible solutions to try before calling Microsoft Technical Support:

- If you ran Express Setup, try running Custom Setup. Setup displays a list of the hardware Setup detects, and you can correct any improper settings.
- If you are using a memory manager like QEMM386 or 386MAX, remove its command line from your CONFIG.SYS file and delete as many lines loading device drivers and TSRs as possible from your CONFIG.SYS and AUTOEXEC.BAT files. If necessary, boot your system with a DOS disk that contains no device drivers or TSRs, and then retry Setup.
- Read the text file on your installation disk for information about any known incompatibilities between one of your system components and Setup. The text file includes information about overcoming many such problems.

Problems Starting Windows

If Setup seems to have installed Windows properly on your system but Windows will not boot, here are some possible solutions to try before calling Microsoft Technical Support:

- Reboot your machine to make sure that changes in the CONFIG.SYS and AUTOEXEC.BAT files have taken effect.
- Check your AUTOEXEC.BAT file to make sure that the Windows subdirectory is in your system path. Ensure that your path is no more than 127 characters long—the limit imposed by DOS. If you need help editing your path, consult your DOS manual.
- Remove from your CONFIG.SYS and AUTOEXEC.BAT files the lines loading device drivers and TSRs that are not related to Windows. For example, keep in CONFIG.SYS the line that loads HIMEM.SYS, and keep in AUTOEXEC.BAT the line that loads SMARTDrive.

Freeing Up Hard Disk Space

If you run short of hard disk space, you can delete unessential Windows components from your system. Elements you can delete without disabling Windows include the README files, Windows accessories like Calculator and Notepad, games, screen savers, wallpaper, and other files. By deleting these files, you can free nearly 1M of hard disk space. To remove Windows components from your system, you must use Windows Setup. Follow these steps:

1. Open the Main group (double-click the Main group icon, or press Alt-W and choose the number that corresponds to the Main group).
2. Launch Windows Setup (double-click its icon or move the highlight to the Setup icon and press Enter).
3. Open the Options menu.
4. Choose Add/Remove Windows Components. Windows displays the Windows Setup dialog box.

As shown in figure 2.15, you can delete five groups of components from your system. These groups include the README files, Accessories, Games, screen savers, and wallpaper and miscellaneous files. To remove a complete group of components, all README files, for example, follow these steps:

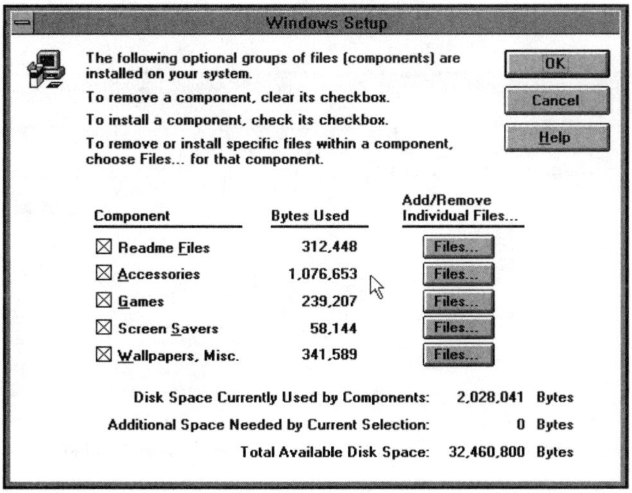

Fig. 2.15.

The Windows Setup dialog box.

1. Clear the check box next to the component group you want to remove.
2. Choose OK.

You also can remove specific files from any of the groups; for example, you can remove the Calculator and the Calendar from the Accessories group but leave Notepad and the other Windows utilities. To remove specific files, choose the Files button next to any of the five groups of components. The Accessories dialog box opens (see fig. 2.16). Follow these steps:

1. Use the mouse or the keyboard to highlight files in the scrolling list box labeled Install These Files on the Hard Disk.
2. Choose the Remove command button.
3. Choose OK. The files are removed from disk.

To reinstall these Windows components, start Windows Setup from the Main group and open the Options menu. Choose Add/Remove Windows Components. Regardless of whether you deleted an entire component group, or just a few files from a component group, follow these steps:

1. Choose the check box next to the component group you want to reinstall.
2. Choose the OK button.

   Setup prompts you for the Windows installation diskettes that contain the files needed to reinstall the deleted files.

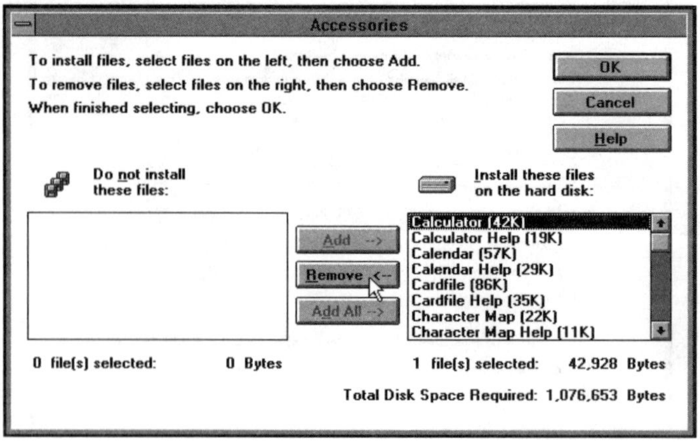

Fig. 2.16.

Removing specific Windows Accessories files.

3. Insert the requested disks, as you are prompted, into your floppy disk drive.
4. When you have reinstalled all desired files, choose the OK button to exit the dialog box.

Summary

In this chapter, you learned to run the Windows 3.1 Setup program. You learned about the system requirements for Windows 3.1, how to prepare your system for Setup, gathering information about your system prior to running Setup, the differences between Express and Custom Setup, and how to run Setup in Express and Custom modes. You also learned about using SMARTDrive with Windows 3.1, and some troubleshooting techniques in case Setup doesn't run properly or Windows will not run after Setup.

3

CHAPTER

Customizing Windows 3.1

The Windows 3.1 Control Panel is an interior decorator's dream. If you want to change the color of text in WordPerfect for Windows or Lotus 1-2-3 for Windows, use Control Panel. If you want to set up your serial port for use with a modem, use Control Panel. Use Control Panel to decorate your Windows desktop with color, wallpaper patterns, and images. Change the graphics picture icons Windows uses to represent programs and functions. Set the mood with music. Display an animated screen saver when Windows is running but not being used. Decide how fast the mouse pointer moves across the screen, or configure the pointer so that it leaves "trails" as it moves. Set an invisible grid to align objects. Change icon spacing or title wrapping, and set the cursor blink rate. Adjust the keyboard repeat rate and delay. Change the system date and time. Sign on and off your network. Set telecommunications parameters.

Literally, the entire graphical world of Windows is at the tip of your mouse pointer in Windows Control Panel. Using Control Panel, you can specify not only the way Windows looks, but the way it works.

This chapter focuses on what has changed in Control Panel from Windows 3.0 to Windows 3.1. Figure 3.1 shows Control Panel.

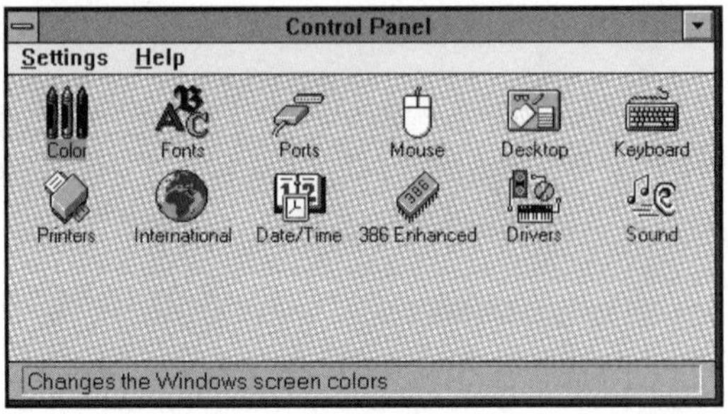

Fig. 3.1.

Windows 3.1 Control Panel.

Control Panel has so many changes from Windows 3.0 that users who are upgrading to Windows 3.1 should consider taking this brief tour, even if they are familiar with the features of Windows 3.0 Control Panel. Many new Windows 3.1 capabilities have been added to existing Control Panel icons. In this chapter, you learn about the following:

- Understanding Control Panel's central function as the Windows configuration center
- Customizing the color, look, and feel of Windows
- Changing the look of your documents, and Windows itself, with fonts
- Managing COM ports
- Setting mouse options
- Customizing the Windows desktop
- Configuring the keyboard
- Configuring your printer or plotter
- Choosing the language Windows works in
- Setting your system date and time
- Fine-tuning your 386
- Enabling Windows new ComPort capabilities
- Using multimedia music and sound
- Customizing networking capabilities

A Quick Tour of Control Panel

Each icon in the Windows 3.1 Control Panel accesses a group of functions that control the way Windows looks, runs, and works. Depending on your system configuration, Control Panel can have a different number of icons. For example, if your system is a 386 but not connected to a network, you most likely will see the 12 icons displayed in figure 3.1. If you are running a 286, the 386 Enhanced icon does not appear. If your 386 is connected to a network, Control Panel probably will display an extra icon. Following is a description of the main icons in Control Panel and what they enable you to do:

- *Color.* Change the color of virtually any element of Windows—from the desktop to window borders, the title bar, the menu bar, highlighted items, dimmed items, and the color of text and background in applications. Also change the colors in Windows programs.
- *Fonts.* Add or remove TrueType fonts, printer fonts, and cartridge fonts.
- *Ports.* Specify basic settings, such as the baud rate and data, parity, and stop bits for your serial ports. You can also specify advanced settings that determine the base I/O address and the interrupt-request line (IRQ) used to send information to a serial port.
- *Mouse.* Customize the way you use your pointing device. For example, adjust how fast the pointer moves across the screen, set the double-click speed, swap functions of the left and right mouse buttons, and enable mouse trails so that you can more easily follow the mouse on a laptop's LCD screen.
- *Desktop.* Choose patterns or images to decorate the desktop, specify a screen saver, set an invisible grid to help you align objects on the desktop, specify icon spacing and title wrapping, and set the cursor blink rate.
- *Keyboard.* Adjust the keyboard repeat rate and delay.
- *Printers.* Install and configure printers and activate Print Manager.
- *International.* Set language, keyboard layout, currency format, number format, measurement, date format, time format, and other options.

- *Date/Time.* Change your system's date and time.
- *386 Enhanced.* Optimize Windows for your 386 and manage your virtual memory options.
- *Drivers.* Install, remove, and configure drivers for multimedia applications and other devices.
- *Sound.* Assign sounds to system and application events and turn on or off Windows warning beep and system sounds.

Although Windows 3.1 has many changes that make it more powerful and useful, users who are familiar with Windows 3.0 will find that most changes seem natural and easy to learn. In fact, the intuitive nature of the Windows interface has been improved in Windows 3.1. This chapter can help you make a quick start. It provides a hands-on introduction to using Control Panel to customize Windows 3.1.

New Color Choices

Windows 3.1 Control Panel enables you to change the colors of many screen elements that you could change in Windows 3.0 only by adding little-known entries to WIN.INI, the Windows system configuration file. Control Panel now also includes several new color schemes, including some designed to save power on laptops equipped with LCD screens.

This section covers Control Panel's new color settings. It assumes that in using Windows 3.0 you have already learned the basics of choosing a color scheme, changing the color of a specific screen element, and creating and using custom colors. If you do not know these procedures, Control Panel's Colors option provides extensive on-line help.

Control Panel now provides more than 20 color schemes. You can use or modify the existing color schemes, or create and save your own color scheme. When selecting a color scheme, consider the following points:

- A color scheme that uses only solid colors might increase the speed at which Windows updates your screen. The Windows Default and several other schemes use only solid colors.
- If you have a laptop with a Plasma screen, you might want to use the Plasma Power Saver color scheme. This scheme uses darker colors, which require less power than bright colors. If you are using an LCD screen, colors might appear in reverse video. In this case, you might want to use an LCD color scheme. The names of these schemes begin with *LCD*. Some systems with LCD screens enable you to configure your video so that the colors are not reversed.

Although Windows 3.0 allowed you to change most elements of a color scheme, you couldn't change all colors using Control Panel. You were forced to enter obscure numeric codes in WIN.INI to change the colors of many screen elements. The screen element colors that now can be changed from within Control Panel include:

- The window frame (the dark edge on both sides of the window border)
- The scroll bars
- The button face (the main surface of command buttons)
- The button shadow (a button's dark edge)
- The button highlight (a button's lighter edge)
- The disabled text (text used for dimmed/unavailable buttons and menu choices)

When you first begin experimenting with new colors for these screen elements, you might want to try changing one element at a time, and then change others only after you are satisfied with the first. Although button faces in purples or greens might seem like a good idea when viewed inside Control Panel, you could quickly tire of such a decorating scheme when using Windows day after day. To make the new color changes, follow these steps:

1. From Control Panel, open the Colors dialog box. The Color Schemes box shows the name of the current color scheme, and the sample screen shows the colors for the current scheme.
2. Click the Color Palette button to expand the Color dialog box (see fig. 3.2).

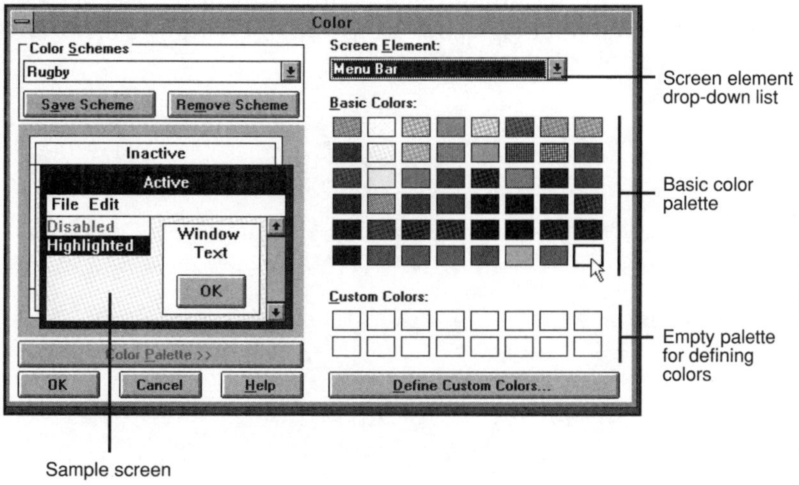

Fig. 3.2.

The Color dialog box with a palette of basic colors.

3. Click the Screen Element drop-down list to view a list of screen elements you can recolor. (You also can use the mouse to click the screen element whose color you want to change, but this method is difficult when you are changing many of the screen elements that now can be recolored in Windows 3.1.)
4. Click the screen element whose color you want to change.
5. In the Basic Colors palette, click the color you want to use for the screen element you have chosen. You may then choose additional screen elements that have colors you want to change. If you want to use a custom color, use the Define Custom Colors command button to define the color before you actually choose the screen element.
6. Click OK when you have made all the color changes you want to make. You return to the Control Panel widow.

Managing Fonts

Different fonts, font sizes, and font styles are an integral part of today's complex and sophisticated business documents. Using the right font can help you create the exact impression you want in your printed documents, whether you are writing a one-page business letter in WordPerfect for Windows or composing a complex annual report with numerous graphics elements in Aldus PageMaker. Windows also uses various fonts to display information on-screen.

Control Panel gives you a single, central place from which you can manage the fonts used in Windows and Windows programs, including the new TrueType fonts included with Windows 3.1. You use Control Panel's Fonts dialog box to add or delete fonts, as well as preview fonts installed on your system (see fig. 3.3). Using fonts in Windows 3.1 is covered in detail in Chapter 6.

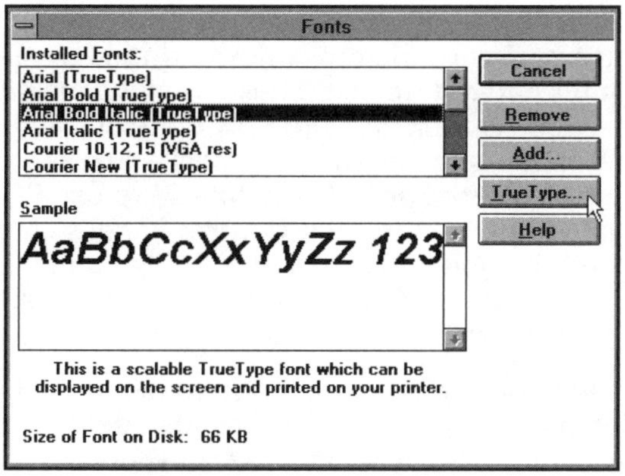

Fig. 3.3.

Control Panel's Fonts dialog box.

Using Control Panel To Manage COM Ports

Windows 3.1 is designed to eliminate a shortcoming of previous versions of Windows—the inability to use COM 3 and COM 4 on most machines. This shortcoming often resulted in Windows users having to choose among devices like a mouse, a modem, and a scanner when those users actually needed all three.

Windows 3.1 also has a powerful new capability that enables you to use COM ports 1 and 3 or 2 and 4 at the same time. On most machines, you cannot use COM 1 at the same time as COM 3 or use COM 2 at the same time as COM 4, due to a conflict between these ports and the interrupt-request lines (IRQs) the ports need to handle data.

These changes in Windows 3.1 might seem highly technical, but they are basic for someone who uses more than two devices that require the computer's serial ports.

Most computers include at least two COM ports, or serial ports: COM 1 and COM 2. Your computer also may include COM 3 and COM 4. If you are unsure, consult your computer for the manual configuration of your COM ports.

TIP

If your computer includes only two COM ports but you need to connect more than two devices that use COM ports, you can purchase an inexpensive plug-in card that adds these ports on most systems.

You use Control Panel to specify settings for each COM port on your system. These settings determine how information is transferred between your computer and the device. These settings include standard settings—such as baud rate, parity, and flow control—and might include more advanced settings—such as the base port address and IRQs used to send information to a serial port. If you intend to use COM 1 and COM 2 only, you need only ensure that Control Panel's standard settings are correct for your machine and the device being connected to your serial port. If you intend to use COM 3 and COM 4, you also might need to change the advanced settings.

The following sections provide a basic guide to using the COM ports on your system under Windows. These sections also detail Control Panel's advanced settings, which enable you to use COM ports 1 and 3 or 2 and 4 at the same time.

Learning COM Port Basics

To connect a device through a COM port to your computer, you must know how your computer and the device are configured to transmit data. Consult your computer documentation and the user manual for the device to gather the required information. You need to know the following basic information to configure a COM port in Windows:

- The COM ports on your system and the available port. For example, ensure that COM 1 is not already being used by an internal modem if you plan to use COM 1 to connect a serial mouse.
- The IRQ used by each port. On most machines, the IRQ for COM 1 is the same as the IRQ for COM 3, and the IRQ for COM 2 is the same as for COM 4. For more on setting IRQs, see "Using Advanced Settings" later in this chapter.
- The COM ports that the device can use. Some devices recognize only COM 1 and COM 2. Others also work on COM 3 and COM 4.
- The baud rate, or transmission rate, that your device uses. Most devices use a baud rate between 300 and 9600.
- The data bits your device uses for each character. Most characters are transmitted in 7 or 8 data bits.

- The parity, or type of error checking, your device requires. Many devices need none.
- The time between transmitted characters, or stop bits, required by your device. Many devices use 1 stop bit.
- The flow control needed by your device. Many devices use Xon/Xoff flow control, also known as software handshaking. Some devices, particularly error-correcting modems, use hardware handshaking, or CTS/RTS.

Configuring a COM Port in Windows

After you gather the necessary basic information about your computer and the device you want to connect to a COM port, you need to configure the COM port in Windows so that the port is prepared for the device you are installing. To configure a serial port in Windows, follow these steps:

1. From Control Panel, open the Ports dialog box (see fig. 3.4).

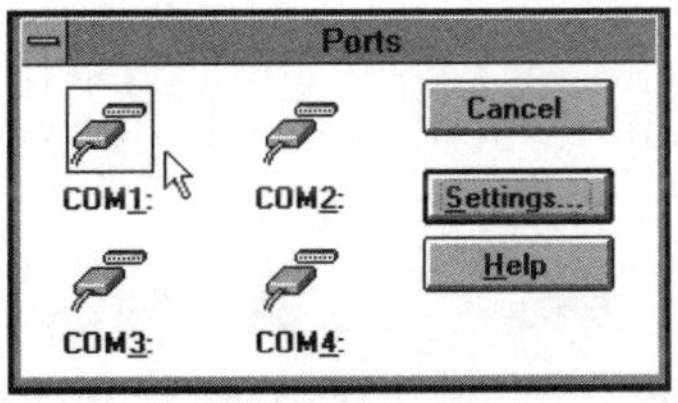

Fig. 3.4.

The Ports dialog box.

2. Double-click the icon for the port you want to use for your device. You see the Settings dialog box for the COM port you have selected. Figure 3.5 shows the Settings for COM1 dialog box.
3. Click the scroll arrow to the right of each setting to display the options for that setting.
4. Set each option to match the device you want to connect to that port. For information about the correct settings, see the documentation for the device and your computer manual.
5. When you have chosen all settings, choose OK. The Settings for COM1 dialog box closes.
6. Click the Ports dialog box's Close button.

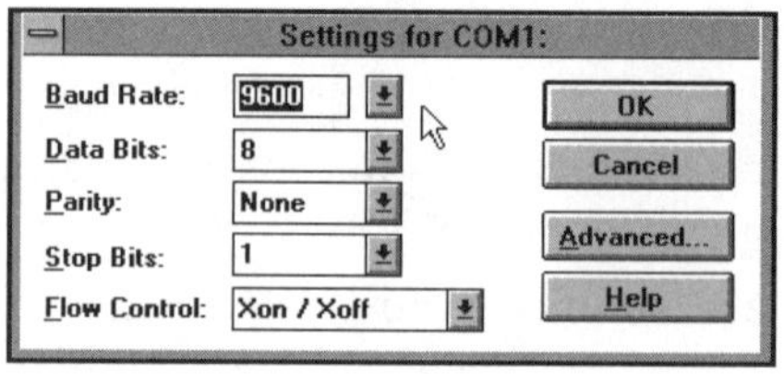

Fig. 3.5.

The Settings for COM1 dialog box.

Using Advanced Settings

Control Panel's advanced port settings enable you to use COM 3 and COM 4 on machines equipped with those ports. Control Panel's advanced port settings also enable you to use COM 1 at the same time as COM 3, or COM 2 at the same time as COM 4. Control Panel accomplishes these things by enabling you to select the base port address and the interrupt-request line (IRQ) for each COM port.

The base port address and IRQ settings for COM 1 and COM 2 are fairly standardized in the computer industry, so if you plan to use only COM 1 and COM 2, you probably do not need to change the base port addresses and IRQ settings for these ports. Common port address and IRQ settings are listed in table 3.1. These addresses and IRQ settings might not be the same as those used by your system or the device you are installing.

Table 3.1 Common Port Address and IRQ Settings

Port	Address	IRQ
COM 1	03F8	4
COM 2	03E8	3
COM 3	02F8	4
COM 4	02E8	3

NOTE

If your machine is based on Microchannel Architecture (MCA) or Expanded Industry Standard Architecture (EISA), it probably can simultaneously access two ports that use the same interrupt. See your computer manual to determine whether you need to make changes in order to use COM 1 and COM 3, or COM 2 and COM 4, at the same time.

If your system has additional serial ports or you install them, or if a device connected to a COM 1 or COM 2 port does not use standard addresses or IRQs, you can use the Advanced Options dialog box to change the settings.

Before you make any changes to the base address or IRQ used by a COM port, you must determine the base address of each port on your system and the IRQ used by each port. You also must determine the COM ports in use and the available IRQs on your machine. Consult your computer manual for this information. You then need to ensure that the device you plan to connect to a COM port can use one of the IRQs available on your machine. For more information, consult the documentation for your device.

To use Control Panel's Windows advanced ports settings to configure a COM port, follow these steps:

1. From Control Panel, open the Ports dialog box.
2. Double-click the icon for the port you want to configure. This step opens the Settings dialog box for the COM port you have selected.
3. In the Settings dialog box, click the Advanced button to open the Advanced Settings dialog box. Figure 3.6 shows the Advanced Settings for COM4 dialog box.

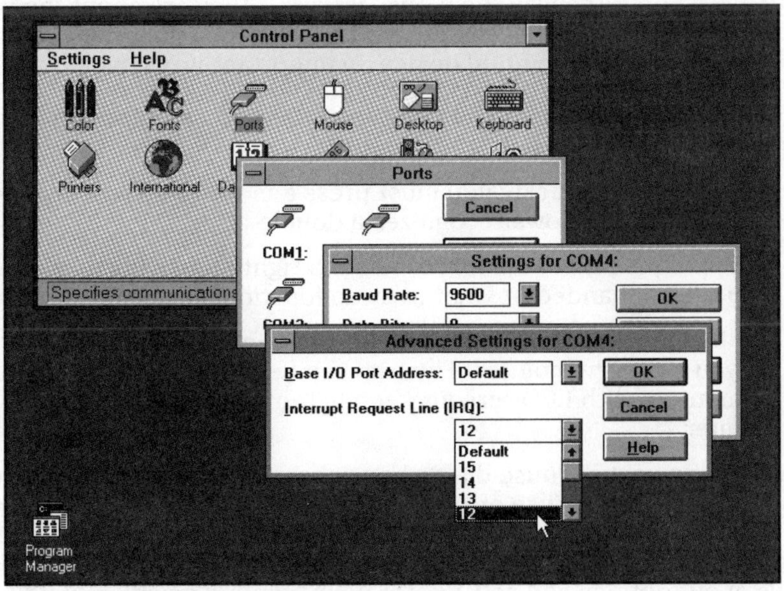

Fig. 3.6.

Selecting advanced settings for COM4.

4. Click the Base I/O Port Address scroll arrow and scroll through the list to choose a port address from the list, or type the correct address in the text box. A change to the base I/O port address does not take effect until you restart Windows. If you change this option, a dialog box appears asking whether you want to restart Windows. To restart Windows, choose the Restart Now button.
5. Click the Interrupt Request Line (IRQ) scroll arrow and choose an IRQ number from the list, or type a number between 2 and 15 in the text box.
6. Choose OK to close the Advanced Settings dialog box. You must also back out of the Ports dialog boxes by choosing OK or Close, depending on the dialog box.

Configuring the Mouse

The mouse is an important device in the Windows icon- and menu-based graphical user interface (GUI). You use the mouse to launch programs by double-clicking their icons, to open menus by clicking the menu bar, to select text in document windows, and to perform numerous other tasks. Most Windows users use the mouse at least as often as they use the keyboard. Because of this intimate association, some Windows users are as picky about the way the mouse works as they are about the Windows colors. Control Panel enables you to customize the way you use your mouse, or other pointing device, in important ways, including

- Adjusting how quickly the pointer moves across the screen when you move the mouse
- Adjusting how quickly you must press a mouse button a second time before Windows recognizes a double-click
- Swapping the functions of the left and right mouse buttons in case you are left-handed or want to swap functions for another reason
- Enabling mouse trails, a trail of mouse pointers left on your screen as you move the pointer. The trail can help users who use laptop computers with LCD screens keep better track of the mouse pointer.

Figure 3.7 shows the Mouse dialog box, where you make changes in the way your Microsoft mouse or other compatible pointing device operates in Windows. The options that appear in the dialog box on your system might be different, depending on the pointing device you are using. For details about options and settings for your pointing device, see its documentation. To use Control Panel to configure your mouse, follow these steps:

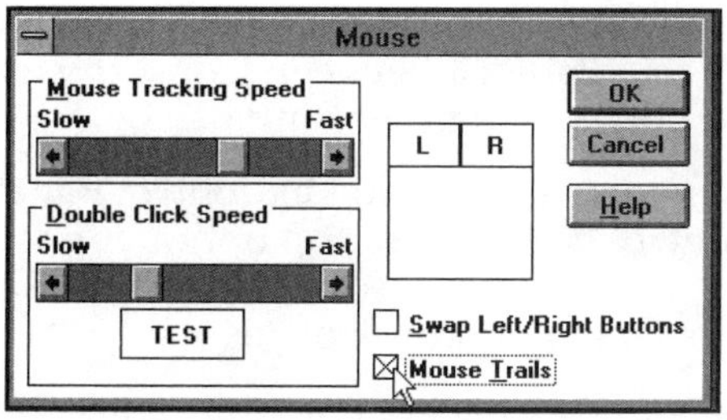

Fig 3.7.

The Mouse dialog box where you configure your pointing device.

1. From Control Panel, open the Mouse dialog box.
2. To change the speed at which the mouse pointer moves across the screen, move the mouse pointer to the Mouse Tracking Speed scroll bar. Click the left arrow to slow the mouse tracking speed or the right arrow to speed mouse tracking, or drag the scroll box to the left or right to adjust the speed.
3. To adjust how quickly you must press a mouse button a second time before Windows recognizes a double-click, move the mouse pointer to the Double Click Speed scroll bar. Click the left arrow for a slower double-click speed or the right arrow for a faster double-click speed, or drag the scroll box to the left or right. This change takes effect immediately. Use the rectangle labeled TEST to try your new double-click speed before returning to Windows.
4. To swap the functions of the left and right mouse buttons, click the Swap Left/Right Buttons check box. This change takes effect immediately. Use the rectangular areas marked L and R to test the function of your mouse buttons before returning to Windows.
5. To enable mouse trails, click the Mouse Trails check box. This change takes effect immediately. You can see mouse trails right away to determine whether they will help you keep track of your mouse pointer. If your video driver does not support mouse trails, the option will be dimmed in the Mouse dialog box.
6. Choose OK to accept your changes and exit the Mouse dialog box.

Changing the Look of Windows Using the Desktop Option

With Control Panel's Desktop option, you can easily customize the look of the Windows background, or desktop, by installing Wallpaper and other patterns, and you can choose an animated screen saver that can be used to password-protect your work. The Desktop option also enables you to specify the distance between icons, the use of multiple lines for lengthy icon titles, and other options.

Although Windows colors are changed in Control Panel's Colors option, the selections in Control Panel's Desktop option are important to making Windows look and run the way you want. The Desktop option enables you to control the following Windows elements:

- Wallpaper and patterns for the Windows desktop
- A screen saver to blank your screen or fill it with animation when Windows is running but not being used
- Icon spacing
- Icon title wrapping
- Cursor blink rate
- Window border width
- The invisible grid used to align windows and icons
- Fast Application Switching

Using Wallpaper and Desktop Patterns

Wallpaper, which is made up of bit-mapped graphics, is a popular way for Windows users to customize the graphical user interface. The Windows desktop is a solid color when Windows is installed, but you can replace the solid color with Wallpaper by using the Desktop Wallpaper option, or you can choose a textured background pattern. Figure 3.8 shows the Desktop dialog box against a background created by a Wallpaper called Arcade, which comes with Windows 3.1.

Using the Windows 3.1 Screen Saver

Windows 3.1 includes a built-in screen saver to reduce the wear on your screen and to password-protect your work from prying eyes. You can configure this screen saver to blank your screen or create moving designs on-screen. The following sections cover the screen saver, including

- How to enable the screen saver
- How to set the time your computer must be idle before the screen saver starts

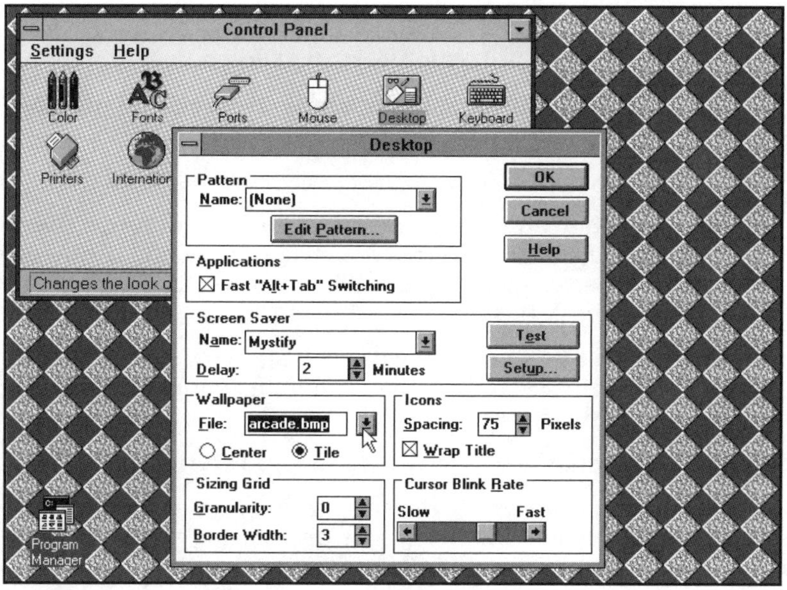

Fig. 3.8.

The Desktop dialog box against a background of Arcade Wallpaper.

- How to choose and test a screen-saver pattern.
- How to set the options in each screen-saver pattern so that the screen saver uses the colors and type of animation you want
- How to password-protect your work using the screen saver

Enabling the Screen Saver

Windows 3.1's screen saver is managed from Control Panel's Desktop option. You can select the screen saver pattern you want to appear on-screen, set the length of time your system must be idle before the screen saver starts, set options for the configurable screen-saver patterns, and password protect your work while you are away.

NOTE The screen saver can operate only if the active application is a Windows program. The screen saver does not work if a DOS program is the foreground application, regardless of whether the DOS program is running full screen or in a window. If you want the screen saver to operate, minimize your active DOS program.

To enable the screen saver, follow these steps:

1. From Control Panel, open the Desktop dialog box.
2. In the Screen Saver area, click the scroll arrow beside the Name list box to open the Name list.
3. Highlight the name of the screen saver you want to use.
4. Click the Test button, making sure that you do not move the mouse on your desk afterward. Your screen will darken and the selected screen-saver pattern will appear. When you want to return to the screen-saver scroll box, move the mouse.
5. Click the Delay box's up or down scroll arrow to increase or decrease, respectively, the number of minutes your computer must be idle before the screen saver appears.
6. Choose OK to enable the screen saver and return to Windows.

When your screen is blanked by the screen saver, you can immediately return to Windows by moving the mouse or pressing any key on your keyboard. If you use the screen saver's password option, however, you must enter your password before the screen blanker will return you to Windows. For more information, see "Setting or Changing the Screen-Saver Password."

If you purchased the Microsoft Entertainment Pack, you can use the screen-saver modules from IdleWild. To use these screen savers, you must place the modules, which have the extension IW, in the same directory as the IWLIB.DLL file. Your Windows subdirectory or Windows System subdirectory is a good place for these files, but you can place them in any directory you want as long as it is on your DOS path.

Choosing Options in a Screen Saver

You can customize some screen-saver patterns. For example, you can change the colors of the pattern, the number of lines the pattern contains, or the text that appears. Because each screen saver is different, the settings you can change depend on the specific screen saver. Only general guidelines on customizing a screen-saver pattern are contained here.

To customize a screen saver, follow these steps:

1. From Control Panel, open the Desktop dialog box.
2. In the Screen Saver area, click the scroll arrow beside the Name list box to open the Name list.

3. Move the highlight to the name of the screen saver you want to use.
4. Click the Setup button to open the Setup dialog box.

   Not all screen savers enable you to make changes. You can customize screen savers that do not display a message box telling you that no settings in the screen-saver module can be customized.

Figure 3.9 shows the Setup dialog box for the Marquee screen saver, which blacks the screen and displays a line of colored type that moves across the screen. The elements of the Marquee Setup dialog box include

- *Text box.* You can replace the text message that comes with Windows with any message you want, such as one that informs fellow workers when you will be returning.
- *Text Example box.* What you type, as well as any editing changes, in the Text box is instantly displayed in the Text Example box.

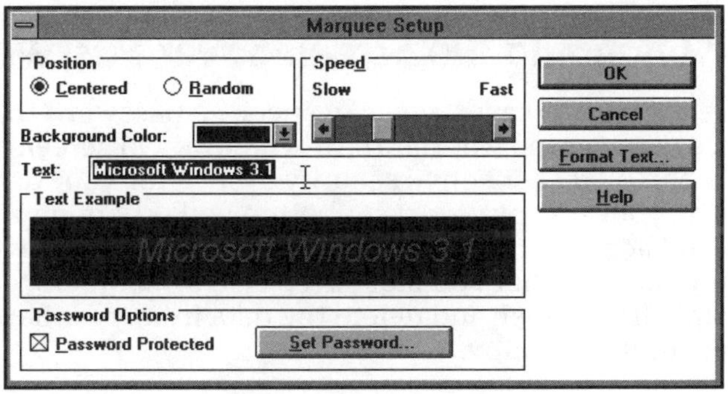

Fig. 3.9.

The Marquee screen saver Setup dialog box.

- *Speed scroll bar.* Set the speed with which the line of type moves across your screen when the screen saver is active. The Text Example box shows the speed the text will move.
- *Position buttons.* Choose whether the line of type will move across the center of your screen each time or appear on various random lines of your screen.
- *Background Color scroll box.* Choose a background color.
- *Password Options area.* Choose Password Protected to require the entry of a password before the screen saver will return Windows to the screen; this option is useful to protect your work from prying eyes. When the Password Protected box is checked, the Set Password button is available for you to enter your password. If the Password Protected box is not checked, the Set Password button is dimmed.

- *Format Text button.* Choosing this button opens the Format Text dialog box shown in figure 3.10. This box enables you to choose the font, font size, and font style of Marquee's line of type, as well as its color and special effects like Strikeout and Underline.

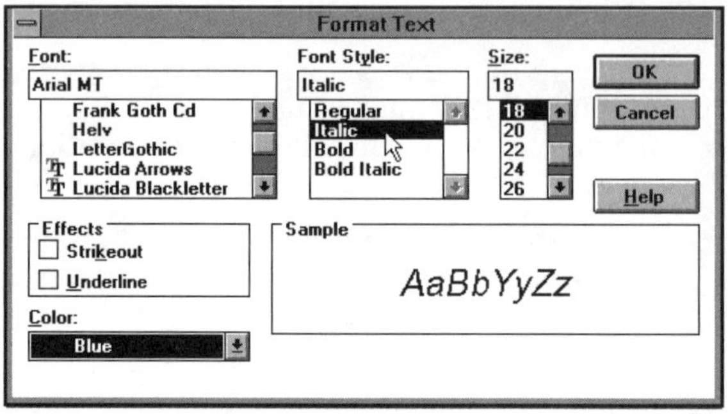

Fig. 3.10.

The Marquee screen saver's Format Text dialog box.

Setting or Changing the Screen-Saver Password

When you use the screen saver, you can specify a password that must be entered before your screen will return to Windows. No screen-saver password is a completely effective security system for your data—merely pressing your computer's reset button and rebooting Windows gives anyone full access to anything on your system. If you have something on your computer that you must keep safe from others, copy that data to a reliable floppy disk and delete the data from your hard disk. And then safeguard the floppy.

The best you can hope the password feature of the Windows screen saver will do is protect your on-screen work from a curious coworker, who sees your computer unattended and wonders what you are working on. If your coworker presses a key or moves the mouse while the password feature is enabled, the screen saver displays a dialog box requesting the password. Remember, too, that this password feature could be a bother as well as a safeguard. You must type the password every time you want to return to Windows from a blanked screen.

To set or change the screen-saver password, follow these steps:

1. From Control Panel, open the Desktop dialog box.
2. In the Screen Saver area, click the scroll arrow beside the Name list box to open the Name list.
3. Move the highlight to the name of the screen saver you want to use.

4. Click the Setup button to open the Setup dialog box.
5. Click the Password Protected check box if it is not checked. The Set Password button is enabled.
6. Click the Set Password button to open the Change Password dialog box.
7. If you are changing your password, type the old password in the Old Password text box.
8. If you are setting your password for the first time, in the New Password text box, type your new password. The password can be up to 20 characters long.
9. In the Retype New Password text box, type your new password again.
10. Choose OK. To return to Windows, choose the OK button in the Setup dialog box and then in the Desktop dialog box.

Disabling the Password Option

Turning on the screen-saver's password option is a quick operation. You can leave the password off most of the day so that you don't have to enter a password every time you are away from your work for a few minutes; then when you need to make a quick trip to, say, the mail room, you can quickly turn on the password function and have some privacy for your work. This section tells how you disable the password option. To disable the password option, follow these steps:

1. From Control Panel, open the Desktop dialog box.
2. In the Screen Saver area, click the scroll arrow beside the Name list box to open the Name list.
3. Highlight the name of the screen saver you want to use.
4. Click the Setup button to open the Setup dialog box.
5. Click the Password Protected check box to clear it. Choose OK. Choose OK again in the Desktop dialog box to return to Windows.

To turn on password protection, follow these same steps and click the Password Protected check box so that the box contains an X.

Wrapping Icon Titles and Changing the Space between Icons

Windows usually leaves adequate space between icons. But if the title for an icon overlaps adjacent icon titles, you can increase the space between icons by using Control Panel's Desktop options. You also can enable multiline icon titles, which make two- or three-word icon title lines narrower by stacking the words.

If you increase the space between icons, the change takes effect for Program Manager icons the next time you use the Arrange Icons command in Program Manager's Window menu or immediately if you select Auto Arrange in Program Manager's Options menu. The change takes effect for minimized program icons the next time you choose the Arrange Icons button in Task List. If you enable multiline icon titles, the icon titles wrap immediately after you close the Desktop dialog box.

When changing the space between icons, keep in mind that Windows measures icon spacing in screen pixels. Adjustments of 10 pixels or more result in a noticeable increase in the space between icons. To change the spacing between icons or enable multiline icon titles, follow these steps:

1. From Control Panel, open the Desktop dialog box.
2. To increase or decrease the space between icons, respectively, click the up or down scroll arrow in the Spacing box in the Icons area, or tab to the Spacing scroll box and type a number.
3. To enable multiline icon titles, click the Wrap Title check box.
4. Choose the Desktop dialog box's OK button to return to Windows.

Adjusting Window Border Width and the Invisible Grid

You use the Desktop dialog box's Sizing Grid area to change two settings that affect how you use windowed programs: the width of the borders that enclose Program Manger, File Manager, and programs when they are running in a window, and the invisible grid that is used to align windows, icons, and other objects in Windows. This section covers making changes to these two settings.

Any changes in the width of window borders affect all windows on your system except dialog boxes—the only window borders that cannot be changed. You might have noticed that the border on a dialog box is different from the border on regular windows. This difference reminds you that dialog boxes cannot be resized and you cannot increase their border width.

The borders of Windows programs and windowed DOS programs are measured in screen pixels on a scale of 1 through 50, with 50 being the thickest. The default window border width is 3. Choosing a size smaller than the default can cause difficulties when you size windows using the mouse.

Adjusting the Cursor Blink Rate

If finding the flashing document cursor on your screen is difficult, particularly on a laptop with an LCD screen, Windows enables you to change the rate at which the cursor blinks. Often, changing the cursor blink rate makes the cursor easier to find on a crowded screen. The cursor is almost like a flashing yellow caution light: the light grabs your attention. Setting the cursor blink rate to an extremely slow speed keeps the cursor on-screen longer, although the cursor also is off-screen longer.

Using Fast Application Switching

Windows' Fast Application Switching option enables you to use a keyboard shortcut (Alt+Tab) to switch quickly between applications. If you activate fast application switching, you can hold down the Alt key and press Tab to display the name of the next application to which Windows will switch. When you reach the name of the application you want, release Alt to switch to that application. If the application is running as an icon, the application is restored. To turn on fast application switching, follow these steps:

1. From Control Panel, open the Desktop dialog box.
2. Click the Fast "Alt+Tab" Switching check box in the Applications area.
3. Choose OK to return to Windows.

Configuring Your Keyboard

Control Panel's Keyboard option enables you to adjust your keyboard's repeat delay and repeat rate. This feature is helpful for users who find that their keyboard responds too slowly when they want repeated characters, or who have problems with characters repeating when they are not wanted. Control Panel's Keyboard dialog box is shown in figure 3.11.

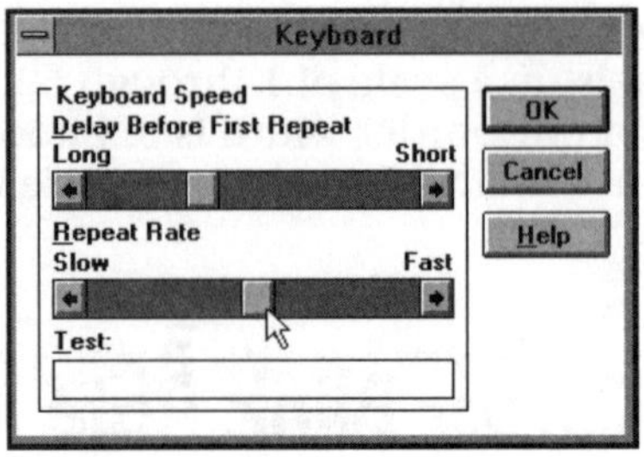

Fig. 3.11.

Control Panel's Keyboard dialog box.

The repeat delay is a measure of how long you must hold down a key before that key is repeated. The repeat rate is a measure of how many times a key repeats if you hold it down.

Using Control Panel To Configure Your Printer

Windows 3.1 offers greatly improved printing capabilities over Windows 3.0. Installing printers and connecting to network printers is now easier and smoother. Print Manager now handles print jobs much more quickly and efficiently, returning control of your computer more quickly. This enhancement enables you to continue work while files are printing. In addition, many printer drivers have been improved.

With Version 3.1, Windows has added support for printing at a baud rate of 19200 on a Hewlett-Packard LaserJet Series II or III printer. With this type of printer, you can increase printing speed dramatically. For more information, see your LaserJet printer documentation.

Control Panel is at the heart of managing printers in Windows 3.1. Control Panel enables you to install a new printer, connect a printer to a port, specify printing options, and connect to a network printer. Depending on your network software, you might be able to use Control Panel to reconnect automatically to all network printers you were previously connected to. Figure 3.12 shows Control Panel's Printers dialog box.

An important new feature of Windows 3.1 is that printer installation and configuration can now be done from Print Manager, as well as from Control Panel. In fact, Print Manager's printer configuration dialog boxes for each printer option are identical to those in Control Panel, so what you learn in these sections also applies to using Print Manager to configure printers.

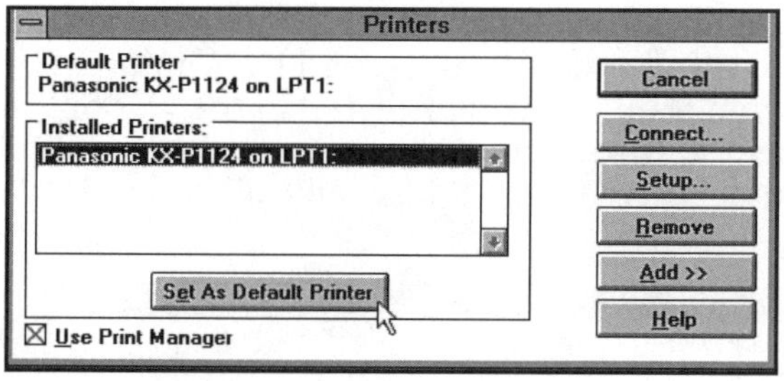

Fig. 3.12.

Control Panel's Printers dialog box.

The Printers dialog box lets you do the following:

- Install one of the more than 200 dot-matrix, laser, and other printers supported by Windows, or install another printer by using a Windows printer driver provided by the printer manufacturer or another source.
- Choose the printer port to be used by each printer.
- Set specific printer options, including printer resolution, paper size, paper source, and landscape or portrait mode.
- Uninstall a printer already installed in Windows.
- Determine which printer will be the default if you have more than one printer installed for use in Windows.
- Receive immediate, context-sensitive help on installing, configuring, or uninstalling a printer.
- Enable Print Manager, which lets you send several print jobs to your printer and continue working while printing continues in the background.

Installing and configuring a printer involves several steps, including choosing the printer in Windows, allowing Windows to copy the correct printer driver from the Windows installation disks (or a disk supplied by the printer manufacturer), and choosing the port. If you need help with functions not covered in this section, the Printers dialog box offers extensive on-line help.

Installing a Printer

1. From Control Panel, open the Printers dialog box.

2. Click the Add button to expand the Printers dialog box so that you can view the list of printers supported by Windows (see fig. 3.13). If the printer you want to install is listed in the List of Printers window, highlight it. If you are using a printer driver supplied by a printer manufacturer, highlight Install Unlisted or Updated Printer.

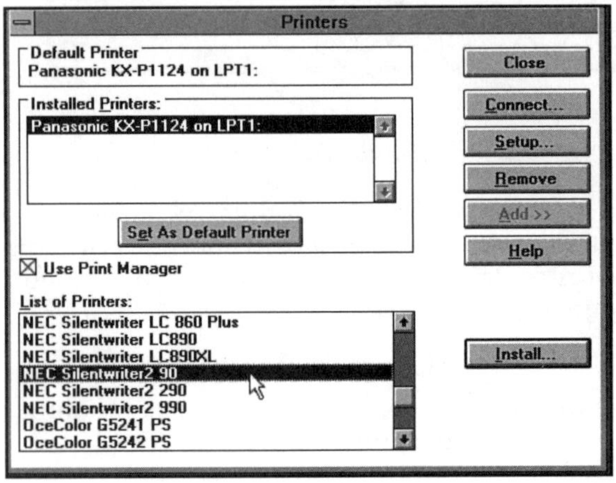

Fig. 3.13.

The List of Printers supported by Windows 3.1.

3. Click Install. Windows prompts you to insert the needed Windows installation disks (or disk from the printer manufacturer). Insert the proper disks into the floppy disk drive, as you are prompted, and press Enter. Windows copies the printer drivers to your system. You must now use Setup to configure the printer.

4. Click Close to exit the Printers dialog box or continue with Setup as described in the next section, "Configuring a Printer."

Configuring a Printer

After you install a printer driver for the printer you want to install in Windows, you still must configure the printer for use in Windows. Printer Setup enables you to choose printer resolution, page size, landscape or portrait page orientation, paper source, and other options. Setup also lets you change the configuration options of an installed printer. To Configure a printer whose printer driver is already installed in Windows, follow these steps:

1. From Control Panel, open the Printers dialog box.

2. In the Installed Printers window, select the printer you want to configure.

3. Click the Setup button. The options in the configuration dialog box differ depending on your printer.
4. Choose paper source, paper size, portrait or landscape orientation, and any other options appropriate to your printer. Some printers have advanced options; you might need to consult your printer documentation.
5. When you have chosen the appropriate options, click OK to return to the Printers dialog box. Click Close to return to Control Panel.

Connecting a Printer

After you install and configure your printer, you must connect the printer to the appropriate port for your system. To connect a printer, follow these steps:

1. From Control Panel, open the Printers dialog box.
2. Click Connect.
3. Select the appropriate LPT or COM port from the Ports scroll list.
4. When you have chosen the proper port, click OK to return to the Printers dialog box. Click Close to return to Control Panel.

Uninstalling a Printer

You use the Remove option from the Printers dialog box to remove a printer from the installed printer list. The printer driver and the fonts used by the printer driver are not removed from disk because they might be used by other installed printers. You can, however, delete the printer driver and fonts from disk using File Manager. To remove a printer, follow these steps:

1. From Control Panel, open the Printers dialog box.
2. In the Installed Printers window of the Printers dialog box, highlight the printer you want to remove.
3. Click Remove. Windows prompts you for confirmation of the operation. Click Yes. The highlighted printer is deleted from the Installed Printers list.
4. Click Close to exit the Printers dialog box.

Choosing a Default Printer

Control Panel enables you to choose a default printer, which is the printer all print jobs are sent to unless you specify otherwise within a certain application. Choosing a default printer speeds printing, so you should choose a default printer unless you use all printers on your system with equal frequency. To choose a default printer, follow these steps:

1. From Control Panel, open the Printers dialog box.
2. In the Installed Printers window of the Printers dialog box, highlight the printer you want to set as the default.
3. Click Set as Default Printer to update your printer configuration.
4. Click Close to exit the Printers dialog box.

Enabling Print Manager

Enabling Print Manager enables you to send several print jobs to your printer and continue work while printing continues in the background. On most systems, Print Manager bypasses MS-DOS to speed printing. You should enable this option unless you have a special reason to use DOS for printing. To enable Print Manager, follow these steps:

1. From Control Panel, open the Printers dialog box.
2. Choose the Use Print Manager check box. The box should contain an X.
3. Click Close to exit the Printers dialog box.

Control Panel now enables you to connect to and disconnect from network printers quickly. Before you can print on a network printer, you must be connected to it. To connect to a network printer, follow these steps:

1. From Control Panel, open the Printers dialog box.
2. Choose the Connect button.
3. Choose the Network button.
4. Enter the network path, port, and any required password. With some networks, you can use the Browse button to choose from all network printers or the Previous button to reconnect to a printer you used previously.

5. Click the Connect button. The Current Printer Connections list adds your new printer.
6. Click the Close button, and then choose the OK button to return to the Printers dialog box
7. Click Close to exit the Printers dialog box.

Disconnecting from a network printer is equally simple using Control Panel. To disconnect from a network printer, follow these steps:

1. From Control Panel, open the Printers dialog box.
2. Click the Connect button to open the Connect dialog box.
3. Click the Network button to open the Current Printer Connections list.
4. Select the printer you want to disconnect from.
5. Click the Disconnect button.
6. Click the Close button, and then choose the OK button to return to the Printers dialog box.
7. Click Close to exit the Printers dialog box.

Choosing International Settings

Control Panel enables you to customize Windows for working in more than 15 different languages—from Danish to Portuguese; use the keyboard layouts, currency symbols, and other options of more than 25 nations—from Australia to Taiwan; and use the date, time and number, formats, measurement systems, and other settings from around the world. Figure 3.14 shows the International dialog box, where these changes are made.

These international settings do not change the language of Windows itself. However, the settings you make are used by all Windows programs and enable you easily to use the proper formats when working in other languages. You can buy versions of Windows in languages other than English. If you are using Windows in English within the United States, you do not need to make any changes to the international settings unless you want to change the date and time format.

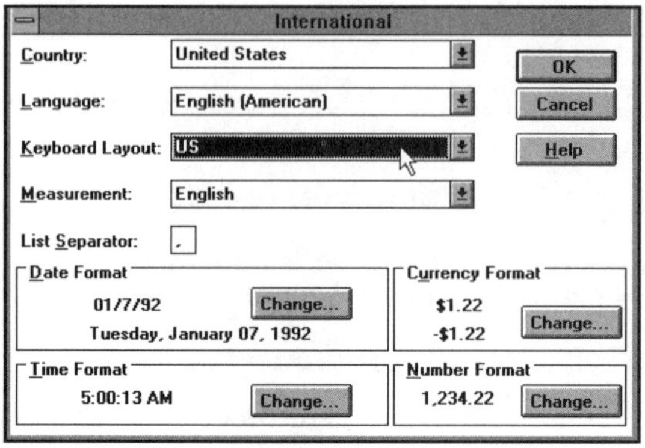

Fig. 3.14.

The International dialog box.

Using the 386 Enhanced Options

Control Panel offers 386 Enhanced mode options when Windows is running in 386 Enhanced mode. These options govern the most advanced capabilities of Windows—the capability to run several different Windows programs at the same time or a mixture of DOS programs and Windows programs, with all these programs continuing to do their work. This capability is called *multitasking*.

To understand multitasking, think of four programs running at the same time on a single computer. All four continue to operate, one perhaps recalculating a spreadsheet and another downloading a file from an electronic bulletin board system. But you can be actually working in only one of these programs at a time. The program in which you are working is running in the *foreground*. The programs that continue to do their work without your active participation are running in the *background*.

Choosing the 386 Enhanced icon enables you to choose how Windows and DOS programs compete for peripheral devices and how much of the computer's resources are allocated to Windows programs when DOS programs also are running. This option also determines how Windows uses *virtual memory*, a scheme in which Windows uses available hard disk space as if it were system RAM, enabling you to multitask a greater number of programs than your system resources alone permit. Windows' virtual memory swapping scheme also speeds Windows operation. Figure 3.15 shows the 386 Enhanced dialog box.

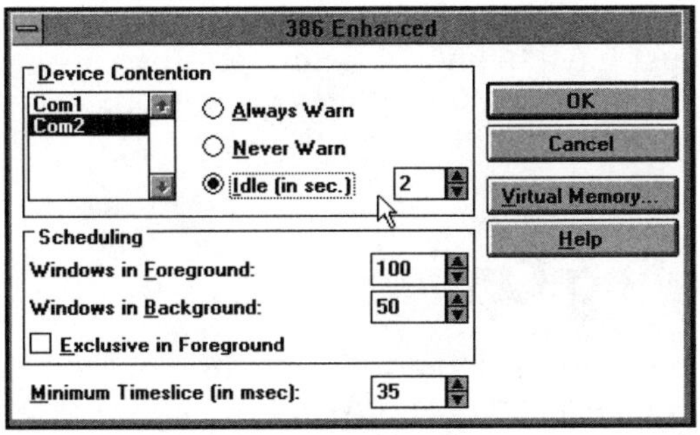

Fig. 3.15.

The 386 Enhanced dialog box.

This section covers several settings that are important when Windows is running in 386 Enhanced mode. These settings are the following:

- *Device Contention* determines how Windows handles the situation when two different programs attempt to access the same COM port or LPT port at the same time.
- *Scheduling* determines the priority Windows gives Windows programs when DOS programs are running at the same time.
- *Minimum Timeslice* determines the smallest amount of the processor's time that is given to a program to do its work before Windows switches to another program.
- *Virtual Memory* governs how Windows uses swapfiles, which it uses to simulate system RAM.

Setting Device Contention Options

The Device Contention options determine how Windows deals with attempts by various programs to access a single port at the same time. If different programs were permitted to access ports at the same time, none of the devices would perform properly. A serial mouse could interrupt a modem, or a scanner could interrupt a fax board. Your choices for Device Contention settings are

- *Always Warn.* If you choose this setting, Windows always warns you when a program attempts to access a port that is already in use. Windows prompts you to choose the program to gain access to the port.
- *Never Warn.* If you choose this setting, Windows never warns you if a program attempts to access a port that is already in use. Use this setting only if you are sure that only one program will use a particular COM port.

- *Idle (in sec.)*. This setting determines the number of seconds that a COM port must have been idle before another program can use that port without Windows' displaying a warning message. Choose a number between 1 and 999 seconds.

The Scheduling Option

The choices you make in the Scheduling section of the 386 Enhanced dialog box affect the performance of Windows and DOS programs when Windows is multitasking. The challenge when choosing Scheduling settings is to balance the needs of Windows programs you are likely to be running at the same time as DOS programs. The Scheduling defaults are adequate for the way most people use Windows.

Virtual Memory Settings

Windows can use either of two swapping schemes to create virtual memory on your system. If you have enough available hard disk space, you can create a permanent swapfile for exclusive use by Windows. This scheme gives Windows the fastest possible access to the hard disk and enables Windows to multitask DOS programs much more quickly and smoothly. The major drawback of this swapping method is that Windows reserves permanent swapfile space for its own use, even when you are not running Windows. If you have limited hard disk space and do not want to allocate any of it permanently to Windows for swapping, Windows can create temporary swapfiles.

During Windows installation, if possible, Setup creates a permanent swapfile based on the type and amount of available space on your hard disk. If Setup cannot create a permanent swapfile, Windows creates a temporary swapfile whenever you start Windows in 386 Enhanced mode.

You use the Virtual Memory option in the 386 Enhanced dialog box to view the current swapping settings used by Windows and to create a permanent swapfile. The Virtual Memory option is new to Control Panel. To create a permanent swapfile in Windows 3.0, you needed to run a separate utility program, SWAPFILE.EXE, from Windows in Real mode.

Before you create a permanent swapfile for Windows, you should use a disk optimization program, like Optune, to defragment your files and move them all to one area of your hard disk. This disk optimization helps Windows locate an appropriate area for the permanent swapfile.

To determine the type of swapfile being used by Windows, follow these steps:

1. From Control Panel, open the 386 Enhanced dialog box.
2. Click the Virtual Memory button. The Virtual Memory dialog box, shown in figure 3.16, displays the type of swapfile currently in use and its size and location.

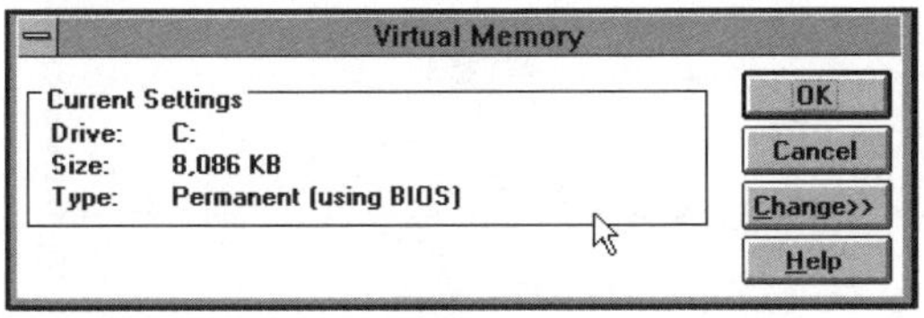

Fig. 3.16.

The Virtual Memory dialog box displays current settings.

3. When you finish viewing your swapfile settings, choose OK to return to Windows.

NOTE

A permanent swapfile actually consists of two files: 386SPART.PAR and SPART.PAR. 386SPART.PAR is a hidden file usually located in the root directory of your boot drive. SPART.PAR is a read-only file located in your Windows directory. Do not delete, move, or rename these files.

To create or change the size of a permanent or temporary swapfile, follow these steps:

1. From Control Panel, open the 386 Enhanced dialog box.
2. Click the Virtual Memory button. The Virtual Memory dialog box opens.
3. Click the Change button to expand the Virtual Memory dialog box. Figure 3.17 shows the expanded Virtual Memory dialog box used to create a swapfile.
4. Click the Drive list in the New Settings area to open the scroll box, and choose the drive where you want to locate the swapfile.
5. Click the Type list in the New Settings area, and choose the type of swapfile you want to use. If you choose None, swapping will not be used the next time you start Windows.
6. Click the New Size box, and type the size in kilobytes for the new swapfile, or press Enter to accept the size recommended by Windows.
7. Choose OK to create the swapfile and return to Windows.

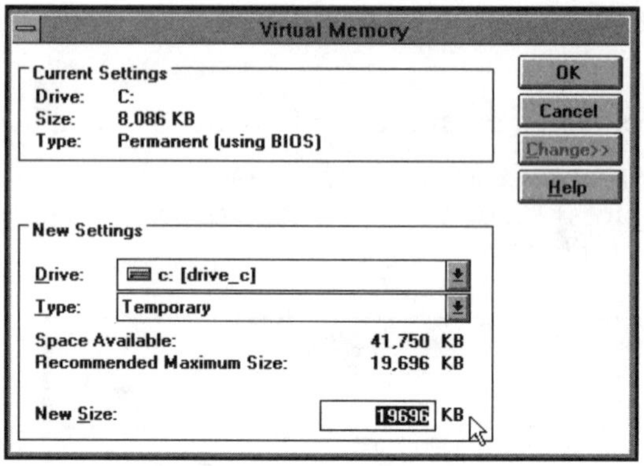

Fig. 3.17.

The expanded Virtual Memory dialog box used to set swapfile options.

Working with Drivers

Often when you add a new device to your computer, a driver is required to enable that device to communicate with Windows. These drivers are often needed with multimedia devices, such as sound cards or video disc players, or pens or pointing devices. Your device will probably include a disk containing the appropriate Windows device driver, although drivers for some devices are included on the Windows installation disks. If necessary, contact the manufacturer of a device about providing a driver. To install a new driver in Windows, follow these steps:

1. From Control Panel, open the Drivers dialog box, which displays a list of drivers already installed.
2. Click the Add button to open the Add dialog box. The Add dialog box lists drivers you can install.
3. Choose the driver you want to install, or if your driver is not listed, choose Unlisted or Updated Driver.
4. The Install Driver dialog box appears, prompting you to insert a disk that contains the driver file. Insert the diskette containing the driver into your floppy disk drive; if the driver is located on your hard drive, type the drive and path name for the driver location but not the driver file name.
5. Choose OK. A setup dialog box appears for the driver if it requires additional settings to work with Windows. The dialog box's Help button displays the information needed to configure the driver.
6. When required drivers have been configured, exit and restart Windows to enable the changes.

Windows does not enable you to install an updated version of a driver that is already installed on your system until you remove the old driver. If you attempt to install the new driver without removing the old one, Windows displays an error message. To remove a driver, follow these steps:

1. From Control Panel, open the Drivers dialog box, which displays a list of drivers already installed.
2. Click the driver you want to remove. A dialog box appears prompting you to confirm the deletion. Click the confirmation button or press Enter.
3. You must exit and restart Windows for the changes to take effect. A dialog box prompts you to do so. If you want to restart Windows immediately, click the confirmation button.

After a driver is installed, you might need to configure it for use with Windows. You can change any driver setting. To change driver settings, follow these steps:

1. From Control Panel, open the Drivers dialog box, which displays a list of drivers already installed.
2. Click the driver you want to configure. If you choose a driver that cannot be configured, the Setup button is dimmed.
3. Click the Setup button. The Setup dialog box appears. Settings in this dialog box vary according to the driver you are configuring.
4. Set the options as described in your device's manual.
5. Click the OK button. You might need to reboot Windows before changes take effect. If so, a dialog box prompts you to restart Windows. To have the new settings take effect immediately, choose the Restart Now button.

For more information about drivers, see Chapter 10.

Using Control Panel To Manage Sound

Control Panel provides several new capabilities to control how Windows works with sound. These features range from warning beeps and other system sounds played through your computer's small speaker to sophisticated sound boards and synthesizers. With the new Windows sound support, you can perform simple sound tasks, such as choosing sounds to play when you start or quit Windows, as well as more sophisticated tasks, such as recording voice annotations to include in a document.

To use sound in Windows, you must already have installed your Multimedia Personal Computer (MPC) compatible sound board or Musical Instrumental Digital Interface (MIDI) device and the drivers that control them. Installing and configuring drivers is covered in the preceding section of this chapter.

The sounds you can assign to system events are stored in files that have the WAV extension. To assign a sound to a system event, follow these steps:

1. From Control Panel, open the Sound dialog box, which is shown in figure 3.18.

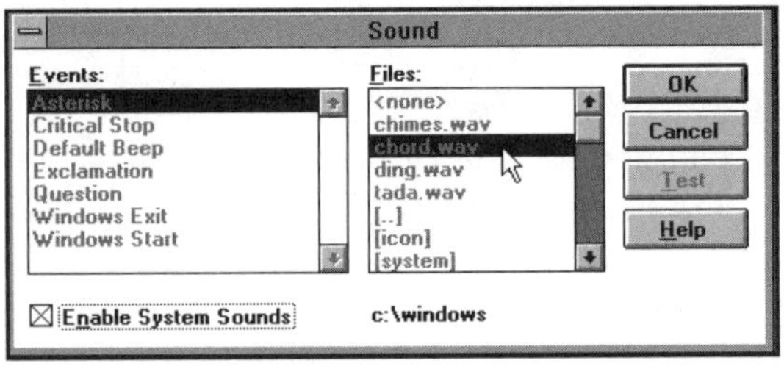

Fig. 3.18.

The Sound dialog box.

2. In the Sound dialog box Events list, choose the system event to which you want to assign a sound.
3. In Sound dialog box Files list, choose the sound file you want to assign to the system event. If you do not want to assign a sound to the event, choose None.
4. Test the sound by clicking the Test button.
5. When you are satisfied with your choice, choose OK.

For more information, see Chapter 9.

T I P If you want to turn off all system sounds, such as the warning beep used when you perform an action Windows doesn't recognize, clear the Enable System Sounds check box.

Choosing Network Options

If you configured Windows to run on a network when you ran Setup and if the network was running when you booted Windows, the Control Panel window includes a Network icon. When you choose the Network icon, Windows opens a dialog box specific to your network. You receive information about your network, and you can change certain settings for your network. On many networks, this dialog box enables you to perform these tasks:

- Sign on and off the network
- Change your user ID and password
- Send messages to other network users
- Restore network connections when you start Windows

For information about network tasks you can perform from this dialog box, see your network documentation and on-line Help (if available) in the dialog box.

Summary

In this chapter, you learned about the important changes in Control Panel for customizing Windows 3.1, including changing colors, managing fonts, using Windows' new COM port capabilities, choosing new mouse options, and changing the look of Windows using the Desktop option. You also learned about using Control Panel to manage printers, setting 386 Enhanced options including virtual memory, working with drivers, managing sounds, and choosing certain network options.

4

CHAPTER

Using Program Manager

The first time you see the Windows 3.1 Program Manager, you will immediately notice some changes from the Windows 3.0 Program Manager. Brightly colored icons appear everywhere. Gone is the plain DOS application icon. More important, Program Manager works faster, enables you to arrange windows more directly, and starts according to your needs. Major improvements include the following:

- Windows 3.1 provides a StartUp group, where you can customize the way you want Windows to start. You can specify the programs to be opened, and each opens upon startup either running in a full screen or minimized as an icon.
- You can use the mouse to drag and drop program icons from one window to another. You can use drag and drop to move or copy items from File Manager to Program Manager.
- Icons are available for DOS applications, including a selection of full-color icons for many program types.
- Help buttons are available in many dialog boxes to provide immediate context-sensitive help. These same Help buttons appear in dialog boxes in other Windows applications, such as Setup, Print Manager, PIF Editor, and Control Panel.
- A reorganized Help facility includes an on-line tutorial where you can practice your mouse moves and learn Windows terminology.

- Program Manager uses less system memory, so you can create more groups than you create with earlier versions of Windows. You might even notice the increased overall speed of Windows 3.1 and the faster screen rewrite as you use Program Manager.

Operating Program Manager

Figure 4.1 shows the various elements of the Program Manager window. Program Manager is the operations center for all applications in Windows and consists of three unique elements: program group windows, group icons, and program item icons.

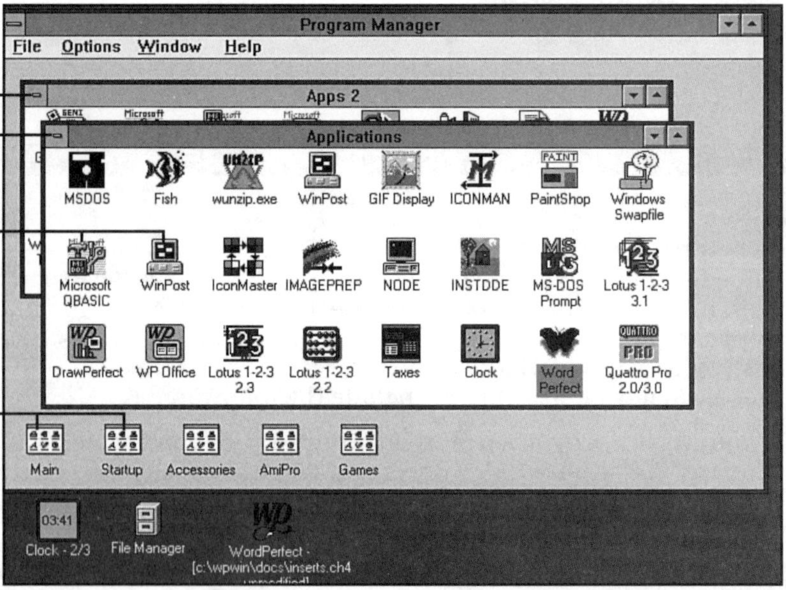

Fig. 4.1.

The Program Manager window.

- *Program group windows.* Program group windows display icons that represent applications you have installed and documents you have created. Several program group windows are created automatically when you install Windows. You can create additional windows that contain related or similar programs and documents. If you use only a few applications, you might only need one or two program group windows. You can give the windows unique names to describe their contents.

- *Group icons.* To better organize your screen, your can minimize an inactive program group window to a group icon. Group icons are displayed along the bottom of the Program Manager window. You can move a group icon to another location in the Program Manager window.

- *Program item icons.* These icons represent programs and documents in Program Manager. If you minimize a program that is running, its icon appears below the Program Manager window along with the name of the active document, and you can move them to another location on-screen.

The familiar Windows groups—Main, Accessories, Applications, and Games—can actually be named anything you want; you can create additional group windows, and you can place applications in any group window. The new StartUp group, however, serves a special function.

Using a StartUp Group

Applications placed in the StartUp group start automatically when Windows is loaded. You add or change applications in this group using the New or Properties commands from the File menu; both of these commands are covered in the section "Customizing Groups and Applications" later in this chapter.

Depending on how each application is configured, placing applications in the StartUp group has the same effect as including each application in the `load=` or `run=` line of the WIN.INI file. Applications can be started and then minimized or left running full-screen. Figure 4.2 shows a StartUp group that contains several Windows applications. Figure 4.3 shows how the screen would look if you started Windows using this StartUp group.

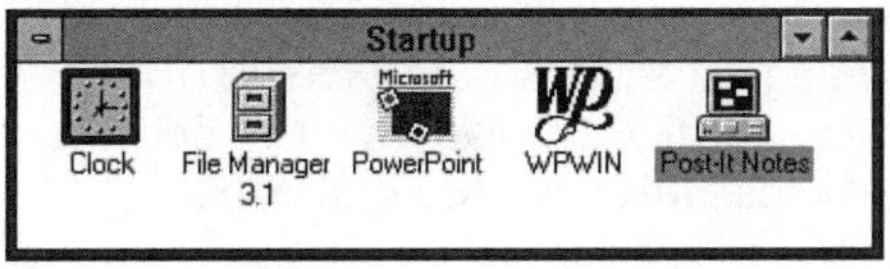

Fig. 4.2.

A StartUp group featuring Windows applications.

The StartUp group is created automatically when you install Windows 3.1. You can add, arrange, and configure applications to customize the group for your needs. If you have deleted this group, you can create a new one. Simply name the new group StartUp, and Windows handles the rest.

Include your frequently used utilities in the StartUp group. If you intend to run Program Manager minimized, you might want to include File Manager, Calculator, and Clock in the StartUp group. Minimizing Program Manager is discussed in the section "Options Commands" later in this chapter.

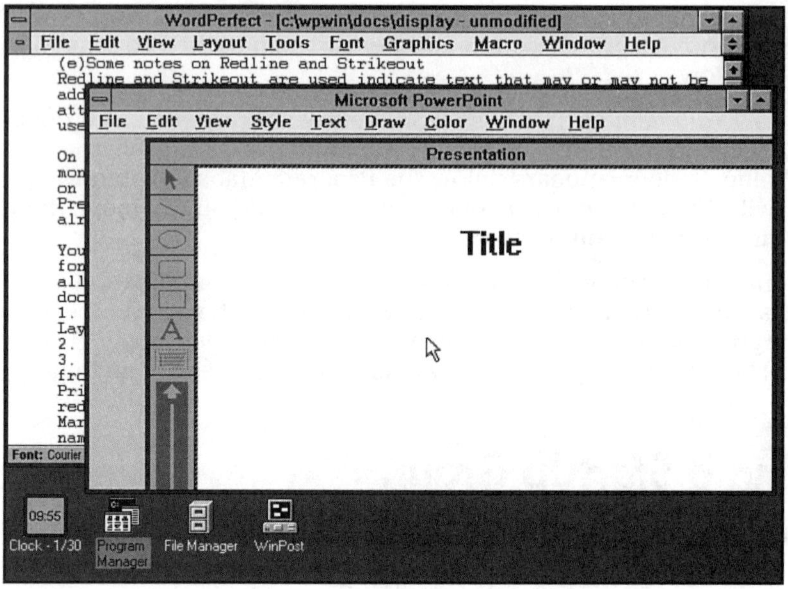

Fig. 4.3.

Applications in the StartUp group open when Windows is booted up.

You can include any program in the StartUp group; the programs then start in the order you placed their icons in the StartUp window. You can include a program with a document or just include the document, provided you have already established the necessary association. (For more information about creating document associations, see Chapter 5.)

A variety of options enable you to configure the StartUp group to meet your needs. You can include a program in as many groups as you want, and the properties that you set for a program or document in one window only apply when the program or document is started from that window. You set these properties using the Properties command from the File menu. (For more information, see the section "Customizing Groups and Applications" later in this chapter.)

In addition to the options that are available from the Properties command, you can use the application PIF file to fine-tune how the document or program starts up.

Using Drag and Drop

Application icons can be installed, moved, or copied into group windows by using the mouse to drag the icon to a new window and then "drop" the icon into the new location. "Drag and drop" is available as an alternative to the New, Copy, and Move commands from the File menu, and it bypasses the dialog boxes available in these menus.

To drag and drop an application icon to a new group window, follow these steps:

1. Point to the icon with the mouse pointer.
2. Hold down the left mouse button. The application icon disappears, and the mouse pointer becomes a black-and-white copy of the icon.
3. Drag the icon copy to the new window and release the mouse button. The original icon now appears in the new window.

The behavior of the mouse pointer is the same as when you move group icons by choosing Move from the group's Control menu. As you move the icon around the screen, the icon changes to the international No symbol (a circle split by a diagonal line) when you cross a portion of the screen where the icon cannot be installed.

To copy an application icon to a new group, follow the same steps, except hold down the Control key while you drag the icon, releasing first the mouse button and then the Control key to drop the icon. When you are copying, the icon remains in its original location while the black-and-white copy of the icon moves to the new group window.

If you change your mind while copying an icon using the drag and drop method, you can cancel the operation by releasing the Control key before releasing the mouse button. Another way to cancel is to move the replica to an area where the icon changes to the international No symbol, and then drop the icon. If you try to return the replica to its original position and superimpose the replica on the original icon, Windows adds another copy of the application to the original group when you drop the replica. If this situation occurs, delete the additional program item by selecting it and choosing Delete from the File menu.

You can add an application to a program group while the group is minimized to an icon, provided its icon is displayed on-screen. Drag the icon replica until it is directly over the group icon, and then drop the icon replica.

You can install a new application in a program group by dragging the application's EXE file from File Manager. You can associate a document with this application by dragging the application's EXE file and the document file from File Manager, even if the files are located in different directories. Windows handles the path statements necessary to make this technique work. You can install just the associated document from File Manager in the same manner. For more information on these operations, see Chapter 5.

Using the Menu Bar

The Program Manager menu bar in Version 3.1 includes several changes from Version 3.0 (again see figure 4.1). You can access a number of commands on the menu bar by using shortcut keys. Saving your arrangement of windows when you exit is now a menu bar option rather than part of the Exit Windows dialog box. And the options available in Help reflect the major rearrangement in the Help program.

The features available using the File, Options, and Windows commands are reviewed in the next sections. Later sections discuss the Help commands and the new tutorials.

File Commands

Table 4.1 lists the commands, and their keyboard shortcuts, available from the File menu.

Table 4.1 File Menu Commands and Shortcut Keys

Command	Shortcut	Operation
New		Creates a new group window or installs an application in a group window.
Open	Enter	Starts an application that has been installed in a group or opens a document associated with an application.
Move	F7	Moves an application to another group.
Copy	F8	Copies an application to another group.
Delete	Del	Deletes a group window or an application.
Properties	Alt-Enter	Changes the way an application is set up to run after it is started, or changes the program icon. The options available in Properties are discussed later in this chapter.
Run		Starts an application, even if it is not installed in Windows.
Exit		Exits the Windows program.

Options Commands

Table 4.2 lists the menu commands available under the Options menu. These commands have no available shortcuts.

Table 4.2 Option Menu Commands

Command	Operation
Auto Arrange	Automatically arranges program and document icons when group windows are resized or icons are moved from window to window.
Minimize on Use	Minimizes Program Manager to an icon whenever another application is run.
Save Setting on Exit	Saves changes from session to session regarding window size and placement, which windows are open, and so on.

In the Options menu, you can still choose to have Windows arrange icons in a group window automatically as you move them from group to group, move them within a group, or resize a group window. Choose Auto Arrange so that a check mark appears by the command. This feature is handy if you are new to using a mouse. You need practice for your double-clicks to open programs rather than just smear icons around the screen. Using Auto Arrange ensures that the icon snaps back into its place if it was moved slightly out of line. This option does not prevent the rearrangement of icons. Choose Auto Arrange again when you want to turn off this feature.

TIP

You can change the horizontal spacing of the icons and the double-click speed of your mouse in Control Panel. For more information, see Chapter 3.

After you tailor the features of Windows so that the utilities and programs you need are at your "mousetips," you might find that you rarely need to access Program Manager. To display Program Manager as a minimized icon when you load Windows, activate Minimize on Use from the Options menu. Then just double-click Program Manager's icon to display the contents of Program Manager. Choose Minimize on Use again to have Program Manager start in a window the next time you start Windows.

After all your windows are sized and placed exactly as you want and your icons are lined up in the order you like, you can save this arrangement by choosing Save Settings on Exit from the Options menu. After you have saved a satisfying layout of windows, check the layout carefully when you next reboot. If the layout works as you want, choose Save Settings on Exit again so that any temporary adjustments you make later will not be saved the next time you exit.

TIP To rearrange the order of the group icons at the bottom of the Program Manager window, simply drag them into place. Then choose Save Settings on Exit from the Options menu.

If you create a new group and want its icon included at the bottom of the Program Manager window, minimize the group's icon, click it, and choose Save Settings on Exit from the Options menu.

If you are an experienced user of Windows, the relocation of Save Settings on Exit will require you to establish new work habits. When this command was in the Exit Windows dialog box, thinking about changes and deciding whether to retain them were part of the process of exiting. With Windows 3.1, you need to choose Save Settings on Exit as soon as you change the arrangement of groups and icons. Fortunately, most changes—such as changes to group and program properties, changes to PIF files, and settings specified in the Setup program—are saved using other methods.

Window Commands

Table 4.3 lists the commands, and their keyboard shortcuts, available from the Window menu.

Group windows are arranged rather haphazardly within the Program Manager window. Windows 3.1 offers you several ways to organize the windows' display. The Cascade command on the Window menu displays the title bar of each window in the group. The Tile command displays the group windows side-by-side like floor tiles.

Arrange Icons enables you to shuffle icons within and between group windows, experimenting with arrangements without regard for neatness. Choose Arrange Icons from the Window menu to have the icons realigned in evenly spaced rows and columns. To realign the group windows, make Program Manager the active window, and then choose Arrange Icons again.

Table 4.3 Window Menu Commands and Shortcut Keys

Command	Shortcut	Operation
Cascade	Shift-F4	Arranges open program group windows in a cascading stack so that the title bar of each is visible.
Tile	Shift-F5	Arranges open program group windows in a side-by-side pattern.
Arrange Icons		Temporarily rearranges icons so that all are returned to evenly spaced rows and columns.
1 Main, and so on		Makes the chosen program group active.

The Windows menu also contains a numbered list of your group windows. You can maximize a group window by choosing the group. A check mark appears by the active group window.

Customizing Groups and Applications

Whether you are installing a program in Windows for the first time using New from the File menu or fine-tuning the way a program runs by using Properties from the same menu, Windows presents the same Program Item Properties dialog box, shown in figure 4.4, for you to fill in.

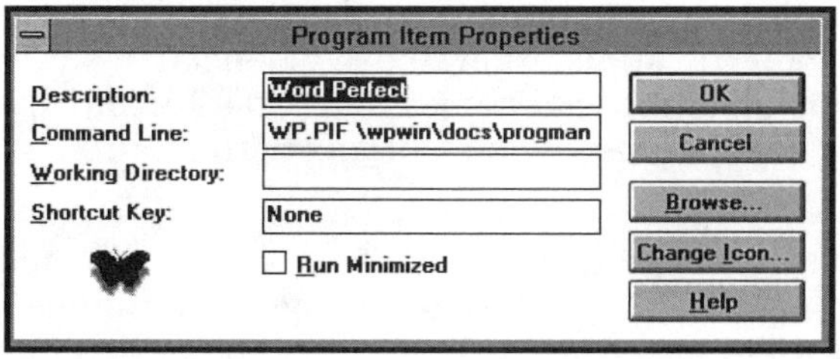

Fig. 4.4.

The Program Item Properties dialog box.

The Description is the title that appears under the program icon. Use the Description text box to shorten names when they overlap in the group window or to specify version numbers when you have several versions of a program installed. Windows names the program for you if you leave this item blank.

TIP You can also open the Program Items Properties box for a new application by holding down the Alt key and double-clicking in a blank area of the appropriate group window. To open the Program Item Properties box for an existing application, highlight the title under the program icon and press Alt-Enter.

TIP If you prefer, you can ask Windows to rearrange the way the titles are placed under program icons using Wrap Title in the Icons section of Control Panel's Desktop. For more information, see Chapter 3.

Use the Command Line text box to specify how Windows should start the application. You can type the PIF file name or the EXE (or COM) file name, insert a space, and then type the path name for a document you want the program to retrieve automatically. If the document is in the same directory as the specified EXE file, you can type just the file name. If you use the PIF file in the Windows directory or have a document subdirectory in your program directory, include the full path to the document. Provide the path name for the EXE file if its directory is not in your path.

Another option is to specify a batch file to start the program. For example, Microsoft Word uses the directory where the program was started as the default document directory. Incorporate this start-up configuration of changing to the appropriate directory into a batch file. Substitute batch files for the Windows PIF file to start other applications, such as the DOS prompt.

In the Working Directory text box, type the full path for the document directory you want the application to use when saving and retrieving files. You can install additional copies of a program and specify a different working directory to use when working with multiple document directories.

The Shortcut Key text box enables you to reserve a shortcut key combination to switch directly to the program when it is running. Hold down the Control key to display the `Ctrl+Alt+` combination and type a letter or number to end the sequence, or hold down the Shift key to display `Ctrl+Shift+Alt+` and type the desired letter or number. Hold down the Control or Shift key while you press the number or letter key else the option will return to `None`.

If you want the program to be minimized to an icon when you start it, activate Run Minimized. You especially will want to use this option for many of the applications you include in the StartUp group.

The Cancel button enables you to exit without making any changes. When you provide incorrect information for the Command Line text box or the Change Icon option, you are notified of the error, but you can still choose OK to exit the box. If you choose OK, you probably cannot start the application until you correct the error. If the Program Item Properties setting worked originally, choose the Cancel button to keep the original setup in effect and exit the box. You will be able to access the application while you troubleshoot the changes you want to make.

To install or change an icon, choose the Change Icon button. Even if the file you specified in the Command Line text box contains an icon, you need to open the Change Icon dialog box to install the icon. After you choose an icon, it appears in the lower left corner of the Program Items Properties dialog box.

The Help button accesses context-sensitive help that includes buttons to obtain glossary explanations of the text boxes and changing icons.

The Browse button is available to help you fill in the Command Line text box. The Browse dialog box shown in figure 4.5 is decidedly more graphical, using opened and closed file folders to indicate the directory levels and floppy, and using regular drive faces in the Drives pull-down menu. A text box provides the list of file extensions used initially. When you access the Browse dialog box from the Program Item Properties dialog box, the extensions provided are EXE, COM, PIF, and BAT. Use the List Files of Type pull-down menu to change this text box entry to *.* for all files.

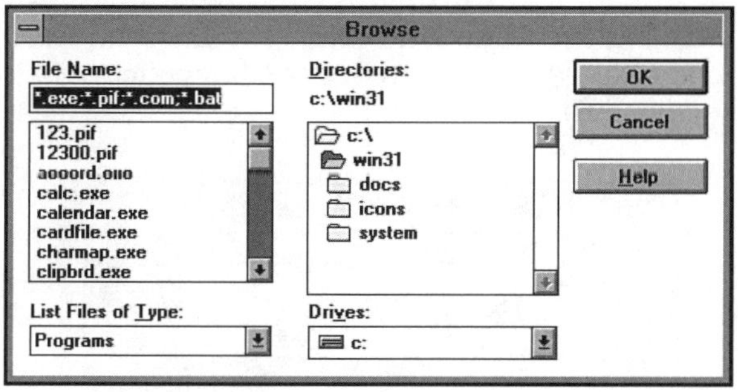

Fig. 4.5.

The Browse dialog box when opened from the Program Item Properties box.

Changing Properties Versus Using PIFs

PIF files provide a wide variety of configuration options, which are discussed in detail in Chapter 8. Anything specified in the PIF file, such as the shortcut key, is subordinate to conflicting information provided in the Program Items Properties dialog box. Further, the PIF file can be used to start one configuration of the program, and Properties can specify a different start-up mode.

Using PIFs and the Properties option from the File menu can be useful when you are setting up the StartUp group. DOS programs that are loaded but not minimized at startup might best be windowed so that several are visible on-screen. The Applications group version can then start another copy full-screen, if you need it.

You cannot specify a document after the program name in a PIF file. You can, however, associate a document with the program by using File Manager (see Chapter 5).

Each time you include a program in another group window, you can customize the program's properties. To set up customized PIF files, you need to create a separate PIF file for each variation.

Changing Icons

Finding, creating, and editing icons to use with applications has become a major source of Windows entertainment for many users. Almost every bulletin board service (BBS) has a directory of these icons. Some collections contain as many as 1,700 icons designed by users. Pursuing this sideline in Windows 3.1 is now easier than ever.

The basic steps for installing an icon are as follows:

1. From the File menu, choose New or Properties.
2. Choose Program Item or Properties to open the Program Item Properties box. Fill in the Command Line text box with the file name; then choose Change Icon to open the Change Icon dialog box shown (see fig. 4.6).

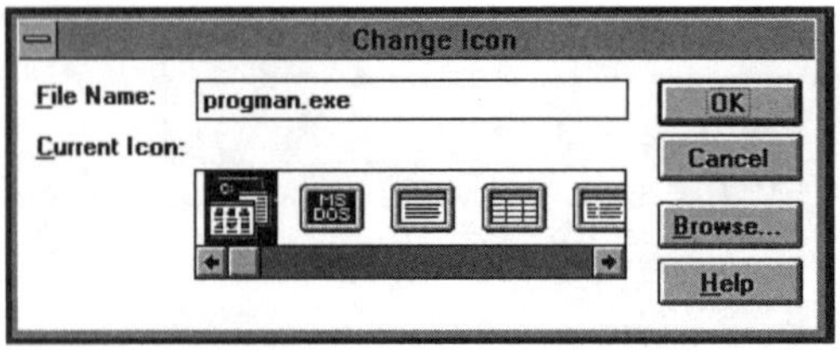

Fig. 4.6.

The Change Icon dialog box.

3. To search for possible icon files, choose the Browse button. The familiar Browse dialog box appears with the suggested selection of files being *.ICO, *.EXE, and *.DLL (see fig. 4.7).

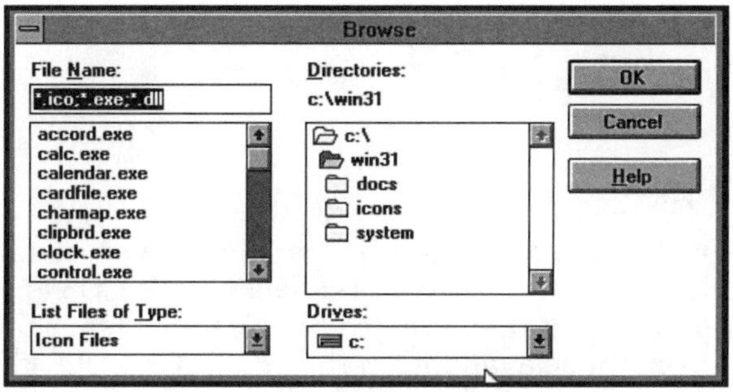

Fig. 4.7.

The Browse box now contains a list of possible icon sources.

If you are changing an icon and do not find one you like, choose Cancel to exit the Change Icon dialog box. If you need assistance, choose the Help button.

4. Choose OK or press Enter to add a selected icon to the program item.

EXE File Icons

Every Windows application includes an icon in the program EXE file. In fact, some EXE files include several icons, and all are displayed in the Current Icon display box (again see fig. 4.6). Highlight the icon you want to use and choose OK twice.

Some programs have icons in several EXE files, such as in their Install, Spell, License Registration, Thesaurus, and Macro Recorder subprograms. You can use File Manager at any time to place EXE files in a group window in order to see what icons are available. Check the EXE files on the original program floppy disks also. The AmiPro group window in figure 4.8 shows the icons for some of the EXE files included on the program disks. Refer to Chapter 5 for information on using File Manager.

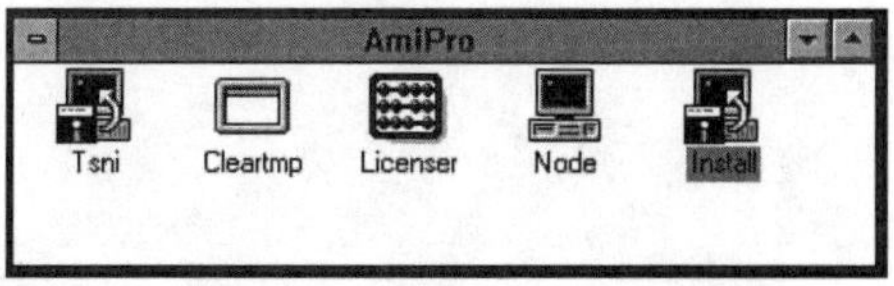

Fig. 4.8.

A selection of icons from EXE files on the AmiPro program disks.

When you find an icon you want to use, include the file EXE name in the File Name text box of the Change Icon dialog box and choose OK or just double-click the icon.

The icon from the EXE file appears in the lower left corner of the Program Item Properties box. Choose OK to finish arranging icons. You can use the icon from an unrelated application by specifying the icon in the Change Icon dialog box.

PIF File Icons

PIF files for DOS applications might be installed as you install programs in Windows 3.1. When Setup recognizes and installs DOS applications in the Applications group, it then creates PIF files for them and assigns icons to them from those available in the MORICONS.DLL file or the PROGMAN.EXE file. You can also use the icons from these files for applications you manually install or in place of the icons the programs have in their files.

Many of the icons that Windows uses in PIF files are included in the PROGMAN.EXE file. You can also use icons from PROGMAN.EXE for other applications.

PROGMAN.EXE Icons

If the application EXE or PIF file you have named does not contain an icon, a box appears to notify you that no icon is available in that file and that you can choose an icon from PROGMAN.EXE. Your only choice is OK. The Change Icon dialog box appears, and the PROGMAN.EXE icons are displayed in the Current Icon box. Figure 4.9 shows some of the icons from PROGMAN.EXE.

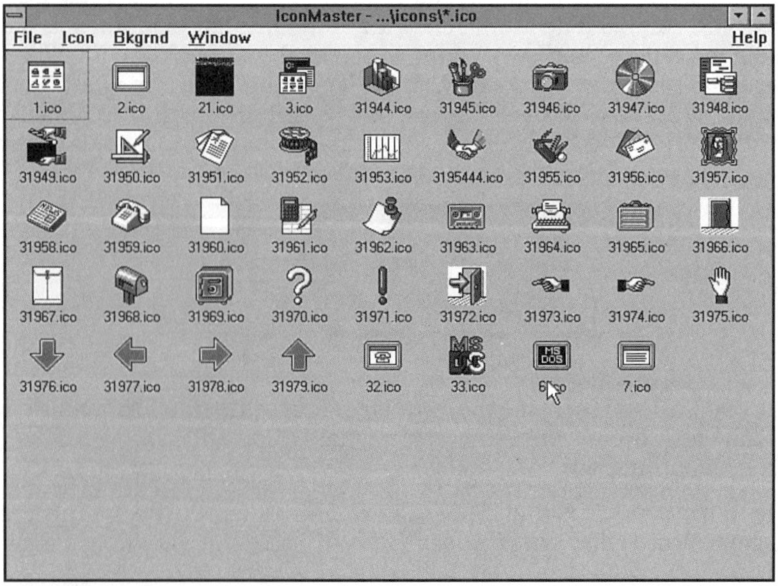

Fig. 4.9.

Some of the icons included in PROGMAN.EXE.

When you want to change an icon, you can choose one from PROGMAN.EXE. Type *PROGMAN.EXE* in the File Name text box of the Change Icon dialog box (again see fig. 4.6), and then choose OK to retrieve the icons into the display box. Scroll through the icons in the Current Icon display. When you find one you want to use, make sure that it is highlighted and then choose OK twice.

Custom Icons

If you have individual icon files (identified by the extension ICO), type the icon file name in the File Name text box of the Change Icon dialog box (again see fig. 4.6). When you first choose OK, the icon appears in the display box. If this icon is the one you want to use, choose OK twice.

Icon Libraries

Included with Windows 3.1 is a library of more than 100 icons in a DLL file named MORICONS.DLL. To use an icon from this library, type the file name in the File Name text box of the Change Icon dialog box (again see fig. 4.6). Scroll through the icons until you find one you want to use. When the icon is highlighted, choose OK twice.

Software is available for you to create a DLL file of your personal icon creations. Alternatively, if you have software that inserts icons into an existing DLL file, copy MORICONS.DLL to another file name and add your favorites to this new DLL file. Many of these programs are available as shareware, and the registration fees are quite small. Icon Master, a well-known icon manager that works with ICO, EXE, and DLL files, has a paint-style icon editor to fine-tune or create your own icons. It is available on most bulletin boards that offer Windows shareware.

Getting Help

Help, which is still your reliable source for information about how to manipulate the boxes, buttons, icons, and other features available in Windows, has been rearranged significantly.

The most visible change is that the Help display is larger so that you can see sizeable amounts of Help information without having to change to a full-screen display. The text area of the Help window is also increased because the command buttons now display only the text of each command, which substantially reduces the size of the buttons.

The Windows Help program (WINHELP.EXE) is a separate Windows application that provides the framework for the help text in Windows applications. After you upgrade to Windows 3.1, you will see the same format in all your other Windows programs. There are some exceptions—primarily program versions that predate Windows 3.0.

Remember that many topics are now available by choosing the Help button provided in various dialog boxes. The help topic that is displayed relates to the specific part of the program you are using.

The Help Menu

You access the Windows Help program through the Program Manager menu bar. The Help program has been rearranged and now offers new tutorial features. When you select Help, the following selections are available:

- Contents provides a list of the topics available about Program Manager. The list is divided into How To, Commands, and Keyboard. Choose an underlined topic to access information about the topic.
- Search for Help On opens the familiar Search dialog box (see fig. 4.10). You choose a topic from an alphabetical list in the upper list box to see a display of related topics in the lower text box. You can type one or more letters to move the highlight bar directly to that portion of the alphabet. Highlight a topic in the lower box; then choose the Go To button.

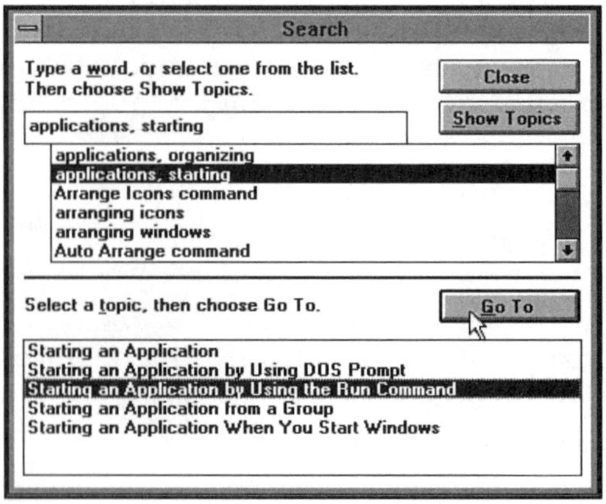

Fig. 4.10.

The Search box showing a list of topics pertaining to starting an application.

- How to Use Help provides a list of topics on using the Help program. The list is divided into Introduction, How to, Commands and

Buttons, and Keyboard. Choose any underlined topic to see an explanation of the feature and learn how to use it.

- Windows Tutorial replaces the former Basics topics with interactive on-line tutorials. The Windows Basics tutorial covers opening, closing, and minimizing programs, as well as resizing windows. One of the last screens in the Windows Basics tutorial is a dialog box containing up and down buttons, check boxes, radio buttons, and text boxes where you can practice changing ingredients for ice cream sundaes and seeing the effect of each change on total calorie count. The Mouse tutorial takes you through clicking every part of the "screen" to disassemble it, and then dragging each screen element back into place.
- About Program Manager is the standard Windows display of the program name and version number, your registration information, and the program serial number. Also included are the Windows operating mode, the bytes of memory free, and the percent of system resources available.

The Help Menu Bar

The lone addition to the Version 3.1 Help menu bar is that you can set up Help so that it remains on top of the screen. When you want to work in a Windows application and view its Help at the same time, activate Always on Top. Resize the Help window so that your work is still visible, or minimize the Help window; its icon will stay on top of your application window. To turn off this feature, deactivate the option.

The Command Buttons

The command buttons under the Help menu bar are sized to contain only the text for their function, and include helpful changes (see fig. 4.11). History and Glossary buttons access a window of information that can be left on-screen as you work in other parts of Help.

Choosing the Contents button displays the original Contents screen for the Help feature you are using. This display can be the contents for Program Manager, for How to Use Help, or for a specific Windows application.

The Search button opens a Search dialog box identical to the one available using Search for Help On from the Help pull-down menu. Only the topics pertaining to the section of Help where you are working are available. Refer to the discussion earlier in the section "The Help Menu Bar."

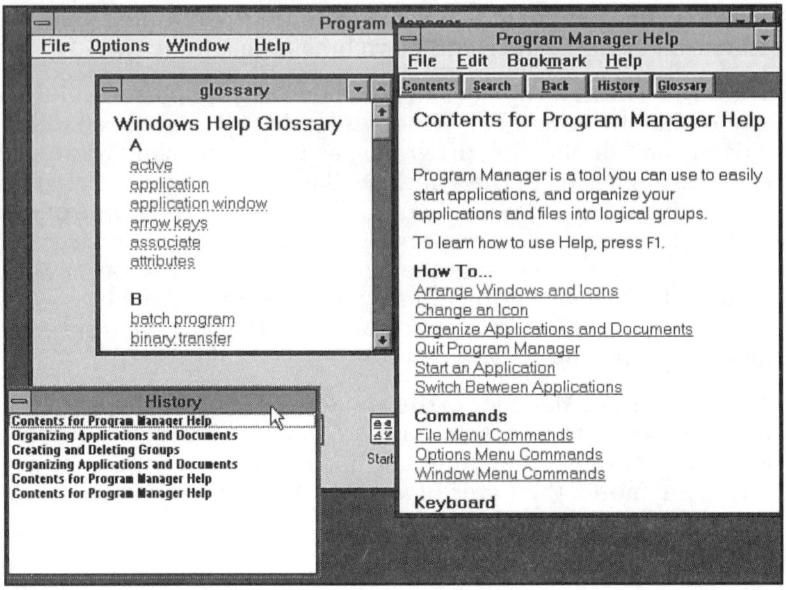

Fig. 4.11.

Help Glossary and History can be arranged so that you can see them while you use Help.

Choosing the Back button returns you to the topic you viewed before the current topic. This button is especially handy when the preceding topic has several references at the end of the text. You can open the first reference, go back to the original topic, open the second reference, and so on.

As you use Help in various Windows applications during one work session, it keeps a record of the last 40 Help screens you have used. Choosing History opens a window listing this record by topic name preceded by the name of the application or help file. Choose any topic in the list to return immediately to that screen, even if that application is not running at the time.

The Glossary contains a list of Windows terms, each term accessing a display of its definition. Words that appear in Help topics displayed in green with a broken underline can be chosen to display their Glossary definition. The Glossary also contains a number of terms not found in Help topics.

The main reason computer manuals can be difficult to read is that these books use terminology that is new to many readers. Try leaving the Glossary window open as you read manuals for Windows applications. Definitions for many terms are suddenly at your fingertips.

From time to time, browse buttons appear at the end of the row of buttons. Their appearance indicates that the topic is in sequence with others that appear before or after the current topic. Choosing the back (<<)

or forward (>>) button moves you to the preceding or next topic, respectively. If either button is dimmed, you have reached the beginning or end of the connected topics.

You can choose the back button from the keyboard by pressing the comma and the forward button by pressing the period.

Protecting Your Work

With Windows 3.1, you can dress up the screen, use icons. and customize program operation. After you have made your changes, you will want to develop strategies to protect your efforts from accidental deletion or corruption. The following ideas can get you started.

- Make backup copies of all your INI, GRP, PIF, ICO, and user-created DLL files frequently. Set up a subdirectory in Windows and name the subdirectory BACKUPS or something similar. Write a batch file that performs this backup job for you.

> **CAUTION:** Windows offers no warning if you choose to delete a group without moving the applications in the group to other locations. If you back up your GRP files frequently, you can copy the deleted GRP file back to the Windows directory. Then use New from the File menu to reinstall the group with all its applications and their configurations intact.

- When you find that you are no longer making changes to a certain file, consider write-protecting the file so that it will not be changed unintentionally. Alternatively, write-protect the backup files after they are saved to the BACKUPS subdirectory.
- If you have changed any of the files during a work session, do not back up the files immediately. Restart Windows or review the icon or restart the program with a new PIF to be sure that the change does what you want. Then back up the changed files.

Summary

In this chapter, you learned about the Program Manager features added to Windows. These features include operating and customizing Program Manager to suit your needs and work environment, as well as how to use the enhanced Help system.

5

CHAPTER

Managing Your Work with File Manager

The Windows 3.1 File Manager has undergone substantial improvement, as is immediately apparent by File Manager's on-screen appearance. File Manager features a single window with a directory tree in the left pane and the contents of the highlighted directory in the right pane. As you open other directory windows, you see similar displays of directory contents accompanied by the directory tree. Windows 3.1 File Manager also includes the following changes:

- File Manager now can interact with Program Manager, enabling you to install programs and documents by dragging and dropping the file icons from File Manager into the appropriate group window in Program Manager.
- You can drag and drop files from File Manager to Print Manager, as well as embed and link files in the same fashion.
- Dialog boxes are easier to work with. File Manager provides extra buttons, such as Browse (to locate specific files or change directories) and Help (to access context-sensitive support).
- You can cancel a procedure if you need to change conditions or execute a different task.
- You can customize the display in such ways as moving the bar that splits each directory window or setting up a display font from the Font dialog box.

- As you complete tasks in File Manager, directory window contents are updated automatically to reflect your changes.
- File Manager now works faster—both its operating speed and the speed at which the screen is redrawn.
- Keystrokes have been added or changed to accommodate improved features.

This chapter does not discuss all the preceding features. Rather, it highlights the major changes and explains how you can best use Windows 3.1 File Manager.

Viewing the File Manager Layout

The standard window in File Manager, referred to as a *directory window*, contains a *directory tree area* in the left pane and a list of the contents of the selected directory in the right pane (called the *directory contents area*). You can choose to display windows containing only the directory tree or only the contents of a directory.

Several terms have been changed and details have been added to accommodate this layout. Figure 5.1 shows the parts of the split window display. Table 5.1 summarizes the new or modified features of the File Manager window.

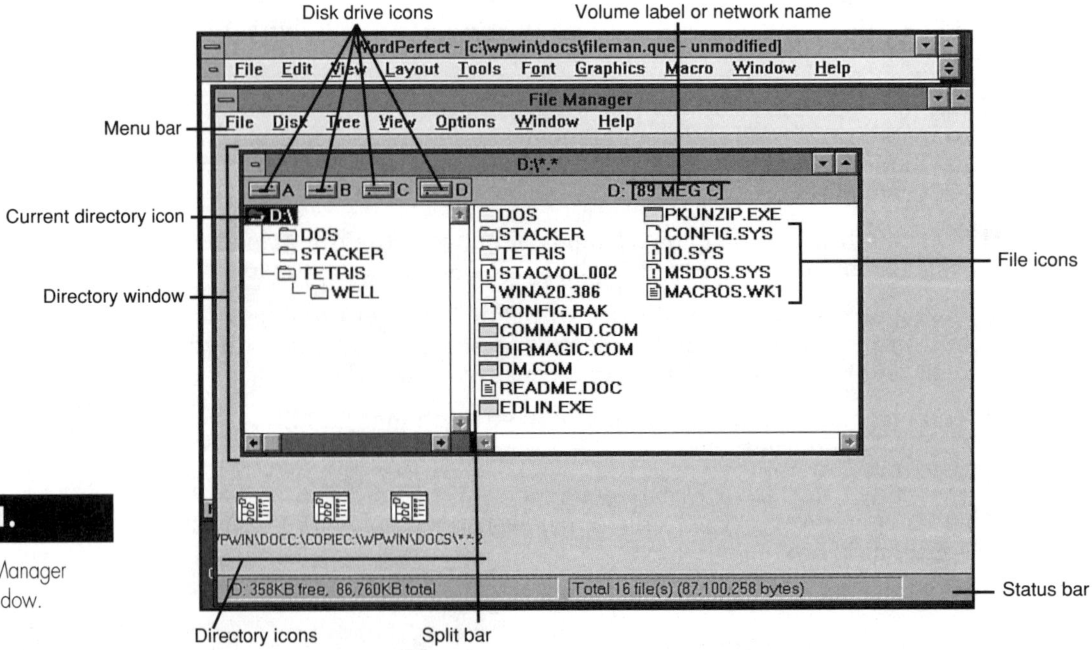

Fig. 5.1.

The File Manager initial window.

Table 5.1 New Features in File Manager

Feature	Definition
Volume label or network name	The label assigned to the displayed disk, which appears in brackets to the right of the drive letter. If you choose a network drive, its name is displayed instead of the volume label.
Current directory icon	The open file folder icon, which represents the current directory.
Split bar	The line that divides the directory window into two panes; you can move this line to customize the size of the panes.
Up icon	When chosen, changes the directory display to show the parent of the current directory.
Status bar	The bar at the bottom of the File Manager window. When the directory contents area is active, the status bar displays on the left the number and total bytes of selected files and on the right the total number of files and total number of bytes they contain. When the directory tree area is active, the left area displays the drive letter, the total bytes free, and the bytes used in the root directory.

In addition to the directory and current directory icons, figure 5.1 also illustrates several types of file icons. These icons include

- The executable file icon, which represents EXE, COM, BAT, and PIF files.
- The system/hidden file icon, which includes the two system files necessary for the operation of the disk operating system and any other files where the system or hidden attributes of the file have been turned on.
- Associated document icons, which represent files that are associated with an application.
- Other document icons, which represent any other files. These files can be unassociated documents or program files that are not executable, such as drivers, fonts, icons, and overlays.

The only major changes to the menu bar are found in the layout of the View and Help menus. Help has been reorganized in the same manner as it was reorganized in Program Manager (see Chapter 4). The View menu and its commands are explained in the section "Customizing the Directory Window Contents" later in this chapter.

Using the Keyboard and Mouse in File Manager

File Manager provides a variety of ways to accomplish every task. You use the menu bar to perform most jobs with the mouse or the keyboard. You can use the mouse, alone and in combination with keys, to select, move, copy, and launch. Additionally, the keyboard provides access to a number of shortcuts and speed keys.

Because of the differences in layout, some familiar keyboard and mouse operations have undergone subtle changes from Windows 3.0 to 3.1.

Using the Keyboard To Move Around

At times when using Windows 3.1, you might prefer to use the keyboard rather than use the mouse. Table 5.2 describes the key presses available to move around in directory windows.

Table 5.2 Keyboard Movement Shortcuts

Key	Action
Tab	Cycles the active area inside the directory window from the drive icons to the directory tree pane to the directory contents pane and moves up and down a tree of directories or list of files.
Ctrl-,	Moves between the same-level subdirectories of one directory, moves to the first subdirectory in the next lower directory level (the child directory), and moves from the current subdirectory directly to the parent directory.
letter	Selects the first directory starting with *letter*.
PgUp, PgDn	Moves through the directory tree or directory contents one screen at a time.

Key	Action
Home	Moves to the first directory or file in either section of the window.
End	Moves to the last directory or file in either section.

Changing Disk Drives

The current directory window can display the contents of any of your disk drives. To change to another drive, use either of these methods:

- Press Ctrl-*letter* to change to the *letter* drive.
- Click the appropriate drive icon.

Selecting Files and Directories

To select a file or a directory, you need only to move to the appropriate section of the directory window and highlight or click the file or directory. You can select more than one file or directory several different ways.

You cannot select multiple directories in the directory tree area. If subdirectories are displayed in the directory contents area, however, you can select multiple directories and rename, move, copy, and delete them in the contents area.

To select multiple *adjacent* files or directories, use either of these methods:

- Click the first file or directory name; then press and hold the Shift key and click the last adjacent name.
- Select the first file or directory; then press and hold the Shift key and use the arrow keys to extend the selection.

To remove the highlight from the selected files, move the cursor or press Ctrl-\.

To select multiple *nonadjacent* files or directories, use either of these methods:

- Ctrl-click each file name until all are selected.
- Press Shift-F8; then move to a file name and press the space bar. Continue highlighting files, pressing the space bar each time, until all desired files are selected.

To deselect one or more of the multiple files, repeat the same select process to toggle off the highlight.

To select files using the DOS wild cards, follow these steps:

1. From the File menu, choose Select Files.

   The Select Files dialog box opens (fig. 5.2).

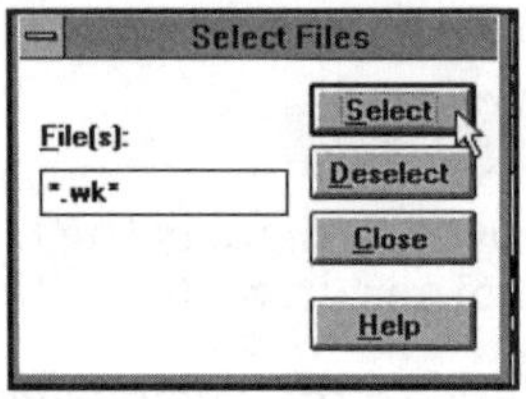

Fig. 5.2.

The Select Files dialog box.

2. In the File(s) text box, type the file name using standard DOS wild cards, and then press Enter. You can see the specified files boxed in the directory window behind the dialog box.
3. If the boxed files are the ones you want, choose Select. The boxed file names are highlighted.

If necessary, you can move the Select Files dialog box so that you can preview your file selections before you close the box.

Alternatively, follow these steps:

1. From the View menu, choose By File Type.

   The By File Type dialog box appears.

2. In the Name text box, type the file name using standard DOS wild cards.
3. Choose OK. The directory window now contains only the files you specified.
4. Press Ctrl-/ or use the mouse to select all files now displayed.

To deselect all files, use either of these methods:

- Press Ctrl-\.
- In the Select Files dialog box (again see fig. 5.2), choose Deselect.

Expanding and Collapsing Directories

When you first open File Manager, the directory tree contains a list of the directories in the root directory of the selected drive. In Windows 3.0, the directory tree window opened with all directories and one level of subdirectories displayed; icons of directories that could be expanded or collapsed contained a + or –. The default directory display in Windows 3.1 is simply a tree of the directories contained in the root directory; the display does not indicate whether any subdirectories exist.

You can change the display so that the directory icons show a + or – to indicate that the directory can be expanded or collapsed. To activate this feature, activate the Indicate Expandable Branches command from the Tree menu.

To expand a directory to show one level of subdirectories in the directory tree, use one of these methods:

- Select the directory and press the + (plus) key.
- Double-click the directory icon.
- Select the directory; then choose Expand One Level from the Tree menu.

To expand a directory to display all the levels of subdirectories it contains, use one of these methods:

- Select the directory and press the * (asterisk) key.
- Select the directory; then choose Expand Branch from the Tree menu.

To collapse a directory, use one of these methods:

- Double-click the directory icon.
- Select the directory and press the – (minus) key.
- Select the directory; then choose Collapse Branch from the Tree menu.

To collapse a multilevel directory display, select the highest level parent directory, as illustrated in figure 5.3.

You might prefer to have the directory tree display all the subdirectories of all directories. Use either of these methods:

- Press Ctrl-*.
- From the Tree menu, choose Expand All.

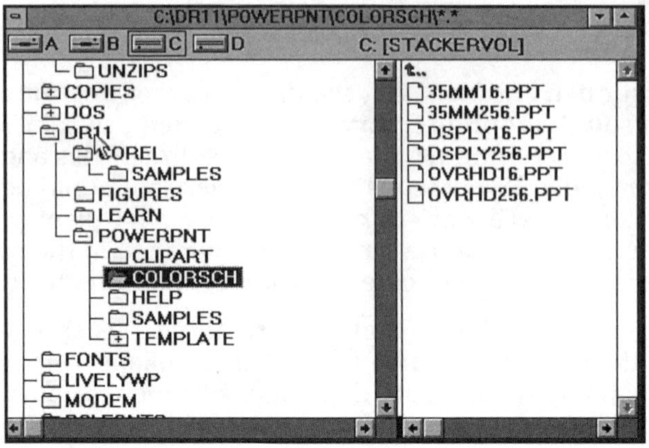

Fig. 5.3.

Double-click the highest level parent directory to collapse the entire branch.

Windows has no "collapse all" command. However, expanding all directories changes the display only in the current directory window. To return to a collapsed list of directories, close the directory window and then open it again, or close the window and use the directory tree in another window to continue your work.

Working with Multiple Windows

The first time you use File Manager, it opens with a directory window displaying the contents of the Windows 3.1 directory. The windows that are open when you exit File Manager are displayed the next time you open File Manager.

You can work with multiple directories in several ways, including changing directories in a window, opening and arranging additional document windows, and closing directory windows when you no longer need them on-screen.

Opening Multiple Windows

To open several directory windows at the same time, use one of these methods:

- Double-click a drive icon. A directory window opens, displaying the directory tree for the root directory of that drive.
- From the Windows menu, choose New Window. When the directory window opens, select the directory you want displayed.

If you have File Manager running full-screen and the active window maximized, each additional window you open completely covers the preceding ones; to switch between them, follow of these methods:

- Press Ctrl-F6 to toggle through the windows in order.
- From the Window menu, select the window you want.

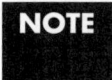

NOTE When you open multiple windows of the same directory, a number appears after the directory name in the title bar of the window to indicate its numeric order.

To open a window displaying only the directory contents, use either of these methods, whether the directory you select is in the directory tree or the directory contents area:

- Press and hold the Shift key and double-click the directory icon.
- Select the directory; then press Shift-Enter.

When several windows are open, only one window is the *active* window. To make a different window active, use one of these methods:

- Click part of another window to make it the active window. Click the outer edges of the window. Clicking the list area makes the window active *and* selects the nearest file or directory.
- Double-click a minimized window icon to make it active.
- Press Ctrl-F6 to cycle through the windows. If you want to activate a minimized window, press Enter when the highlight reaches the title of the minimized window.
- From the numbered list of open windows on the Window menu, choose the window you want to make active.

Arranging Windows

As you open more directory windows, arranging them so that a portion of each is visible on-screen becomes increasingly difficult.

One way to arrange the windows so that the title bar is visible is to have them cascade like a fan of playing cards (see fig. 5.4). To arrange the open directory windows this way, choose Cascade from the Window menu.

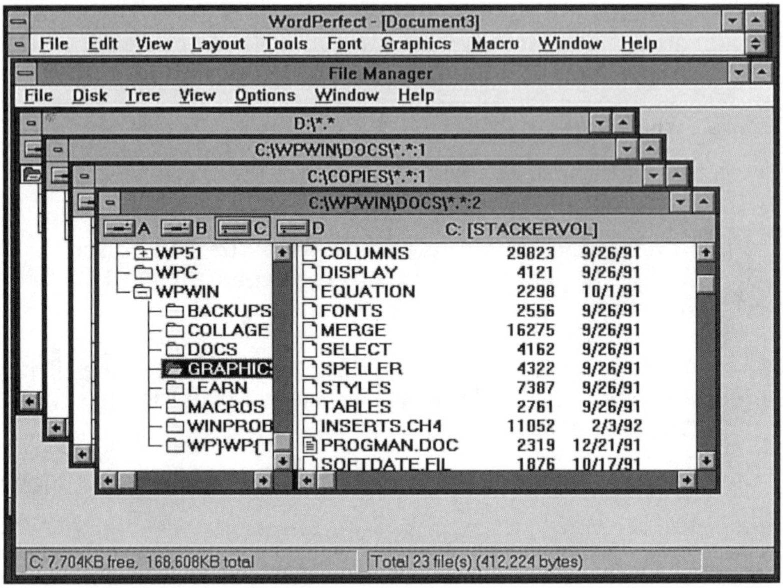

Fig. 5.4.

Cascaded windows in File Manager.

You might prefer to have a portion of the contents of each window on-screen. If so, choose Tile from the Window menu to arrange the windows in a floor-tile pattern (see fig. 5.5).

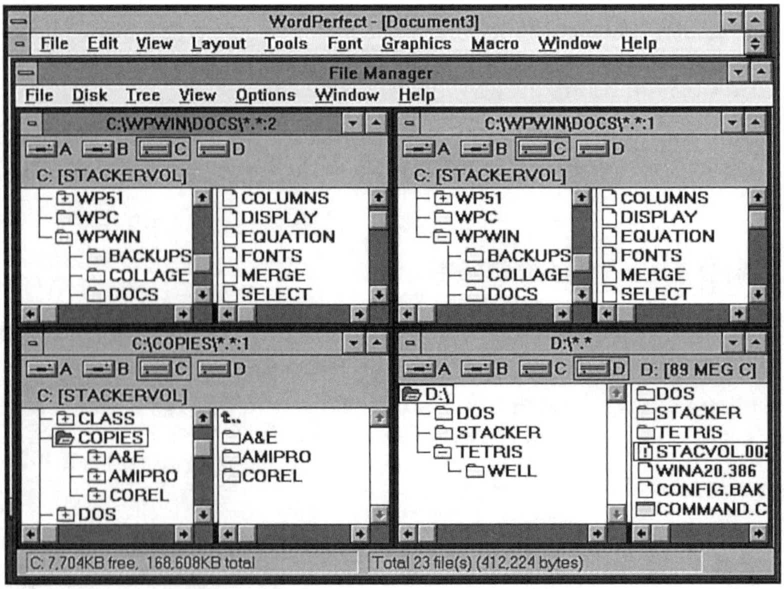

Fig. 5.5.

Tiled windows in File Manager.

As more windows are tiled, the program focuses on keeping the directory area, rather than the contents area, displayed. The default tile arrangement is to tile a few windows vertically, and then add a second row when you reach four open windows. To tile windows side-by-side, press the Shift key while you choose Tile. Figures 5.6 and 5.7 show the difference in vertical and horizontal tile arrangement.

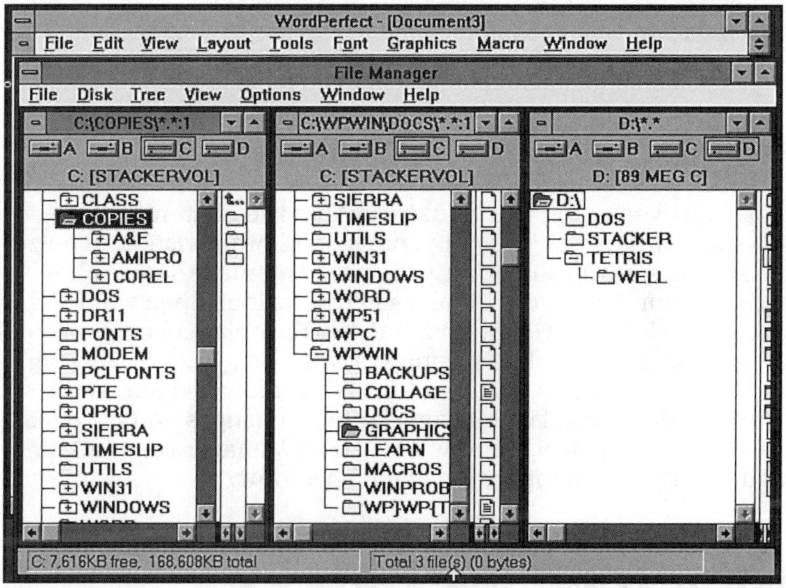

Fig. 5.6.

The default vertical tile arrangement.

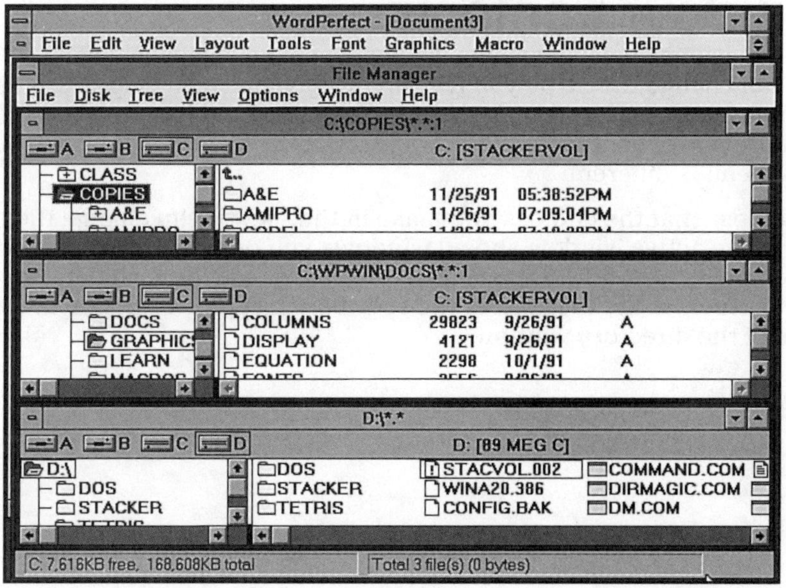

Fig. 5.7.

A horizontal tile arrangement.

TIP When you minimize a window, it is reduced to an icon and placed at the bottom of the File Manager window. As you continue to minimize and maximize, the row can become disheveled. To tidy up the row of icons, choose Arrange Icons from the Window menu. The spacing of the icons within File Manager is controlled by a grid in Control Panel. Refer to Chapter 3 for information on changing the spacing of the icons.

Refreshing Window Contents

A major improvement in File Manager is that the contents of directory windows are updated as you copy, move, and otherwise reorganize your drives. As you save files in other programs and make some other changes on your drives, the displays in the various open windows in File Manager occasionally are not updated. This problem occurs particularly when you change the disk in a floppy drive, when you are working with a network drive, and when a Search Results window is open. To be sure that the data display in File Manager reflects changes you have made, choose Refresh from the Window menu. File Manager reads all directories and updates the information in each window.

Customizing the Directory Window Contents

You can change the display in the directory window to emphasize different information. Customizing the way files are listed has changed little from previous versions of Windows, but accessing commands from the View menu is different.

Remember that the choices you make in the View menu change the display in the active window and all windows you open in the future until you change the conditions again. These changes include all details you modify, such as the location of the split bar, except the outside dimensions of the directory window.

Setting Up the Window Layout

In the default layout, the directory tree area is larger than the directory contents area. You can move the *split bar*, the single line dividing the two areas, the same way you move the sides of the window. To adjust the position of the split bar, follow these steps:

1. Position the mouse pointer over the split bar so that the cursor changes into a double arrow.
2. Drag the double arrow until the heavy line is positioned where you want to divide the two areas; then release the mouse button.

To move the split bar using the keyboard, follow these steps:

1. From the View menu, choose Split.
2. Use the left- or right-arrow key to move the split bar (now a thick line) across the window.
3. When the bar is positioned where you want it, press Enter.

The default view of the window displays both the directory tree and directory contents area. However, you can opt to view only the directory tree or only the directory contents. To change the view in the directory window, follow these steps:

1. Make the window you want to change the active window.
2. From the View menu, choose Tree Only to display only the directory tree.

   Choose Directory Only to display only the contents of the selected directory.

When working with only the directory tree displayed, you can expand and collapse the tree. You can also change to a different drive. To display the contents of a directory, you must open a new window. For instructions on opening new windows, see the section "Working with Multiple Windows" earlier in this chapter.

When the active window contains only the directory contents, you can move to a parent directory by choosing the up icon in the upper left corner of the window. To display the contents of a subdirectory, double-click the directory name or select it and then press Enter. You can open additional windows from either window (see "Opening Multiple Windows" earlier in this chapter).

Displaying File Information

The file names displayed in a window can be limited to files of one or more types, or the displayed files can be limited by name. The display can include any subdirectories, all program files, document files, and other files, or you can exclude any type of file. You can also specify file name restrictions to limit the files of any type that are included in the window.

To specify the type of files to display in the active window, follow these steps:

1. From the View menu, choose By File Type.

   The By File Type dialog box opens (see fig. 5.8).

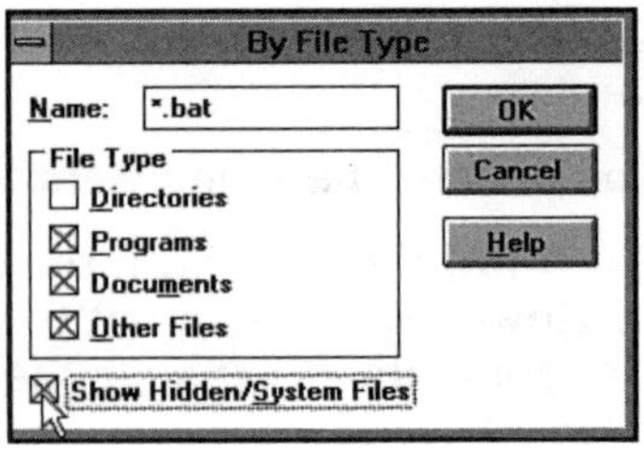

Fig. 5.8.

The By File Type dialog box.

2. In the File Type area, activate the file types you want included.
3. If you want hidden files included in the display, activate Show Hidden/System Files.
4. When you finish specifying types, choose OK.

In addition to the types of files, you can use file names to select the files you want displayed. To select files by name, follow these steps:

1. From the View menu, choose By File Type.

   The File Type dialog box appears (see again fig. 5.8).

2. In the Name text box, type the name conditions, using the DOS wild cards, as appropriate.
3. Choose OK.

After you decide which files to include in the window, you can ask File Manager to provide more information about them. To display the name, size, date and time last modified, and file attributes, choose the All File Details command from the View menu. If you want to select the information to be displayed, choose Partial Details from the View menu. The Partial Details dialog box opens (see fig. 5.9).

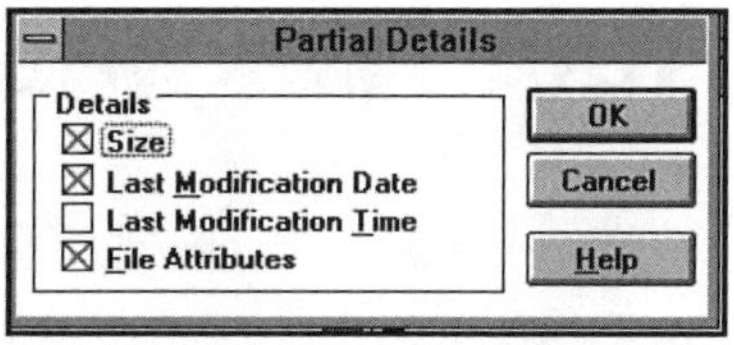

Fig. 5.9.

The Partial Details dialog box.

The Partial Details dialog box provides a check list of items you can display about the files in the directory window. You can activate the following options: Size, Last Modification Date, Last Modification Time, and File Attributes.

Sorting Your File Display

As with any good file manager, you can sort the list of files displayed in directory windows into an order that is convenient for you. For easy selection of the files modified during the work day, choose to sort by date. Sorting files by type places them alphabetically by extension—handy if you are looking for the BAT files or your data files.

To sort files in a directory window, open the View menu. Then choose one of the following options:

Sort by Name

Sort **b**y Type

Sort by Si**z**e

Sort by **D**ate

A check appears by the sort method you choose, and all subsequently opened windows are sorted in that order. Sorting by date last modified, as shown in figure 5.10, can be helpful when performing weekly file backups.

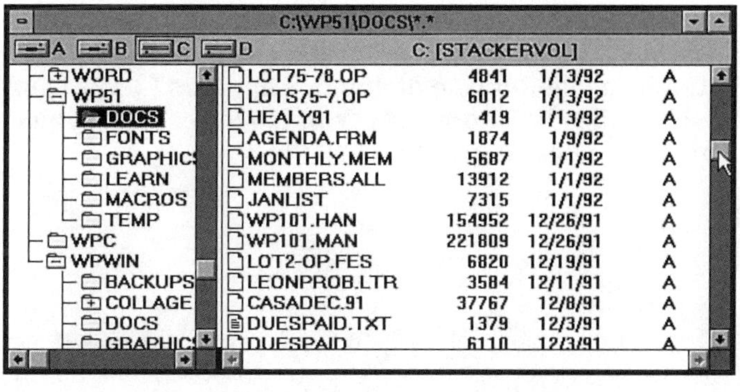

Fig 5.10.

A directory window sorted by date modified.

Managing Your Files and Directories

After you are comfortable with File Manager windows and the process of selecting, you might want to begin rearranging and managing files and directories.

Copying Files and Directories

You can copy one or more files to another directory on the current drive or to another drive. You can also copy directories to another location or drive. After you select the files or directory you want to copy, use either of these methods to complete the operation:

- Press and hold the Control key while you drag the files to the destination directory or drive icon.
- From the File menu, choose Copy; then enter the destination information in the To text box and choose OK.

When you release the mouse button, the Confirm Mouse Operation dialog box inquires whether you are sure you want to copy the files or directories to that destination. When you use the menu bar, choosing OK in the Copy dialog box starts the copy process.

Copying directories is just as simple as copying files if you remember the basics of directory structure and the window layout. You can select multiple directories only if they are listed in the directory contents window. If you want to select directories in the root directory of your drive, first select the root directory at the top of the directory tree. You can copy (or move) directories only if the action creates new subdirectories in a different directory.

To copy one or more directories, follow the procedures you use to copy files.

If files with the same file name already exist at the destination you specify, the Confirm File Replace dialog box appears (see 5.11). You can confirm individual files by choosing Yes or No for each, or you can choose Yes to All to confirm replacing all files.

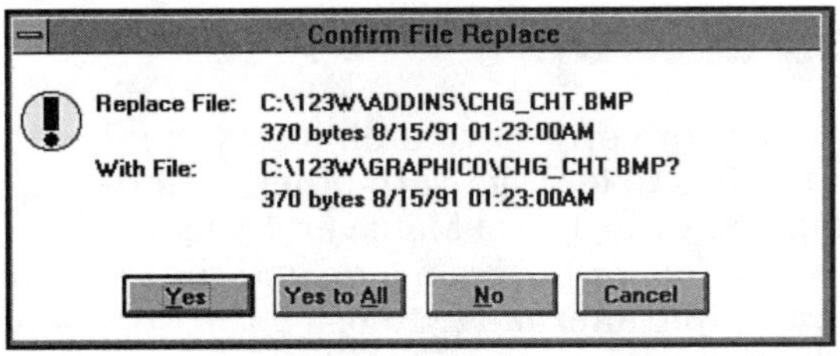

Fig. 5.11.

The Confirm File Replace dialog box.

Whether you are copying multiple files or one or more directories, you can halt the copy process at any time by selecting the Cancel button in the Copy dialog box (which remains on-screen) or by pressing the Esc key.

You can copy files into the same directory if you give them different names. If you use the Rename command from the File menu, only the file name is changed. By using Copy and specifying the same directory but a different file name, you have both the original file and the copy with a new name. You can use Copy to copy and rename multiple files by using DOS wild cards when assigning new names. For example, if you select several files with the extension TXT, you can copy them to *.DOC.

Moving Files and Directories

You can move one or more files or directories to new locations. After you select the files or directories, follow either of these methods:

- Drag the file or directory icon to the new directory or drive icon. The Confirm Mouse Operation text box appears. If the instructions are correct, choose OK.
- From the File menu, choose Move. Then enter the destination directory path or the drive in the To text box and choose OK.

You can also change file names when moving one or more files by providing a new file name or using DOS wild cards (see the previous section, "Copying Files and Directories").

As with Copy, you can cancel a lengthy move operation by selecting the Cancel button in the Move dialog box or pressing the Esc key.

Using Drag & Drop

You can install, move, or copy file and directory icons within File Manager and can cause files to interact with other Windows applications, such as Print Manager or Program Manager, by using the mouse to drag the icon to a new window or program icon and then dropping the icon. *Drag and drop* is a simple alternative to using the Copy and Move commands on the File menu.

To move files or directories, follow these steps:

1. Select the files or directories you want to move.
2. Point to one of the highlighted files.
3. Press and hold the left mouse button. The mouse pointer becomes an icon of a document with the upper right corner folded down. If you are moving multiple files or directories, the icon is a stack of three documents (see fig. 5.12).
4. Drag the icon to the desired location; then release the mouse button.

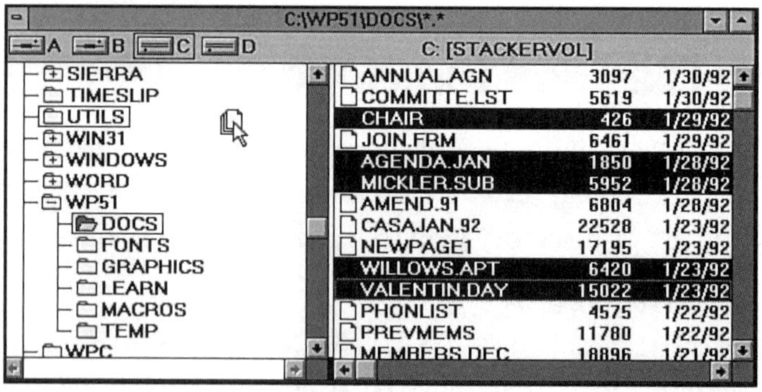

Fig. 5.12.

Documents being moved from C:\WP51\DOCS to C:\UTILS.

As soon as the file icon is moved into the directory tree area, the icon by the highlighted files or directories disappears, indicating that the files or directories are being moved rather than copied. As you move the icon around the screen, the icon changes to the international No symbol (a circle cut in half by a diagonal line) while you are crossing any portion of the screen where you cannot drop the files.

When you move into the directory tree area, the nearest directory on the directory tree is boxed. Moving the icon (now the pointer) up and down the tree moves the box so that you can select the destination directory.

To copy files or directories, follow the same steps, except hold down the Control key while you drag the icon; first release the mouse button and then release the Control key to drop the icon. As you move the icon out of the document contents area, copies of the file icons remain at their original locations and a + appears in the center of the moving icon.

Using either method, if the destination is another drive, you can only copy files or directories. If you try to move to another drive, the process changes to copy when you reach the drive icon.

Using drag and drop, after you begin copying, you can change to moving by releasing the Control key before you release the mouse button. The reverse is also true. To change from move to copy, press the Control key while you are still holding down the mouse button. To cancel either operation, move the icon back to the directory contents pane or outside the directory window and drop the icon.

Using drag and drop to install applications into Program Manager or to print documents is discussed in the section "Interacting with Other Windows Programs" later in this chapter.

Deleting Files and Directories

To delete files or directories, begin by selecting the files or directories you no longer want. After selecting, follow these steps:

1. From the File menu, choose Delete. You also can press the Delete key.
2. Choose OK in the Delete dialog box.
3. Confirm the deletion of each file by choosing Yes or No in the Confirm File Delete dialog box, or choose Yes to All to delete all the files you selected without further confirmation.

To stop the delete process, choose the Cancel button in the Delete dialog box.

Renaming Files and Directories

When you rename a file or directory, that item remains at its current location and the name is changed. To retain the original file or directory, use the Copy command.

You can rename multiple files and directories by using the DOS wild cards to change common elements. After you select the file or directory to rename, follow these steps:

1. From the File menu, choose Rename.

   The Rename dialog box opens.

2. In the To text box, type the new name, using wild cards for multiple files.

3. Choose OK.

Creating Directories

You can create a new directory in File Manager. To create a new directory, follow these steps:

1. Select the directory that you want to be the parent directory of the new directory you are creating.

2. From the File menu, choose Create Directory.

3. In the Name text box, type the name of the new directory.

4. Choose OK.

You do not have to select a specific directory when you create a directory. You must then, however, type the full path beginning with a backslash (\) before the new directory name.

Changing File Attributes with Properties

Files can have one or more of four attributes. The directory window in figure 5.13 contains files displaying each of the following attributes:

- The *archive* attribute (A) is used by various copy and backup programs to keep track of which files have been backed up. The archive attribute is on when a file is created or modified and is turned off by various copy and backup programs to indicate that the file has been copied.

- The *hidden* attribute (H) keeps the file from being displayed. You can display hidden files in a directory window by using the By File Type command from the View menu. The hidden attribute provides one way to keep a file confidential, although it is not as effective as using a password. The hidden attribute is off when a file is created.

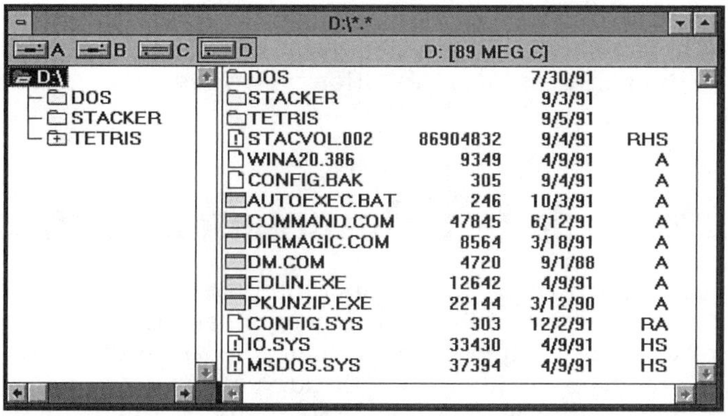

Fig. 5.13.

The root directory D:\ includes files with different attributes.

- The *read-only* attribute (R) specifies that the file cannot be edited or changed. Use read-only to prevent changes in form files or to protect your AUTOEXEC.BAT and CONFIG.SYS files from accidental corruption. The default for the read-only attribute is off.
- The *system* attribute (S) designates two files that DOS uses, along with COMMAND.COM, to operate your computer. Like hidden files, system files are hidden from view. Some programs, such as the Stacker disk compression utility, create their own system files.

You can change file attributes from File Manager by using the Properties command. To change attributes for one or several files, follow these steps:

1. From the File menu, choose Properties.

   The Properties dialog box opens (see fig. 5.14).

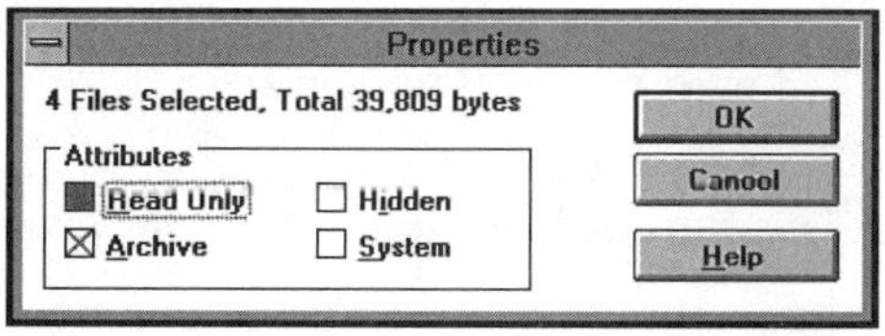

Fig. 5.14.

The Properties dialog box.

2. Activate or deactivate each attribute you want to change.
3. Choose OK.

If you have selected multiple files and their attributes are not all the same, only those attributes that are the same for all selected files will be available for modification in the File Properties dialog box. Those attributes that are mixed for the selected files will have their boxes filled with gray, to indicate that they cannot be changed.

If you are operating on a network, you might find more than these four attributes displayed in the Properties box. Consult your network manual or network administrator for information on working with network attributes.

Conducting File and Document Searches

At times, you might "lose" files. A typographical error when naming a file is a common reason for lost files. File Manager can also lose files easily. Suppose, for example, that you are moving a file to another directory window and you drop the file icon in the area at the top of the directory contents area. If a subdirectory icon appears first in the list of contents, the file you are moving might end up in that subdirectory.

Anyone can accidently misplace a file or directory. Use the Search command from the File menu to locate your file or directory on the disk. Follow these steps:

1. Select the drive you want to search.
2. From the File menu, choose Search.

   The Search dialog box opens (see fig. 5.15).

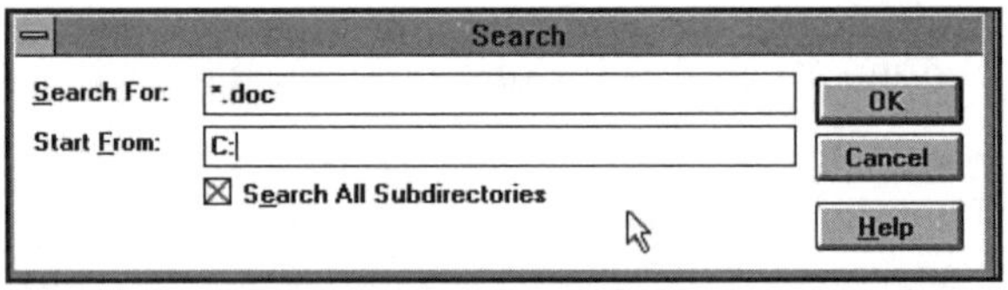

Fig. 5.15.

The Search dialog box ready to search the C drive.

3. In the Search For text box, type the file name or a portion of the file name, using DOS wild cards, if necessary.
4. In the Start From text box, type the name of the directory you want searched, if it is different from the active directory.
5. If you want to search only one directory and not its branches, deactivate the Search All Subdirectories option.
6. Choose OK.

To search an entire disk, you must select the appropriate root directory name, such as A:\ or C:\. If you type the name of a directory, such as C:\WIN31, only that directory and its subdirectories are searched.

While searching, File Manager displays a count of directories searched in the left end of the status bar. When the search is completed, a Search Results directory window like the one in figure 5.16 appears, and the status bar displays a count of the total files found.

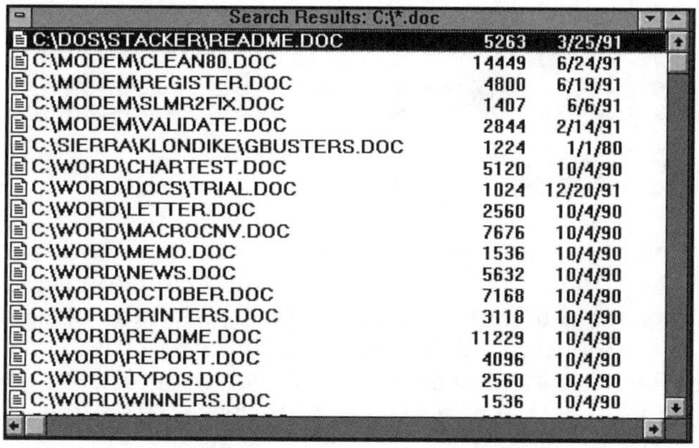

Fig. 5.16.

The Search Results window displays the results of a search.

You can interrupt a search in progress by pressing Esc. The Search Results window then appears, displaying the files found so far, and the status bar displays the number of files found.

You can also rename a file in the Search Results window. To rename a file in the Search Results window, follow these steps:

1. Select the file; then choose Rename from the File menu.

   The Rename dialog box appears.

2. In the To text box, type the entire new path name for the file. The Search Results window is not restricted to the contents of a single directory and cannot, therefore, provide the path for you.

3. Choose OK.

4. From the Window menu, choose Refresh if you want the information in the Search Results window updated to reflect the new file name.

If you want to continue to use this window, it can be minimized to an icon. When maximized later, the window might need to be refreshed again.

Although the Search Results window seems to behave in all respects like a directory window, you cannot move or copy files or directories to this window. Unlike other windows, the Search Results window does not represent a location to go to. All the files in the window include complete path names, however, so you can copy or move files *from* this directory window. After you move a file from the directory window to another location, you are asked whether you want to update the search window information.

Associating Documents with Applications

When a document is associated with an application, Windows is informed that the application uses a specific file extension for data files. The associated data file can then be used to launch the application. When you select the data file and use any command that starts an application, Windows checks to see whether the document extension is associated with an application and, if it is, Windows starts the application and retrieves the document.

After the association has been created, you can treat a data file as if it were a program. For example, you can install a document in a Program Manager group, enabling several copies of the application to be running, each copy working with a different document. The document will show the icon of the application with which it is associated and will show the first part of its file name (before the extension) for the title.

To associate a document with an application, follow these steps:

1. From the File menu, choose Associate.

   The Associate dialog box opens (see fig. 5.17).

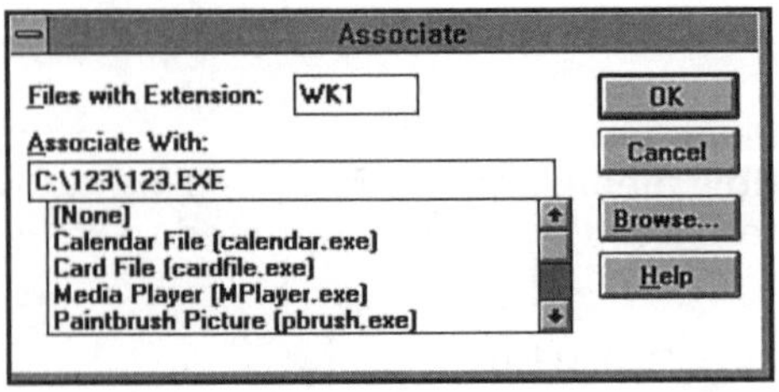

Fig. 5.17.

The Associate dialog box.

2. In the Files with Extension text box, type the extension you want to use.

3. In the Associate With text box, type the path name (full path and EXE or COM file name) for the application. Choose Browse if you need help locating the directory and file. Refer to Chapter 4 for information on using the Browse dialog box.
4. Choose OK.

You might find that a program you install later automatically provides a file extension you have already associated with another application. If the new program creates an association during installation, that association prevails over your earlier specification. In this situation, follow the preceding steps to provide a new extension to associate with the first program.

You might need to remove the association between files and an application. To remove the association, follow the steps to create an association but enter *none* in the Associate With text box.

Interacting with Other Windows Programs

With Windows 3.1, you can drag and drop programs and files into some other Windows application programs. Programs and associated documents can be dragged directly from a directory window to a group window in Program Manager. To print a file created by some programs, you no longer have to open its application. Just drag the file to Print Manager.

Installing Applications in Program Manager

You can install new applications from File Manager to Program Manager by using drag and drop. Program Manager must be open, and the destination group icon or window must be visible. Select the EXE, COM, BAT, or PIF files you want to install from the File Manager window; then drag it to its destination. If you have established document associations, you can drag a document file to the appropriate Program Manager group window to install the document.

Using this method does not take care of all the decisions you might want to make about the program properties. Installing directly from File Manager also does not always install the icon you want to use. You must change program properties from within Program Manager. (See Chapter 4 for more information.)

Printing Files

To use drag and drop to print files, the application you use to create the document must support printing in Print Manager. In addition, Print Manager must be open, although it can be minimized to an icon. Finally, the file you want to print must be associated with the application.

After an application and its associated documents have been set up to work with Print Manager, select the file or files you want printed and drag them to the Print Manager icon or window.

TIP

An easy way to tell if you can use drag and drop to print a document is to check in the Associate With list box (again see fig. 5.17). Applications that support printing from File Manager are added to this list box as each application is installed.

Managing File Manager

You can further customize File Manager so that it better meets your individual needs and working habits. You can limit the number of confirmation messages you must click, choose not to save the changes you have made in File Manager, and select the font used in the directory windows.

If you use File Manager to launch applications, you can choose to have File Manager minimized while the application is running. You can even choose to have File Manager, rather than Program Manager, be the shell for Windows.

Turning Off Confirmation Messages

After you become comfortable with using File Manager to perform your disk housekeeping jobs, you might find that the various confirmation messages are more of a hindrance than a help. To turn off these messages, choose Confirmation from the Options menu. The Confirmation dialog box opens (see fig. 5.18).

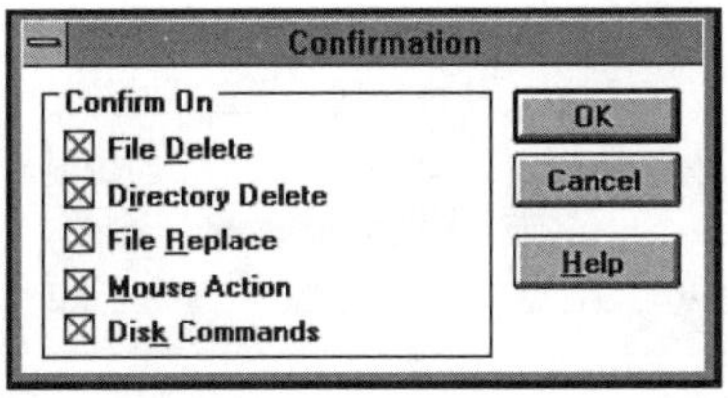

Fig. 5.18.

The Confirmation dialog box.

You can eliminate confirmation messages only in those areas where you no longer require protection. The Mouse Action confirmation, for example, is helpful to verify whether you are copying or moving. The File Delete confirmation is particularly tedious, but the Directory Delete confirmation can prevent a major disaster, especially if you do not have the software to undelete a directory. Deactivate each type of message you no longer want displayed; then choose OK.

Turning Off Save Settings on Exit

The changes you make using the Options menu are automatically saved from session to session. After you configure confirmation messages, for example, those settings remain until you change them.

Other changes, such as the way you view windows and which windows are open by default, also are saved from session to session. To turn off the save option, deactivate the Save Settings on Exit option from the Options menu. Turning off this setting is particularly useful when you are in the middle of some serious experimenting. To escape from a muddle, turn off Save Settings on Exit and exit; then restart File Manager with your previously saved layout. Remember to turn this feature back on. Because this option is in the Options menu, the change to this feature is saved automatically.

Changing the Display Font

New to Version 3.1 is the capability to select and customize the font used in the directory windows. Choose Font from the Options menu to open the Font dialog box (see fig. 5.19).

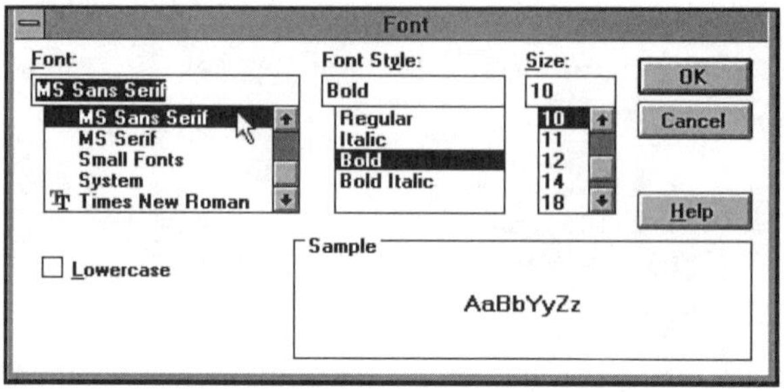

Fig. 5.19.

The Font dialog box with a font preview area.

First, choose the typeface you want to use. When considering styles, you might find that a boldfaced font will be the easiest on your eyes after a long day of work. Italic type makes the individual characters more ragged in appearance, and they take up more space in the directory windows. A 10-point font size is comfortable for most users, but you can choose a larger size and increase the size of the directory windows if you have vision difficulties.

In the Font dialog box, the Font list box displays the available fonts. When you select a font from this list, its appearance is previewed for you in the Sample box. Next, you select the style of the font from the Font Style list box. The available styles are regular, bold, italic, and bold italic, but not all styles are available for every font. The contents of the Font Style list box change to reflect the styles available for the font you have selected.

You also need to select a size for the font. The available sizes are displayed in the Size list box. As with styles, the sizes from which you can choose change to reflect the sizes available for the font you have selected.

Finally, you can choose to display the information in lowercase or uppercase. Activate the Lowercase option to use only lowercase text. Deactivate Lowercase to return to uppercase text.

As you continue to make changes to the base font, your selection is previewed in the Sample box. When you find a font appearance you like, choose OK. The font you select remains in effect until you choose a different configuration.

Using File Manager as Your Windows Shell

If you find that you spend most of your time in File Manager rather than in Program Manager, try using File Manager as the shell to be started when you open Windows.

The shell is specified in the SYSTEM.INI file, and the default is PROGMAN.EXE. Here are the first several lines found in one SYSTEM.INI file. Yours might be different; each one is customized at installation.

```
[boot]
shell=progman.exe
mouse.drv=MOUSE.DRV
network.drv=
language.dll=
sound.drv=MMSOUND.DRV
comm.drv=COMM.DRV
system.drv=SYSTEM.DRV
```

Use Notepad or a file editor program to change the second line to read

```
shell=winfile.exe
```

If you don't use Notepad, be sure that you use an editor that will save the file as an ANSI text file.

Minimizing File Manager

If you launch applications with File Manager, particularly if you are using File Manager as your shell, you might prefer to have it minimized while applications are running. Although the language of the command is the same as the language of minimizing Program Manager or specific applications, choosing to minimize File Manager "on use" causes it to minimize when an application is started. To use this feature, activate the Minimize on Use option from the Options menu.

Working with Floppy Disks

Most of the floppy disk tasks that require you to exit a program are available from File Manager's Disk menu. Do not use these tasks to check on File Manager's speed improvement. Floppy disk tasks are always slow, and any intermediary program, such as Windows, makes the job seem even slower.

Copying Floppy Disks

You can copy the contents of one floppy disk to another. Although not clear from the command's name, the Copy Disk command on the Disk menu is actually the same as the DOS DISKCOPY command and therefore works only with identical disk sizes. To copy the contents of one disk to another, follow these steps:

1. From the Disk menu, choose Copy Disk.

   The Copy Disk dialog box opens (see fig. 5.20).

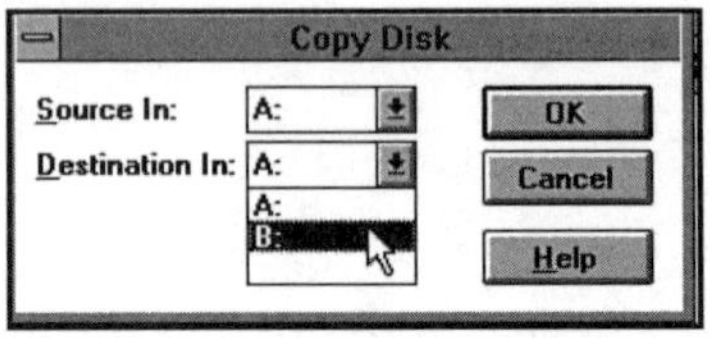

Fig. 5.20.

The Copy Disk dialog box with the Destination In menu displayed.

2. In the Source In list box, select the letter of the source drive. You also can select the drive from the pop-up menu.
3. Enter the letter of the destination drive in the Destination In list box or select the drive from the pop-up menu.
4. Choose OK.
5. Follow the prompts that tell you where and when to insert or replace source and destination disks.

File Manager checks the destination disk while copying, and then formats it, if necessary, without prompting you. High-density disk copying takes several passes to complete.

To copy the contents of a floppy disk to a blank formatted floppy disk of a different size easily, open File Manager windows for each drive, select all the files on the source disk, and drag and drop them onto the destination disk. (Unlike the Disk Copy command, this method does require that the destination disk already be formatted, and it will not copy the volume label from source to destination.) This method does not require multiple passes or shuffling disks for high-density disks.

NOTE

If you insert an unformatted disk of the wrong capacity when you are using Copy, Windows still will format the destination disk without prompting. Windows tries to format the destination disk as if it were the same capacity as the source disk. If formatting seems to be taking an unusually long time, this error might be the problem. Choose the Cancel button to interrupt the format process.

Labeling Floppy Disks

If you want to assign a volume label to a disk that has already been formatted, follow these steps:

1. Select the disk drive you want to use to label the disk. The drive should appear in the active directory window.
2. Insert the floppy disk into the selected drive.
3. From the Disk menu, choose Label Disk.

   The Label Disk dialog box opens.
4. Type the volume name in the Label text box. Your label can contain up to 11 alphanumeric characters, no spaces, and no punctuation except hyphens (-) and underscores (_). Choose OK.

Making System Disks

You can transfer the DOS system files to a floppy disk to make a self-booting floppy disk. Follow these steps:

1. From the Disk menu, choose Make System Disk.

   The Make System Disk dialog box opens.
2. In the Copy System Files to Disk In text box, type the drive letter.
3. Insert the floppy disk into the selected drive and choose OK.

If your hard disk has several partitions, do not overlook step 1. Make sure that you are in the partition containing the system files. In addition, File Manager is sometimes unable to find the system files when your hard drive is using file compression utilities.

Formatting Disks

File Manager can format your floppy disks and add volume labels and system files in the process, if you want. To format a floppy disk, follow these steps:

1. Insert the disk to be formatted into the appropriate drive.
2. From the Disk menu, choose Format Disk.

   The Format Disk dialog box opens (see fig. 5.21).

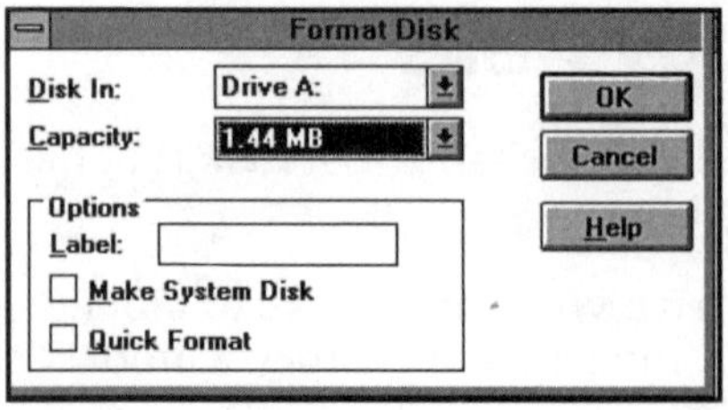

Fig. 5.21.

The Format Disk dialog box.

3. In the Disk In text box, type the drive letter.
4. In the Capacity list box, select a disk capacity.
5. Enter a volume label in the Label text box, if you want.
6. Choose Make System Disk if you want the DOS system files transferred to the floppy disk.
7. Choose Quick Format if the disk has been formatted and you want only the File Allocation Table and Root Directory formatted without reformatting individual sectors.
8. Choose OK to start running the formatting process.

If you use File Manager regularly, you will eventually try to work with an unformatted floppy disk. When this happens, Windows has kindly replaced the old `general failure to read drive...` message with some variation of the dialog box shown in figure 5.22.

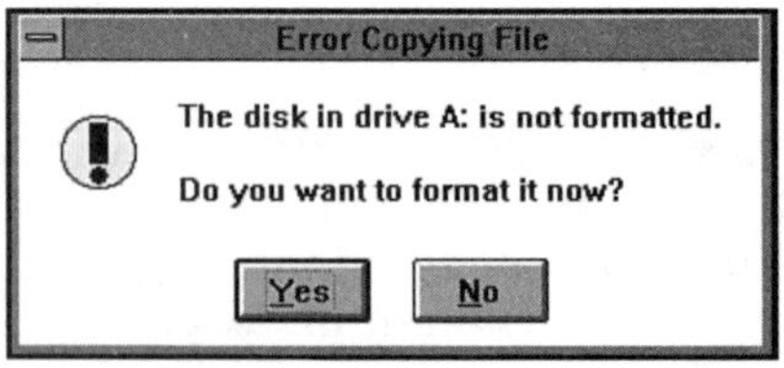

Fig. 5.22.

The Error Copying File dialog box.

If you want the disk formatted, choose Yes. The Format Disk dialog box appears for you to specify the drive letter and the capacity of the disk.

Working with Network Drives

Windows 3.1 works more seamlessly with networks than did Version 3.0. If your computer is connected to a network, you can use any network drive, provided that you know the server it is connected to and you have authorization to the server. Depending on the network you are using, you might be able to browse through the drives that are available.

Windows 3.1 remembers connections that you established. If you established network connections in previous Windows sessions, they are reconnected. Connections made in File Manager are treated like any other drive or subdirectory on your local hard disk. You might start programs from the server, or use drag and drop with a file as you normally would.

The next few sections enable you to manage connections to a network server. They explain how to attach and detach a server, *map* a directory on a network drive to a drive letter, and delete a mapped directory.

NOTE Because Novell networks are widely used, this book focuses on the steps for using a Novell network. Other networks will work somewhat differently.

Attaching a Network Drive

Before you can access a network drive, you must attach Windows to a network server. After you attach to the server, you can select the *path* to work from. A path consists of the name of the server and the subdirectory on the network drive. After you select the correct path, you then assign, or *map*, the path to a drive letter. To attach to a server, follow these steps:

1. From the Disk menu, choose Network Connections.

   The Network - Drive Connections dialog box opens.

2. Click the Browse button.

   The Browse Connections dialog box opens.

3. Click the Attach button.

   The Attach File Server dialog box opens.

4. Select the correct server from the File server drop-down list box. Type your user name in the User name text box. Type your password in the Password text box. Click OK when you are finished.

   The attached server appears on the Servers/Volumes list box.

5. In the Servers/Volumes list box, select the server to attach to. You see all the directories that you have access to in the Directories list box.

6. Select a directory to use for your path from the Directories list box. Click the OK button when finished.

You have successfully selected a path to use from the server. To use the path with File Manager, however, you need to map the path as a drive letter.

NOTE Clicking on the Set Root button makes the network path a volume.

Mapping a Network Drive

Mapping a network path using Windows is similar to mapping directories in DOS. To map a network path, follow these steps:

1. Select the path from a server on the network by either typing the path in the Path text box, or Browsing for a path.
2. In the Data drives list box, select a drive letter that is not currently being used.
3. Click the Map button. The path from the Path text box appears in the Data drives list box, following the drive letter you selected.

You can remove a mapped drive. Simply select the mapped drive in the Data drives list box, and then click the Map Delete button. Click OK to delete the Network device mapping, or click Cancel to keep the map.

Detaching a Network Server

After you finish using a server, you can detach from the server. Be careful, however, not to detach from a server that contains the Windows environment. To detach from a server, follow these steps:

1. Click the Browse button.

   The Browse Connections dialog box opens.
2. Click the Detach button.

   The Detach File Server dialog box opens.
3. Select the server from the File server drop-down list box.
4. Click OK. Any connections that you had to the server will be lost.
5. Click Cancel to return to the Network - Drive Connections dialog box. Click Close.

Summary

In this chapter you learned about the enhancements and changes to the Windows 3.1 File Server. You learned how to work with those enhancements, such as drag and drop icon manipulation and View options, to customize File Manager to fit your working environment and preferences.

6

CHAPTER

Using TrueType Fonts

Earlier versions of Microsoft Windows brought a modicum of font fluency to the screens of IBM and IBM-compatible computers. A *font*, in Windows' terminology, is the distinctive named design of a typeface, such as Helvetica or Times Roman. By using multiple fonts, any Windows user can transform those drab, dot-matrix printouts of the past into attention-getting documents that look as though they were professionally typeset.

A welcome advance, Windows' multiple on-screen fonts nevertheless brought some irritating problems with them. With Windows 3.0, as with earlier versions of Windows, problems arose in two areas: on the screen and at the printer.

On-screen, you didn't really see your font or font size choices; you saw only simulations. If you chose a printer font, such as Avant Garde, Windows used a generic screen font, such as MS Sans Serif, to display the font on-screen. Furthermore, you were limited to the font sizes listed on your applications' font menus. You could choose from a good variety of built-in sizes (8, 9, 10, 11, 12, 14, 18, 24, 36, 48, and 72 points). If you chose an unsupported font size (such as 53 points), however, Windows displayed the closest supported size. In short, Windows didn't really show you how your document would appear when printed. The program showed you only a simulation of the document's printed appearance, and this on-screen simulation could vary significantly from the printed document.

At the printer, your documents printed beautifully with the printer font you chose—*unless* the printer didn't support this font for some reason (such as not having the correct font cartridge). That problem could happen easily if you took your document home to print it after hours, only to find that your home printer didn't have that Garamond font that printed so nicely at work. What it really came down to with Windows 3.0 was WYSINWYG—What you see isn't necessarily what you get—unless you added a third-party scalable font package, such as Adobe Type Manager (ATM) or Bitstream's Facelift for Windows.

Here is some excellent news for anyone who has struggled with these problems and doesn't have ATM or FaceLift: with Version 3.1's new TrueType technology, you get all the benefits of multiple fonts with *neither* of these shortcomings.

The TrueType fonts you see on-screen are exactly the same as the ones you see when your document is printed. If you choose the Arial font, for instance, you see on-screen exactly the same Arial that you see on your printed document. Furthermore, TrueType fonts are *scalable*, which means—in brief—that you can choose any font size you like, and you see that exact font size on-screen (see fig. 6.1). That statement is true, moreover, even if you choose huge, odd-numbered font sizes, such as 63 or 109 points.

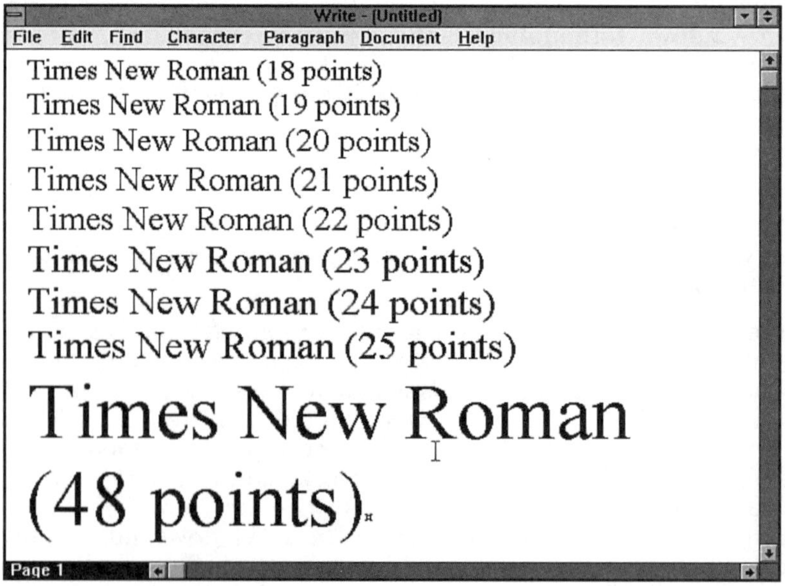

Fig. 6.1.

Sample TrueType font sizes.

TrueType fonts print on any Windows-supported printer—no special cartridge, soft font, or built-in font support is necessary. The document that prints so nicely on your Hewlett-Packard IIp prints just as attractively on your DeskJet at home. With TrueType, your documents become much more portable. You can exchange your document with colleagues or co-workers, who can print the document on their systems without going through the hassle of reformatting the fonts.

Is TrueType a major advance and a significant reason for upgrading to Windows 3.1? You bet. TrueType brings to your system the same benefits as Adobe Type Manager (ATM) or FaceLift, add-on programs that work only with compatible fonts, but—unlike these programs—TrueType is included gratis with Windows 3.1. Now that Windows supports TrueType, third-party font suppliers will begin to offer a variety of TrueType fonts, which you can add to the four fonts included with Windows.

Like all products of truly advanced technology, TrueType is extremely easy to use—and what's more, TrueType hides the complexity of the computer system. You don't have to worry about whether the screen font matches the printer font or whether the printer *has* the right font. You just choose the font, create your document, and print. You can forget about the details, which is the way a computer ought to work.

If TrueType is so easy to use, why does this book have a chapter on TrueType? TrueType is such a marked departure from previous Windows font technology that you will surely need some guidance as you upgrade your system. Several questions arise. Should you continue to use your printer's soft fonts or cartridge fonts? Does TrueType have any disadvantages? Can you use TrueType with ATM? In this chapter, you find answers to these questions and many more. Here's a quick overview of what the chapter covers:

- "Looking at TrueType Fonts" introduces the four TrueType fonts packaged with Windows 3.1: Arial, Courier New, Symbol, and Times New Roman.

- "Deciding Whether To Use TrueType" gives you a basic comparison of TrueType with other fonts. The advent of TrueType brings yet another font technology on the scene, complicating an already confusing picture. In this section, you learn how to distinguish TrueType technology from other font technologies, including screen fonts, printer fonts, cartridge fonts, and soft fonts. You learn just what advantages and disadvantages TrueType has, compared with other font technologies.

- "Using TrueType Fonts" gets down to the procedural nitty-gritty. You learn how to distinguish TrueType fonts from fonts based on other technologies, how to view samples of TrueType fonts on-screen, and how to combine TrueType and other fonts in a single document. You also learn how to print with TrueType fonts—which is pretty easy, as you will discover.

- In “Managing TrueType Fonts,” TrueType fans learn how to turn off all other fonts so that they don’t appear in application menus (and don’t consume memory), and TrueType foes learn how to disable TrueType.
- “Adding More TrueType Fonts” teaches you how to install TrueType fonts that you can purchase from third-party suppliers.

TIP If you’re quite happy with the printer fonts you have been using and their screen equivalents, you can disable TrueType fonts to conserve memory. For instructions, see “Managing TrueType Fonts” later in this chapter.

Looking at TrueType Fonts

When you install Windows 3.1 using Setup, the program installs five TrueType fonts: Arial, Courier New, Symbol, Times New Roman and Wingdings. Table 6.1 lists and describes these fonts, and figure 6.2 shows examples of three of them. These fonts appear in Windows applications menus, and you can use them right away.

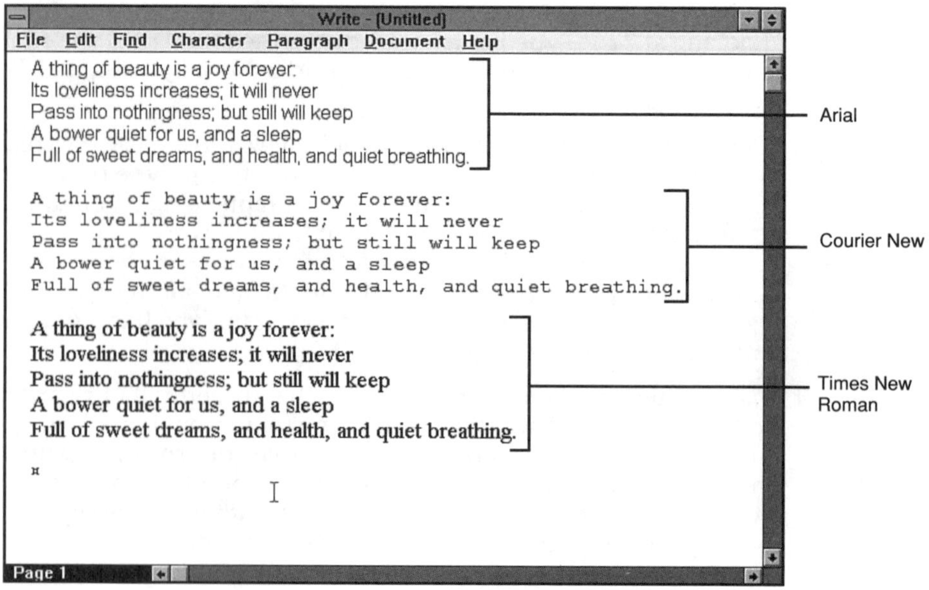

Fig. 6.2.

Samples of the TrueType fonts that come with Windows 3.1 (Arial, Courier New, and Times New Roman).

Table 6.1 TrueType Fonts Supplied with Windows 3.1

Font Name	Description
Arial	A sans serif font similar to Helvetica.
Courier New	A monospaced font that closely resembles the typescript of a fine office typewriter.
Symbol	A serif font, based on Times New Roman, that contains Greek characters and mathematical symbols.
Times New Roman	A narrow serif font similar to Times Roman. Times New Roman packs more words on a line without sacrificing readability.
Wingdings	A font, like Zapf Dingbats, that enables you to create various fun symbols, such as scissors, circled numbers, and clocks, to name a few.

The nucleus of Windows 3.1's TrueType font package contains two major building blocks for good typographic design: Arial, a *sans serif* font, and Times New Roman, a *serif* font. (A *sans serif* font doesn't have serifs, those little cross strokes at the end of each stroke of a character.)

The clean, dramatic Arial font is a fine choice for *display type*, such as titles, headings, subheadings, or banners (see fig. 6.3). With its wide character spacing, Arial isn't the best choice for *body type* (the main text of your document). Arial works well for charts, lists, tables, and spreadsheets.

A serif font that combines readability with impressive beauty and clarity, Times New Roman is an excellent choice for the main text of your document (again see fig. 6.3). Times New Roman packs more words on a line than Arial does, but without sacrificing readability—a testament to the font's excellent design. Equally at home with an authoritative financial report or a Shakespearean sonnet, Times New Roman reveals what you have been missing with those "generic" screen fonts in previous versions of Windows (see fig. 6.4).

The Symbol font, based on Times New Roman, provides Greek and mathematical symbols necessary for writing body text in a variety of scientific and technical fields. While composing text with Times New Roman, you switch to Symbol when you need one of the special characters this font contains. The character you insert blends seamlessly with the Times New Roman design.

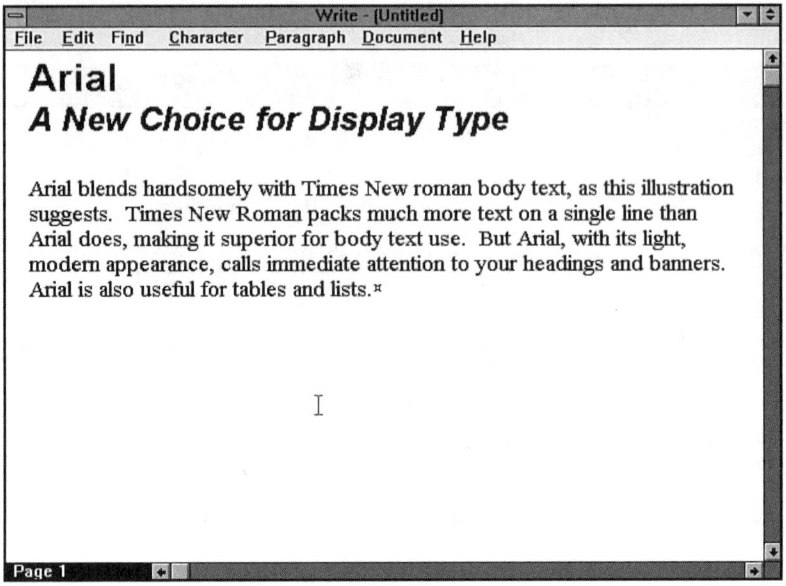

Fig. 6.3.

An example of the Arial font for heads and Times New Roman for body type.

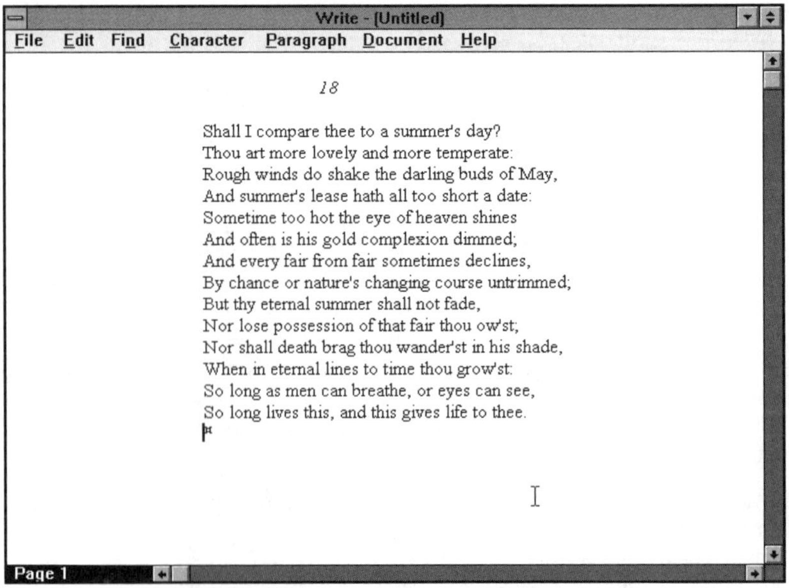

Fig. 6.4.

A Shakespearean sonnet set in Times New Roman.

NOTE The Symbol font is not designed for writing in Greek. The Greek characters included in the Symbol font are suitable for technical, mathematical, and scientific purposes, but you need more Greek characters to compose a document in Greek.

Should you need to emulate the output of a fine office typewriter, Courier New fills the bill (see fig. 6.5). Courier New suggests immediacy and personal attention, as if the document were hand-typed on a typewriter and tailored to the situation. Courier New is also useful when you need to align text by the font's fixed character spacing. Unlike Arial and Times New Roman, every character in Courier New has exactly the same width. Arial and Times New Roman are *proportionally spaced* fonts, which means that wide letters, such as *w* and *m*, get more space than thin ones, such as *i* and *l*. In other words, Courier New is a *monospaced* font.

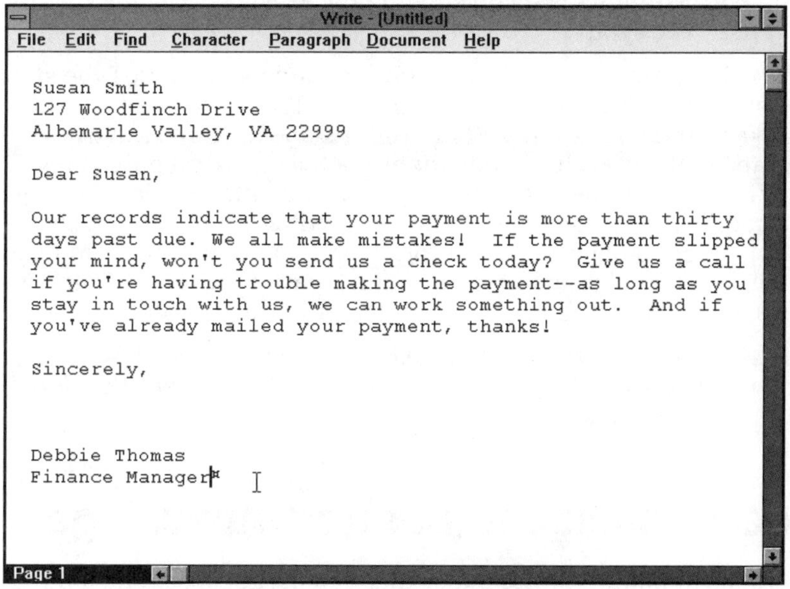

Susan Smith
127 Woodfinch Drive
Albemarle Valley, VA 22999

Dear Susan,

Our records indicate that your payment is more than thirty days past due. We all make mistakes! If the payment slipped your mind, won't you send us a check today? Give us a call if you're having trouble making the payment--as long as you stay in touch with us, we can work something out. And if you've already mailed your payment, thanks!

Sincerely,

Debbie Thomas
Finance Manager

Fig. 6.5.

A sample of the Courier New font.

As you are creating a document, you might want to use special characters to draw attention to part of your document. For example, you can use boxes (❒ ❑ ■), arrows (➲ ➔ ➘ ⇨), scissors (✄), circled numbers (❽ ④), and more. You use the Wingdings TrueType font to create these special characters. If you are familiar with PostScript, you might have seen or used the Zapf Dingbats font, which provides similar characters. Wingdings provides most of the characters available in Zapf Dingbats.

Deciding Whether To Use TrueType

More than a few Windows users feel an aversion to the subject of fonts—and for good reason. Too many font technologies are around, and learning all the terms invented for them is something of a pain. There are printer fonts, screen fonts, cartridge fonts, soft fonts, PostScript fonts, ATM fonts, and more. You wouldn't be alone if you were to exclaim, "The heck with this! I'll just use Courier."

One of the nicer aspects of TrueType is that if you feel bewildered by the forest of fonts, you can disable all other fonts and use just TrueType. (You learn how to disable all other fonts in the section "Managing TrueType Fonts" later in this chapter.) If you take this route, you can forget about what distinguishes TrueType from other font technologies. You can also forget about screen fonts, printer fonts, and all the rest. You can just create documents and print them. An appealing option, isn't it? With Windows 3.1, you should now exclaim, "The heck with this! I'll just use TrueType."

Even so, there are good reasons to understand where TrueType stands in the broader context of font technologies. TrueType is terrific, but you might want to take advantage of a printer's special font resources. For typographically intensive applications such as desktop publishing, for instance, you might need a font that's not available in a TrueType version. Under such circumstances, understanding what distinguishes TrueType technology from other font technologies can come in handy. If you would rather skip the details and just learn how to use TrueType, go to the section "Using TrueType Fonts" later in this chapter.

In this section, you learn what makes TrueType so special—and what you stand to gain by choosing TrueType fonts over other fonts resources in your system.

Understanding the TrueType Advantage

No personal computer system designer can escape from one monstrously inconvenient fact: The technology needed to produce fonts on-screen is completely different from the technology used to produce fonts at the printer. Windows 3.1 faced this same dilemma.

TrueType overcomes the limitations of Windows 3.0 by providing *outline font* technology, both for your screen and your printer. You see exactly the same type on-screen that appears when you print your document, and what's more, any Windows-compatible printer can print the TrueType font you have chosen.

Here's how TrueType conquers the distinction between screen fonts and printer fonts. Each TrueType font is stored in the form of complex mathematical equations, which are capable of drawing an outline of each character. After the outline has been drawn, the display or printing device then fills in the character at the device's highest possible resolution. That technology explains why TrueType fonts work just as well with screens as with printers, despite the differences between screen and printer technologies. The TrueType font generator says, in effect, "Here's the outline of this character. Now you just fill it in the best you know how." For this reason, TrueType fonts can work on a huge variety of screens and printers, despite variations in *resolution*, the density of the dots with which a printer or screen fills in the characters.

Because each TrueType character is generated by a mathematical equation, TrueType fonts can be sized just as you please. For this reason, TrueType fonts are called *scalable* fonts. The best way to understand the advantages of a scalable font is to understand the disadvantages of the screen fonts provided with Windows. These fonts are *bit-mapped fonts*. A bit-mapped font is made up of individual characters, each of which has been created out of tiny, individual dots. Bit-mapped fonts take up huge amounts of disk space because the disk must contain one complete set of such characters for each font size you want to use. (Common sizes include 9, 10, 12, 14, 18, and 24.) Worse, you cannot choose a font size other than the ones stored on disk, at least not without causing hideous distortions. With scalable fonts, you can choose any font size you want.

To put the TrueType advantage another way, TrueType technology is *device independent*. This term means that TrueType isn't tied to the specific capabilities of a given brand or model of display device or printer. TrueType just generates the outlines and leaves to the screen and printer the job of filling in the outlines. Of course, the better your screen and printer, the better the results you get. But you don't have to invest heavily in displays and printers to get outstanding results with TrueType. An ordinary VGA monitor and an entry-level laser printer, such as a Hewlett-Packard IIp, will produce outstanding results.

Here's a quick summary of the benefits of TrueType:

- With a TrueType font, you can choose any font size you want, and Windows 3.1 displays the font size accurately.
- The font you see on-screen looks exactly the same as the font you see on your printed document.
- No special screen or printer resources are needed to display and print TrueType fonts. TrueType technology automatically tells the screen and printer to display and print the font at the device's highest possible resolution.

- If you prepare a document with TrueType, you can print the document on any Windows 3.1 system without having to change the fonts.

These benefits are indeed impressive. TrueType is sure to become the standard font technology for Windows systems.

Understanding the Disadvantages of TrueType

Terrific as TrueType is, it does have disadvantages. Here's a short list of the shortcomings of TrueType for Windows 3.1 users:

- *TrueType prints slowly on some printers.* Some dot-matrix and inkjet printers produce TrueType output much more slowly than they print text formatted with the printer's native fonts. If your printer takes a long time to print a document formatted with TrueType fonts, try switching to a printer font to see whether printing speed improves.
- *TrueType limits font availability.* Many non-TrueType fonts are available in the form of cartridges and soft fonts. However, this situation is expected to change as third-party suppliers create more TrueType fonts.
- *TrueType lacks special printing effects.* Unlike PostScript, a popular page-description language that is supported by PostScript-compatible laser printers (such as the Apple LaserWriter NT), TrueType cannot set type at an angle or along a curve or nonlinear path. These effects are frequently used in desktop publishing. For professional desktop publishing applications, PostScript-compatible printers and fonts still have many advantages.
- *TrueType consumes memory.* If your system is short on memory, you might want to disable TrueType (see the section "Managing TrueType Fonts" later in this chapter). But buying more memory is probably better than turning off TrueType. As any experienced Windows user can tell you, you're going to find plenty of other reasons to upgrade your memory besides TrueType. For good performance, equip your system with 4M of memory; for optimum performance, get 8M.

Should You Continue To Use Printer Fonts?

Chances are you have equipped your system with many printer font resources, possibly including *cartridge fonts* (fonts available on a cartridge you insert into a slot in your printer) or *soft fonts* (printer fonts stored on disk and downloaded to your printer when needed). Should you continue to use these fonts after upgrading to Windows 3.1? Here's a list of questions you can ask yourself to help you decide:

- *Do you frequently give your disk files to colleagues or co-workers to print on their systems?* If so, the portability of the basic TrueType fonts will prove advantageous. Your colleagues or co-workers will be able to print your documents on their Windows 3.1 systems without having to redo your font choices. If you seldom give your disk files to others, TrueType has little advantage over printer fonts in this area.

- *Do you format complex documents in which you need to see exactly how characters will appear when printed?* If so, TrueType has a significant advantage over bit-mapped printer fonts: You see your font choices and font sizes on-screen, exactly as they appear when printed. If you just write letters and proposals and care little about the exact on-screen appearance of your documents, printer fonts might serve your needs just as well.

- *Does your printer print TrueType fonts quickly?* With some printers, printing occurs much more rapidly if you choose one of the printer's built-in fonts. If your printer prints TrueType sluggishly, you might prefer to use printer fonts.

- *Do you have a PostScript printer?* PostScript is a complete page-description language that is capable of many special effects. PostScript sets the industry standard for excellence in computer-based typography. In addition, PostScript printers, such as the Apple LaserWriter NT, typically come equipped with several PostScript fonts, such as Avant Garde and Zapf Chancery. Although your PostScript printer can print TrueType fonts, you probably will want to continue using your PostScript printer's fonts.

- *Do you use non-Windows applications?* If you're like most Windows users, you're still using some DOS applications. With these applications, you cannot take advantage of TrueType. You still need printer fonts to print non-Windows application documents. You can disable these fonts within Windows applications so that the fonts don't take up memory when you're using Windows. For more information, see "Managing TrueType Fonts."

Should You Continue To Use ATM?

Many Windows 3.0 users have equipped their systems with Adobe Type Manager (ATM), which provides almost exactly the same benefits as TrueType. If you already have ATM, is there any point in using TrueType? Here's a list of some points you can consider as you try to decide whether to switch from ATM to TrueType:

- *Every Windows 3.1 system has TrueType, but not all are equipped with ATM.* If you want to give your disk files to others for printing on their systems, TrueType is a better choice because all Windows 3.1 systems have TrueType. ATM, in contrast, is an optional add-on program—and with TrueType available, it's a safe bet that fewer Windows users will purchase ATM.
- *ATM requires expensive Adobe fonts; TrueType fonts are cheaper.* At this book's printing, TrueType fonts are roughly 20 to 40 percent cheaper than the ATM-compatible fonts offered by Adobe. As Adobe faces increased competition from independent suppliers of TrueType fonts, however, the firm might be forced to lower its prices.
- *ATM screen fonts provide exact matches for the fonts built into most PostScript-compatible printers.* If your system has a PostScript laser printer, you have a good reason indeed to continue running ATM. Equip your system with Adobe Systems' ATM Plus Pack to get screen versions of the PostScript fonts usually built into PostScript printers.
- *You can run TrueType and ATM together, but both require memory.* Unless your system is equipped with huge amounts of RAM, you might prefer to choose one over the other.

NOTE Although ATM and TrueType are similar from the user's point of view, they use different mathematical strategies to achieve the same goal. For this reason, TrueType cannot use ATM fonts, and ATM cannot use TrueType fonts.

Using TrueType Fonts

Like all products of good technology, TrueType is easy to use. You choose TrueType fonts just as you choose any other font. You can see a preview of TrueType fonts (and other fonts) on-screen. If you want to choose special characters, such as accented characters or symbols, a new feature, Character Map, enables you to choose special characters from an on-screen map rather than fussing with ASCII codes. The sections to follow explore these procedures.

Trying TrueType for the First Time

In the following tutorial, you learn how to choose TrueType fonts with Windows Write. You learn how to distinguish TrueType fonts from printer fonts in the Font dialog box, and you have an opportunity to see how your printer handles the TrueType fonts. You also find out whether your printer takes appreciably longer printing TrueType fonts than printing printer fonts. For this tutorial, you need a watch with a second hand to time printing—or if you prefer, you can activate and display the Clock accessory.

To explore TrueType fonts, follow these steps:

1. In Program Manager, double-click the Accessories group icon.

   You see the Accessories window.

2. Double-click the Write icon.

   Windows starts Write, and you see a blank Write document on-screen.

3. Click the Maximize button to zoom the Write window to full size.

4. Choose Fonts from the Character menu.

   You see the Font dialog box (see fig. 6.6). Note that Write uses icons to distinguish TrueType fonts from printer fonts. In the Sample area, you see a sample of the font that is selected in the Font list box (Arial). The message confirms that this font is a TrueType font.

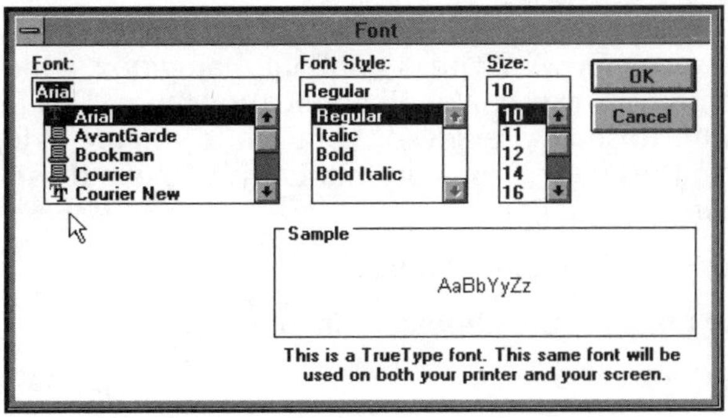

Fig. 6.6.

The Windows Write Font dialog box.

5. In the Font list box, choose Arial.

   Write echoes your choice in the Font text box, just above the list box. The font shown in this text box is the one Write will use after you choose OK.

6. In the Size box, choose 12. In the Font Style box, the Regular option is selected by default. You can choose Italic, Bold, and Bold Italic, if you want.

7. Choose OK.

8. Type a paragraph of text.

   Write creates the text with the font you have chosen. After you have typed some text, you can easily reformat the text just by selecting it and choosing Font from the Character menu. You can choose a different font, font size, or style (such as boldface, italic, or underline).

9. Make three copies of the paragraphs you typed. Format the second with Courier New, the third with Symbol, and the fourth with Times New Roman.

10. Choose Print from the File menu, and when the Print dialog box appears, choose OK. Time printing from the moment you click OK to the ejection of the last page from the printer. Note the time.

11. Select the whole document. Choose a non-TrueType printer font, such as Courier, and print the document again. Time the printing the same way you did in step 10.

Any difference? With many printers, TrueType printing times will be only slightly longer. If the difference is considerable, you may want to consider whether TrueType's advantages are worth the wait.

Viewing Font Samples

A nice feature of Windows Write is the Font dialog box, which previews your font choices on-screen. Not all applications have this feature, however. If you want to see a preview of fonts while you are using an application that doesn't preview them automatically, you can do so by choosing the Font icon in Control Panel.

To preview fonts, follow these steps:

1. From the Main group, choose Control Panel.

   You see Control Panel.

2. Choose Fonts.

   You see the Fonts dialog box.

3. In the Installed Fonts list box, choose the font you want to preview.

   You see a sample of the font in the Sample box (see fig. 6.7). Below the Sample box, you see a message describing the font.

TIP

If you're using an application that doesn't use icons to distinguish TrueType fonts from printer fonts, you can find out quickly whether a font is a TrueType font by choosing Font from Control Panel. The Installed Fonts list box indicates whether the installed fonts are TrueType or printer fonts.

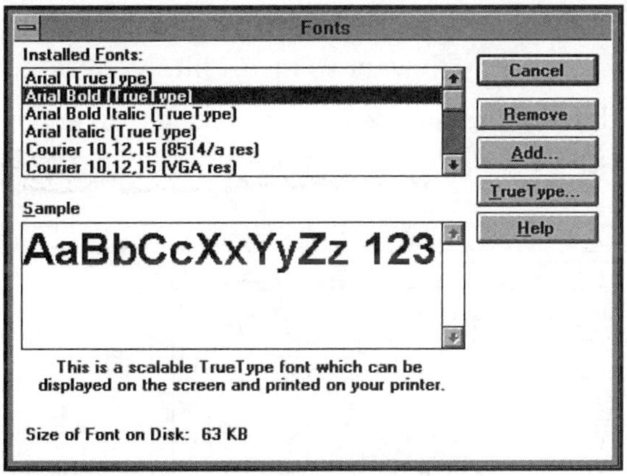

Fig. 6.7.

A sample of the font appears in the Sample box.

Choosing Special Characters

In previous versions of Windows, the only way you could insert special characters, such as accented vowels, was to hold down the Alt key and type an ASCII code—an unsatisfactory method, at best. A nifty new feature of Windows 3.1, Character Map, provides a much easier way to choose special characters.

To insert a special character into your document, follow these steps:

1. From the Accessories group, choose Character Map.

   You see the Character Map dialog box (see fig. 6.8). The grid shows all the characters available with the font selected in the Font list box (Arial in figure 6.8). Note that the right panel in the bottom border shows the Alt key code you can use to enter the selected character directly from the keyboard.

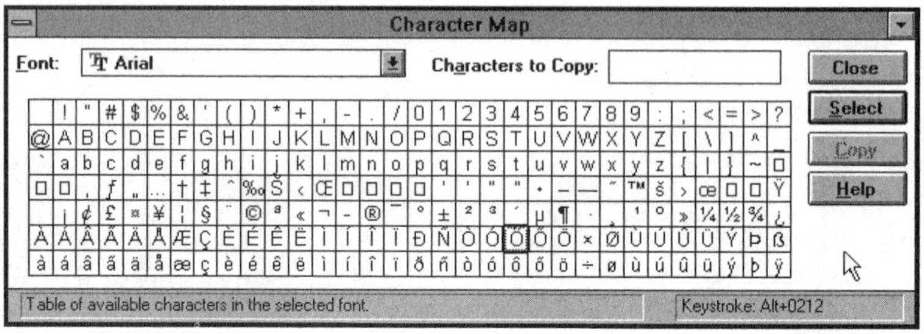

Fig. 6.8.

The Character Map dialog box.

2. In the Font list box, choose the font from which you want to choose the character.
3. Click the character you want to insert into your document.

   If you hold down the mouse button, you see an enlarged view of the character (see fig. 6.9).

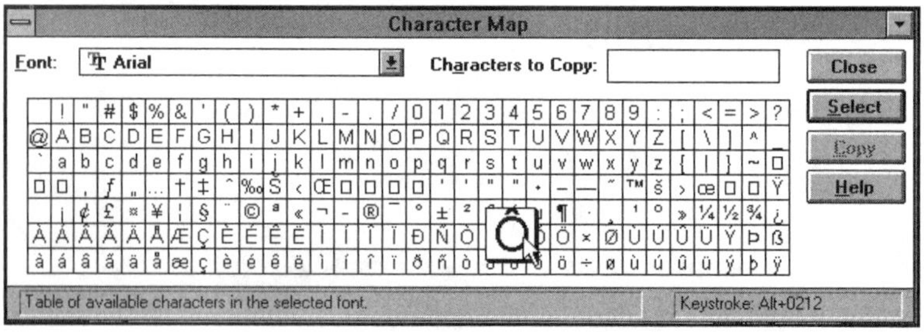

Fig. 6.9.

An enlarged view of a special character.

4. Choose Select to place the character in the Characters to Copy box. Alternatively, just double-click the character.
5. To select additional characters, repeat steps 3 and 4.
6. When you have placed all the characters you want in the Characters to Copy list box, choose Copy to copy these characters to the Clipboard.
7. Choose Close to close the Character Map dialog box.
8. Switch to your document, and position the insertion point where you want the characters to appear.

9. Choose Paste from the Edit menu, or press the Ctrl-V keyboard shortcut.

The special characters are inserted into your document.

Are you curious about the special characters available with TrueType fonts? Figures 6.10, 6.11, and 6.12 show the Character Maps for Courier New, Symbol, and Times New Roman, respectively.

NOTE

In some applications, the inserted characters might lose the font you choose in Character Map. To restore the font, select the character or characters you just inserted, and choose the font from the application's font menu.

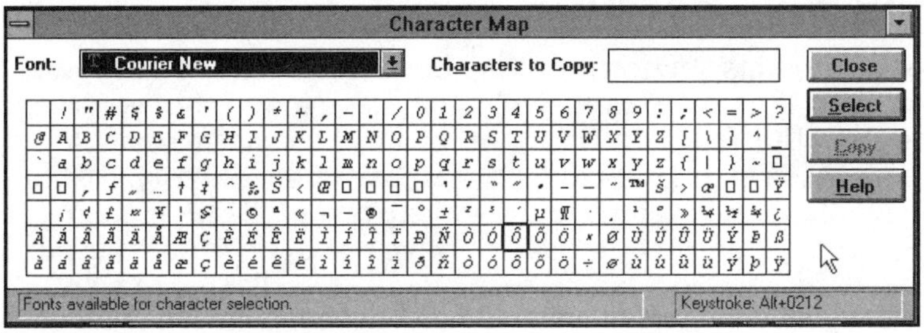

Fig. 6.10.

The character map for the Courier New font.

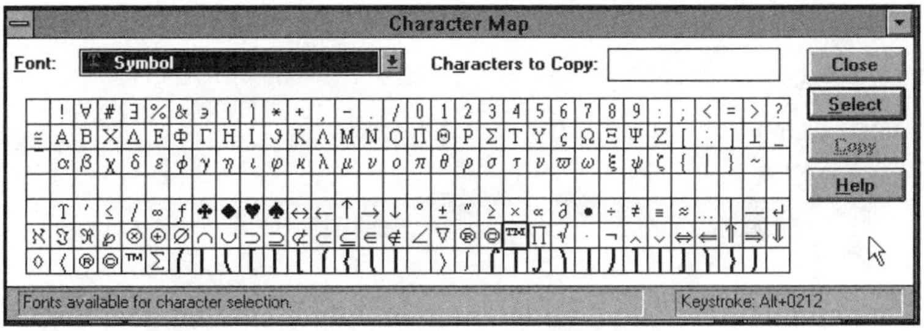

Fig. 6.11.

The character map for the Symbol font.

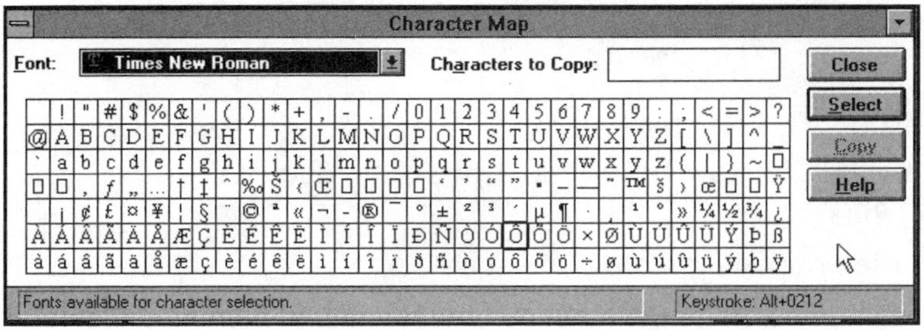

Fig. 6.12.

The character map for Times New Roman.

Managing TrueType Fonts

After you have used TrueType fonts for a while, you might realize that you like them so much that you're not using any other fonts. If so, you can choose an option that shows nothing but TrueType fonts in the font lists of your Windows applications. Alternatively, you might find that you're not using TrueType fonts at all. In this case, you can disable TrueType fonts. Both options conserve memory without actually removing the fonts from your hard disk. You can always change your mind later, and reactivate the fonts you have turned off.

Turning Off All Other Fonts

If you're reading this section, you're a bona fide TrueType convert. You have used TrueType extensively, and have found that you're not choosing any other fonts. In this case, you will be wise to disable non-TrueType fonts, which are taking up memory unnecessarily. Disabling TrueType fonts merely removes the fonts from application menus (and from memory) but doesn't actually remove the fonts from your hard disk. For this reason, you can restore the fonts easily, if you want, at a later time.

To disable non-TrueType fonts, follow these steps:

1. From Control Panel, choose Fonts.
2. From the Fonts dialog box, choose the TrueType button.

   You see the TrueType dialog box (see fig. 6.13).

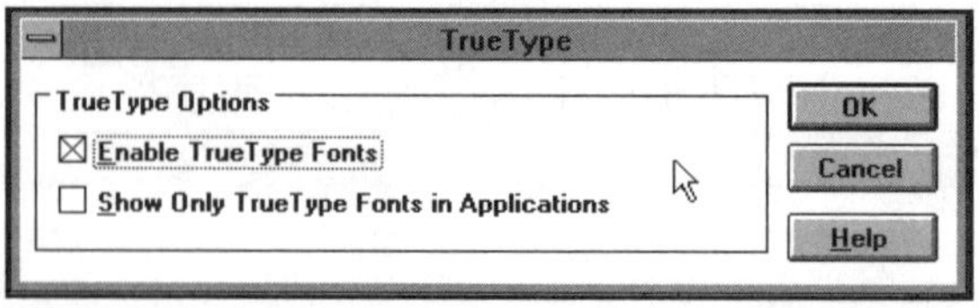

Fig. 6.13.

The TrueType dialog box.

3. Activate the Enable TrueType Fonts check box if it is dimmed.
4. Activate the Show Only TrueType Fonts in Applications check box and choose OK.

   You see the Fonts dialog box again.
5. Close the Fonts dialog box.

After you disable non-TrueType fonts, font lists in most applications show only TrueType fonts. Figure 6.14 shows the font list in Write's Font dialog box after non-TrueType fonts have been disabled. Note that only four fonts—the TrueType fonts—are displayed.

Restoring Non-TrueType Fonts

After you have disabled non-TrueType fonts, as explained in the preceding section, you might want to restore them. Suppose, for instance, that you have decided to create a document which takes advantage of one of your printer's built-in fonts. You can quickly restore the non-TrueType fonts.

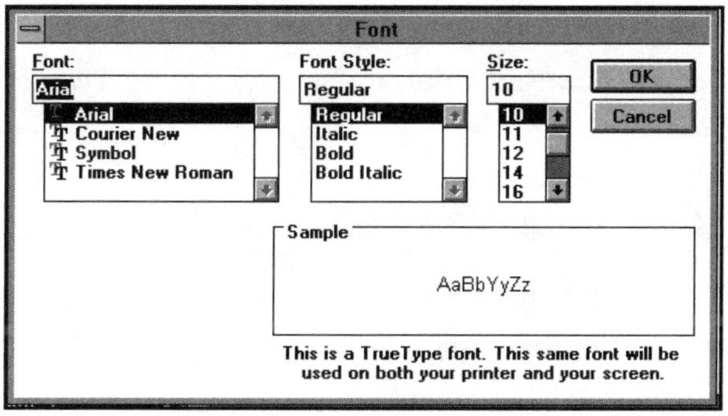

Fig. 6.14.

The Font dialog box showing only TrueType fonts.

To restore non-TrueType fonts, follow these steps:

1. From Control Panel, choose Fonts.
2. From the Fonts dialog box, choose the TrueType button.

   You see the TrueType dialog box.
3. Deactivate the Show Only TrueType Fonts in Applications check box.
4. Choose OK.

   You see the Fonts dialog box again.
5. Close the Fonts dialog box.

You will see printer fonts in your applications' font menus again.

Disabling TrueType Fonts

If you have decided to use your printer fonts and their screen equivalents and have no need of TrueType fonts, you can disable them. Disabling TrueType fonts doesn't remove them from your hard disk; it merely removes them from memory and from your applications' font menus. If you want to activate TrueType fonts in the future, you can do so quickly and easily, as explained in this section.

To disable TrueType fonts, follow these steps:

1. From Control Panel, choose Fonts.
2. From the Fonts dialog box, choose the TrueType button.

   You see the TrueType dialog box.
3. Deactivate the Enable TrueType Fonts check box.

   Windows dims the other option, Show Only TrueType Fonts in Applications.
4. Choose OK.

   You see the Fonts dialog box again.
5. Close the Fonts dialog box.

You will not see TrueType fonts in your applications' font menus.

Disabling and Restoring Fonts Individually

If you find that you're not using one or two of the TrueType fonts, you can conserve memory by removing those fonts from the Installed Fonts list. For example, suppose that you never use Courier or Symbol, but you want to keep Arial and Times New Roman. You can remove just the fonts you're not using by following the procedure given in this section. Removing a font just deletes it from the Installed Fonts list; it doesn't erase the font on disk, so you can restore the disabled fonts later, if you want.

To disable fonts individually, follow these steps:

1. From Control Panel, choose Fonts.
2. In the Installed Fonts list box, highlight the name of the font you want to disable.
3. Choose Remove.

You see an alert box asking you to confirm that you want to remove the font. The alert box contains a check box that enables you to remove the file from disk, if you want. This check box isn't activated.

4. Choose OK to remove the font from the Installed Fonts list.
5. Choose Close to return to Control Panel.

To restore a font you have disabled, follow these steps:

1. From Control Panel, choose Fonts.

   You see the Fonts dialog box.

2. Choose Add.

   You see the Add Fonts dialog box (see fig. 6.15).

3. In the Directories list box, choose the System subdirectory within the Windows directory.

   This directory contains the fonts packaged with Windows.

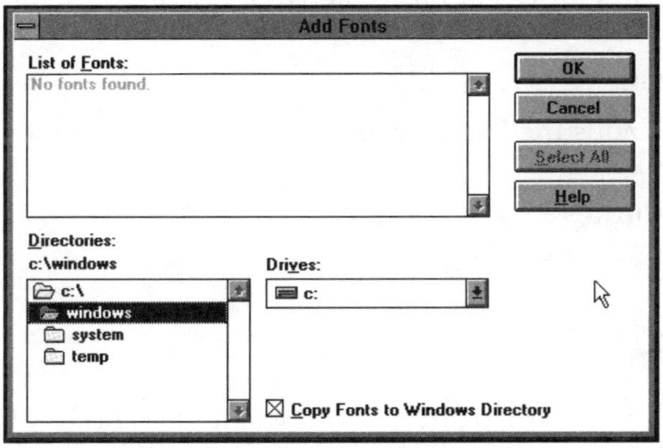

Fig. 6.15.

The Add Fonts dialog box.

4. Highlight the name of the font you want to restore.
5. Choose OK.

   Windows restores the font to the Installed Fonts list box, and you see the Fonts dialog box again.

6. Choose Close.

Adding More TrueType Fonts

Now that Windows supports TrueType, you can expect many font suppliers to offer TrueType fonts for Windows systems. In short order, TrueType will become the standard for Windows fonts, and a variety of font choices will become available. In this section, you learn how to add TrueType fonts to your system.

When you buy a TrueType font, the supplier might include an installation program that adds the font to Windows automatically. If not, you can easily install the font using the following procedure.

To install a TrueType font, follow these steps:

1. From Control Panel, choose Fonts.

   You see the Fonts dialog box.

2. Choose Add.

   You see the Add Fonts dialog box (again see fig. 6.15).

3. Use the Directories list box to activate the drive and directory that contain the font you want to add.

4. Choose OK.

   Windows adds the font to your system, and you see the Fonts dialog box again.

5. Choose Close.

Summary

In this chapter you learned about TrueType fonts—a type of font included with Windows 3.1 that enables you to see on-screen what will be produced from the printer. You learned the advantages—and disadvantages—of TrueType fonts and how to use them in Windows 3.1 to create high-profile documents. You also learned how to disable TrueType fonts if you don't want to use them.

7

CHAPTER

Using Object Linking and Embedding (OLE)

When a new computer feature comes along, many computer users conclude—rightly in most cases—that it's probably too advanced to be of much use to the average user. For this reason, many Windows users will be tempted to ignore Windows 3.1's enhanced *object linking and embedding (OLE)* capabilities. The term suggests a complex, difficult procedure that only a genuine computer freak would want to explore. But that concept is false. As this chapter shows, OLE is actually easy to understand, easy to use, and incredibly valuable for just about any Windows user. If OLE sounds intimidating, read on. You will be glad you did.

To understand why OLE is so valuable, consider the following all-too-likely scenario.

Your boss is clamoring for the bottom line on the analysis you're doing on Excel, and you finally get the answer. Voila! $3,366,722. Clearly, acquiring Bungle Associates is a great idea for your firm. Using the Clipboard, you copy the spreadsheet to your Word document. Only then do you remember that you left something out of your spreadsheet analysis—something *big*. You go back to Excel and make the change, which dramatically affects the spreadsheet's bottom line. All of a sudden, acquiring Bungle Associates doesn't seem like such a good idea. Just then, you're distracted by a phone call, and you forget to recopy the spreadsheet to the Word document. Thinking that you did recopy the spreadsheet, when in fact you didn't, you print the Word document and hand it to your boss. The result? You have given her the wrong figure! Your firm acquires Bungle Associates, but unfortunately, the acquisition lives up to its name.

This scenario helps explain why Windows' object linking and embedding (OLE) capabilities are so important and why you don't have to be an advanced user to be interested in this subject. Without OLE, updating copied information is a hassle—worse, a *manual* hassle. You must start the source application, open the source file, make the changes, and do the copy-and-paste operation all over.

The major advantage of OLE, simply put, is that, should you change any information in the source document, Windows will *automatically* update all the copies you have made of the information, even if you have copied it into documents created in another application. (Both applications, of course, must be OLE-compatible.) OLE provides functionality that is so basic and so useful that knowledge of OLE procedures is rightfully part of the computer skills all Windows users should possess.

Imagine the same scenario using OLE instead of the Clipboard. When you copy the spreadsheet into Word, you use Paste Link—the command that establishes an OLE-based dynamic link. To update the Excel spreadsheet, you just double-click the *copy* of the spreadsheet that you have inserted into the Word document. Windows automatically starts Excel and displays the source spreadsheet. You make the changes in the source spreadsheet in Excel, and then choose Exit from the File menu. The changes you make are *automatically* reflected in the copy of the information in your Word document—and in all other copies of the source spreadsheet, too, as long as you made the copies with Paste Link. With OLE, you don't have to track down all the copies to make the needed changes. In every document that reproduces the Excel spreadsheet, the sad truth about the spreadsheet's bottom line, and about Bungle Associates, appears automatically.

Much more can be said about OLE techniques and procedures, but now you know why they're valuable—and why this chapter is worth reading for virtually every Windows 3.1 user.

What's new about OLE with Windows 3.1? By means of technical capabilities known as *dynamic data exchange (DDE)*, OLE capabilities were built into Windows 3.0; but only OLE-compatible applications (such as the most recent versions of Excel and Word for Windows) could take advantage of the OLE capabilities. That restriction still holds true. To use OLE, you need OLE-capable applications (such as Lotus AmiPro, Microsoft Excel, and Microsoft Word for Windows). What is new about Windows 3.1's OLE capabilities is that four Windows accessories—Write, Paintbrush, Sound Recorder, and Cardfile—are now OLE-compatible. In addition, a new accessory—called Object Packager—lets you embed a file in another document so that it appears as an icon. When you double-click this icon, the source document appears on-screen.

The OLE capabilities of these Windows accessories greatly expand their usefulness, but even so, you're not likely to stop using a full-featured application like Word just because Write is OLE-capable. But read on. Even if you have OLE-compatible applications, such as Excel and Word for Windows, chances are that you, like most users, haven't yet explored Windows' OLE capabilities. For most readers of this book, the new OLE capabilities of these four applications represent an appealing change for learning purposes, because you can now explore OLE in the friendly environment of these simple applications. OLE isn't easy to understand just by reading about it; the best way to learn how to use and apply OLE is to try it with your computer, and the Windows accessories provide the ideal learning environment. This chapter features a tutorial in which you try linking and embedding with the Windows accessories.

Here's a quick overview of what's covered in this chapter:

- In "Understanding Object Linking and Embedding," OLE is defined in plain language from the user's point of view. You learn how to distinguish copying, linking, and embedding, and how to know when one technique is better for transferring information between documents.
- In "Tutorial: Exploring Linking and Embedding," you learn by doing, using the OLE-capable Windows accessories. You see right on your screen what OLE can do.
- "Creating Links and Embedding Objects" covers OLE procedures more generically, in such a way that you can adapt these procedures to all the OLE-capable Windows applications you're using.
- In "Managing Objects," you learn how to gain more control over the embedding and linking processes. You also learn how to manage dynamic links, including copying, breaking, and repairing links.
- "Using Object Packager" describes a new Windows 3.1 accessory, Object Packager, which you can use to *package* linked or embedded documents. A packaged document appears in the destination file as an icon. If you double-click the icon, you see the source document.

NOTE

Bear in mind that not all Windows applications are OLE-capable. If you're not sure about an application, check the documentation that came with the program. Four Windows accessories are OLE-capable (Write, Cardfile, Paintbrush, and Sound Recorder), as are Excel 3.0, AmiPro 2.0, Word for Windows 2.0, and many other popular applications. If your favorite application program isn't OLE-capable, don't despair. Watch for a new version that takes full advantage of Windows 3.1's OLE capabilities.

Understanding Object Linking and Embedding

When an important technological advance in personal computing comes along, the industry seems unable to resist inventing an incomprehensible new term for the new technology. That's true even for advances that, from the user's perspective, are simple and easy to use after you get used to them. Object linking and embedding is a classic example. The term *object linking and embedding* is obscure enough to send any sensible user running for cover. And yet, as you discover in this chapter, the concepts are easy to understand and apply. The underlying technology isn't, but you can leave that to Microsoft!

This section introduces embedding and linking, explains the differences between them in simple language, and indicates when you would prefer one over the other. You will find the following terms useful for this discussion:

- An *object* is simply a whole document or part of a document, such as a part of an Excel spreadsheet or a corner of a Paintbrush drawing.
- A *server application* is a Windows application that's capable of providing an object to other applications. Not all OLE-capable applications can function as servers. Among the Windows 3.1 accessories, only Paintbrush and Sound Recorder are server applications. Write and Cardfile cannot function as servers.
- A *client application* is a Windows application that's capable of receiving an object created by a server application. Not all OLE-capable applications can function as client applications. Write and Cardfile can function as client applications, but Paintbrush and Sound Recorder cannot.
- The *source document* is the document from which you copy an object. You create the source document with the server application.
- The *destination document* is the document into which you paste or embed the object. You create the destination document with the client application.

NOTE Each OLE-capable Windows accessory can function as either server or client, but not both. That's not the norm. Word and Excel, for instance, can function as both server and client applications. Just remember that Paintbrush and Sound Recorder can send, and Write and Cardfile can receive—but not the other way around.

To understand linking and embedding, start by considering the limitations of techniques you have already learned to copy information via the Clipboard: using the Copy or Cut commands to transfer information to the Clipboard, and then using the Paste command to insert the information into a new location. This technique is still available in Windows 3.1, and has its use when there is no need to create a dynamic link between the source document and the destination document. Without OLE, however, you have no other option than to use the ordinary Clipboard techniques in situations where you will be in for a major hassle if imported information needs updating. Such situations arise when you are transferring information from one application to another and, therefore, the destination document's application cannot help you edit the copied information.

Suppose, for example, that you copy a Paintbrush picture to a Write document through the Clipboard. After pasting the picture into your Write document, you cannot alter the picture. If the picture isn't right, you must delete the picture, switch to Paintbrush, make the needed change, and recopy the picture. As you will see, the fundamental advantage of linking and embedding is that *updating* a copied object (such as the Paintbrush picture) is much easier.

Linking

When you link one document with another, you copy an object, just as you copy through the Clipboard. You copy the object from the source document in the server to the Clipboard and then to the destination document in the client application. The only difference is that you use the Paste Link command (instead of Paste) to copy from the Clipboard to the destination document.

NOTE You can link objects only from documents you have saved to disk. Before you copy the object for linking, be sure to save the source document.

When you use Paste Link to copy the object, Windows stores hidden information in the destination document about the object's origin. If you make changes to the source document, Windows uses this information to update the copy of the object in the destination document. If the destination file is open when you change the source document, the change is automatic and instantaneous. If the destination file is closed, you are prompted to update the destination file the next time you open it.

After you create a link, you can easily edit the source document from within the destination document. You just double-click the linked object, and Windows displays the object within the server application. You make the changes you want and save them. When you return to the client application (and the destination document), you see that Windows has updated the copy automatically.

In summary, linking gives you a way of making one or more copies of an object, which you can insert into one or more destination documents. Any change made to the source document is automatically reflected in all the copies.

Embedding

When you link an object, you establish links between the source document and the linked object. The linked object is just an on-screen simulation of the appearance of the real file, the source document. It doesn't contain the hidden information that would be needed to alter the source document. When you want to update the linked object, Windows begins by erasing the copy. It then starts the server application and opens the source document, where you make the changes you want. When you're finished, Windows recopies the information to the destination document.

Embedding is different. When you embed an object, you actually put the object's whole file right into the destination document. The embedded object becomes part of the destination document. When you update the embedded object, it isn't necessary for Windows to display the source document. No other information is necessary. The source document isn't necessary. The embedded object can stand on its own as an editable file. When you double-click the embedded object, Windows starts the server application and gives you all the server application's tools, as if they were an extension of the client application. But you're editing the embedded object, not the source document.

Now that you know the major technical distinction between linking and embedding, you're ready to grasp the big difference between them. The major difference between linking and embedding is that, *with embedding, no link is created between the source document and the destination document.* The embedded object stands on its own. Like linked information, the embedded object is fully editable, but your changes will not affect the source document.

If no link is created between the source document and the destination document, why bother with embedding? Why not just use the regular Clipboard methods? Embedding creates a fully editable copy of the original document; you can modify this copy as much you like without worrying about affecting the original. That capability is advantageous in certain situations. Suppose that you have created a fantastic graphic with Paintbrush, and you want to keep the graphic just the way it is. But you're creating a Write document that calls for a slight modification to the graphic. After embedding the graphic in the Write document, you can modify the embedded graphic as you please, without affecting the original.

In summary, embedding gives you a way of adding a *fully editable copy* of an object to your destination document. You can change the object as you please, calling on the full resources of the server application as you do. But the original version of the file remains undisturbed.

Choosing between Linking and Embedding

Both linking and embedding facilitate the editing and updating of information placed in a destination document. With either technique, you just double-click the object to have Windows start the server application, display the object, and give you all the tools necessary to make the needed change. The difference between the two techniques is simply that with linking, you can create two or more dynamically linked copies of the original, and a change to any one of them is reflected automatically in all the others. With embedding, editing is convenient, but the changes affect only that embedded object.

Linking is useful when you want to maintain one authoritative version of a file, which you might want to copy many times. For example, suppose that you keep your firm's price list in one authoritative Excel spreadsheet. You often copy all or part of this document to Word documents, such as reports or proposals. You always want a change in the Excel spreadsheet to be reflected automatically in all the copies you have placed in Word documents. You choose linking.

Embedding is useful when you want to place just one copy of an object in a file, and you don't want the changes you make to this object to be reflected in the original or any other copies. For example, suppose that you embed your firm's price list in a proposal. Just for this one client, you want to cut all your prices by 10 percent. You don't want this change to be reflected in the original Excel spreadsheet! You choose embedding, and after embedding the object, you double-click it and use Excel to change the prices. The changes you make don't affect the original spreadsheet. Here, embedding is the best choice.

Does the ordinary Clipboard copying technique still have a role to play, now that OLE is available? Windows 3.1 supports Clipboard copying and pasting, with Cut or Copy or Paste, and for good reasons. Many applications don't support OLE, or—like the Windows accessories—can serve only as clients or only as servers. In addition, the Clipboard is useful for text editing within and between documents. Even so, you will be wise to use linking and embedding as often as you can. Using OLE is like expanding the capabilities of your application software by a huge factor.

To illustrate how using OLE expands the capabilities of your application software, imagine a Word document into which you have linked or embedded objects created with PowerPoint, Paintbrush, and Excel. When you double-click the object created by PowerPoint, Windows starts PowerPoint as if it were a subprogram of Word. When you quit PowerPoint after editing the object, you return to Word just where you left off. The same goes for the objects created by Paintbrush and Excel. From your standpoint as user, you're working with just one incredibly powerful program, which can do almost anything you please. In time, you stop thinking about starting and quitting specific applications; you think instead of performing specific kinds of tasks, such as writing or illustrating, using the tools that are seamlessly available to you in what appears to be a totally integrated software environment. That's a pretty dramatic change, and you are no doubt going to love it.

NOTE When you embed an object, you transfer to the destination document all the information the server application needs so that you can update the file. No source document is needed. However, this information takes up much more disk space than a linked copy does. As long as you have plenty of disk space, this need for extra space shouldn't pose a problem, but bear in mind that adding objects can double or triple a file size.

Tutorial: Exploring Linking and Embedding

If you're still not sure that you understand what OLE is all about, rest assured. The best way to understand computer concepts is to try them out. In this section, you learn how to link a Paintbrush graphic with two Write files and a Cardfile document. You make changes to the graphic and see how these changes affect all the linked copies of the graphic. Then you embed the same graphic in a third Write document and alter the graphic. As you will see, the changes you make affect only the embedded object.

To explore linking, follow these steps:

1. Use Paintbrush to create a graphic you can edit easily, like the logo in figure 7.1.

2. Save the graphic with the file name SOURCE1; this file is the source file. This step is very important.

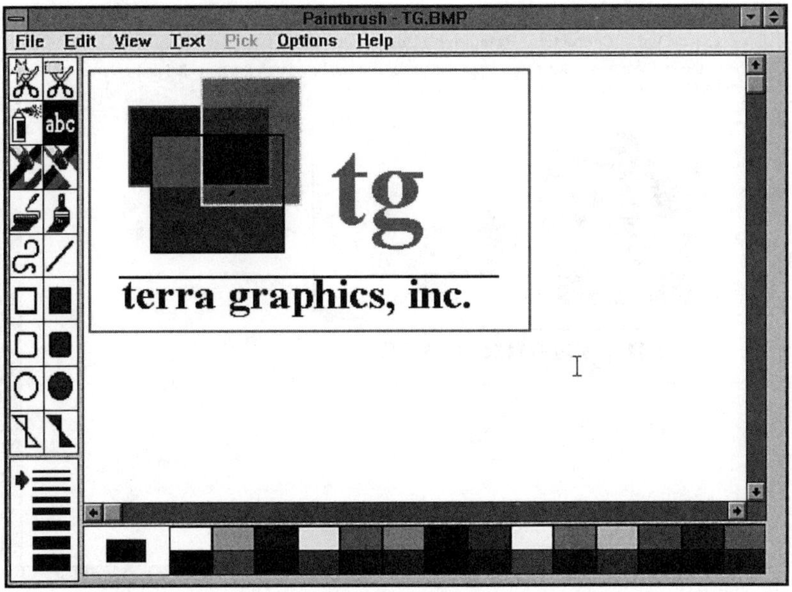

Fig. 7.1.

A graphic created in Paintbrush for linking.

3. Select the graphic, and choose Copy from the Edit menu. You also can press the Ctrl-C keyboard shortcut.

   You have copied the graphic to the Clipboard.

4. Switch to Write.

5. Type a couple of sentences in the new untitled Write document, and then press Enter two or three times.

6. From the Edit menu, choose Paste Link.

   Write inserts a dynamically linked copy of the graphic you just created (see fig. 7.2).

7. Save this Write document, calling it LINK1. This file is the first destination file.

8. Open a new Write document, and repeat steps 5 and 6.

   You have inserted another dynamically linked copy of the graphic you just created.

9. Save this second Write document using the name LINK2. This file is the second destination file.

10. Switch to Cardfile.

11. From the Edit menu, choose Picture.

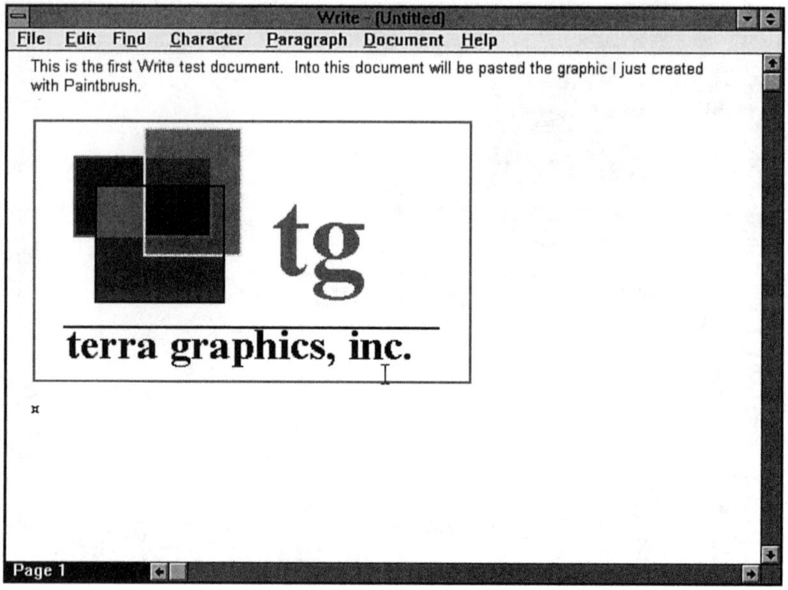

Fig. 7.2.

The graphic inserted into the Write document.

12. From the Edit menu, choose Paste Link.
13. Save the card file using the name LINK3. This file is the third destination file.
14. Now switch to Write, and display LINK2.
15. Double-click the linked graphic.

    Windows displays Paintbrush and the source document. The area that constitutes the object is surrounded by dashes (see fig. 7.3).
16. Change the source document *within the boxed area* of the object, and save the change (see fig. 7.4).

> **CAUTION:** If you make changes outside the area you exported as an object, these changes aren't reflected in the destination documents.

17. Now examine LINK2. As you can see, Windows has automatically updated the object (see fig. 7.5). Save the changes to LINK2.
18. Open LINK1.

    You see an alert box informing you that the document contains links to other documents and asking whether you want to update the links now.

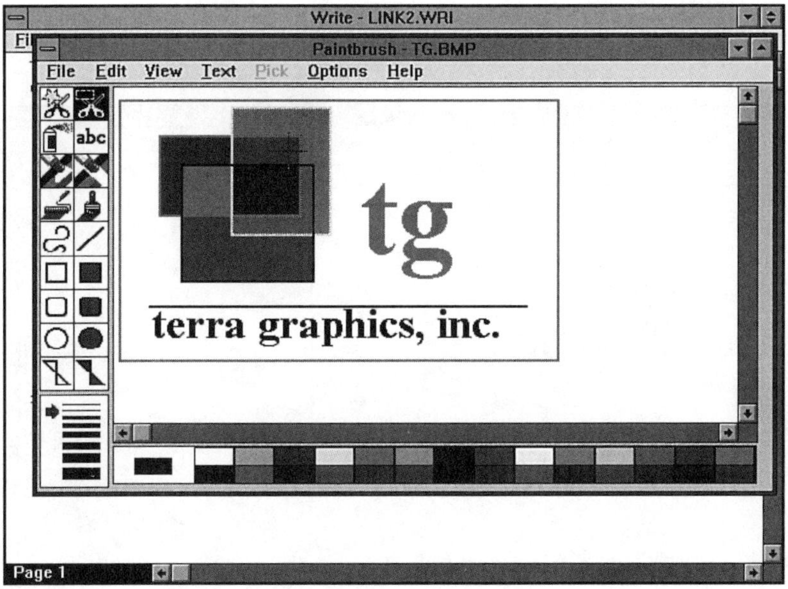

Fig. 7.3.

The graphic object displayed in the source document.

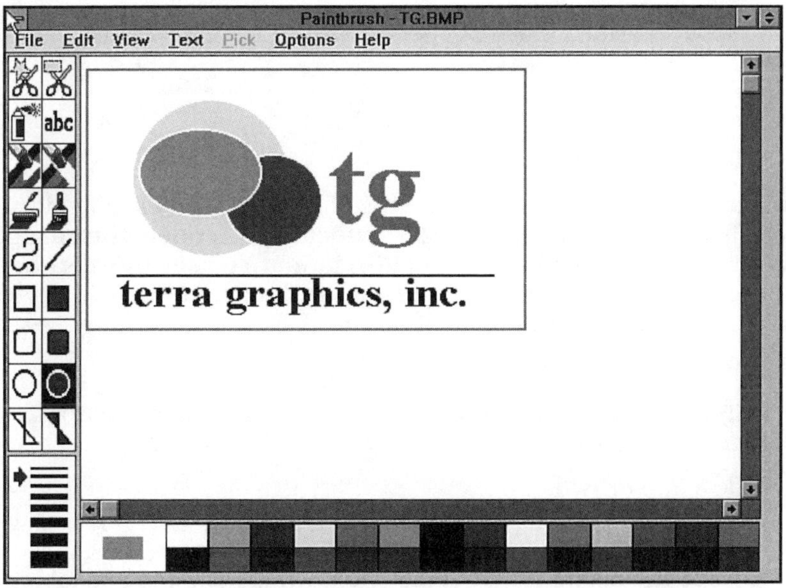

Fig. 7.4.

The edited graphic object in the source document.

19. Choose Yes.

    Windows updates the links. If you choose No, Windows leaves the graphic unchanged. The next time you open this document, you will have another opportunity to update the link, because Windows will redisplay this alert box.

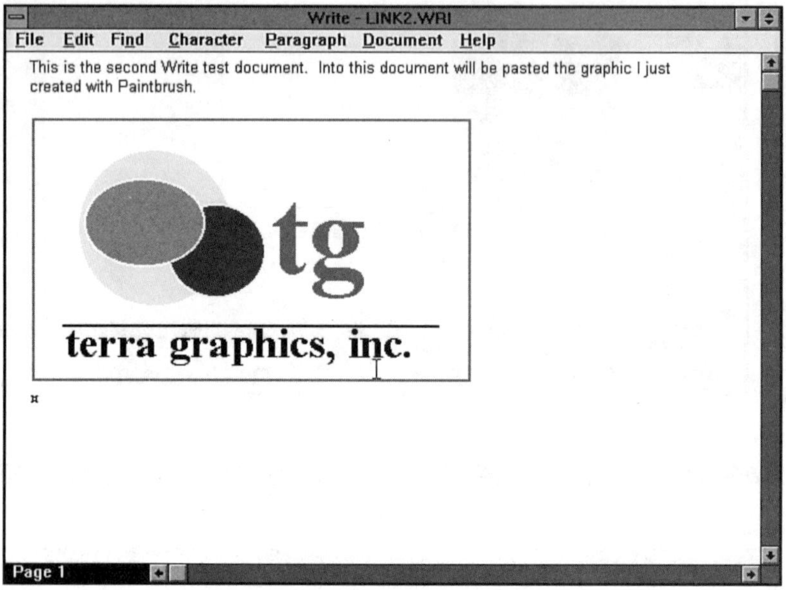

Fig. 7.5.

The changed linked document—LINK2.

20. Save LINK1.
21. Switch to Cardfile.

As you can see, Windows has made the changes to the Cardfile document (LINK3), too. When a destination document is open, the changes occur automatically, without any confirmation. You see the alert box asking you to confirm the update only if the document was closed when you changed the source document.

To explore embedding, follow these steps:

1. Switch to Write, and choose New from the File menu to open a new document.
2. Type a line or two of text.
3. From the Edit menu, choose Insert Object.

   You see the Insert Object dialog box, which lists the available server applications (see fig. 7.6). The applications you see on your screen depend on the Windows applications you have installed. If you have installed all the Windows accessories, you see Package, Paintbrush Picture, and Sound in this list.

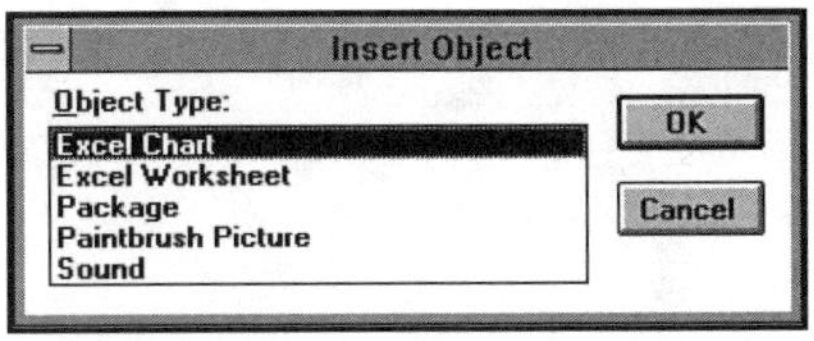

Fig. 7.6.

The Insert Object dialog box.

4. Choose Paintbrush Picture, and choose OK.

   Windows starts Paintbrush.

5. From the Edit menu, choose Paste From.

   You see an Open dialog box.

6. Open the SOURCE1 document, which contains the source graphic you linked in the preceding tutorial.

7. Use the Pick tool to select the portion of the graphic you want to embed.

8. From the File menu, choose Update.

9. From the File menu, choose Exit & Return to [Untitled].

   Windows displays your Write document. You see the embedded graphic (see fig. 7.7).

10. Save the Write document, using the name EMBED1.

11. Double-click the graphic.

    Windows starts Paintbrush and displays the graphic.

12. Make a change.

13. From the File menu, choose Update.

14. From the File menu, choose Exit & Return.

    Windows displays your Write document, and you see the change you have made, such as the change shown in figure 7.8.

15. Save EMBED1.

16. Now open LINK1, LINK2, and LINK3, the documents to which you dynamically linked the SOURCE1 graphic.

As you can see, the pictures in these documents have not been altered by the changes you made to the graphic embedded in EMBED1.

In summary, you have learned three important points from this exercise:

- Both linking and embedding enable you to update the imported object quickly and easily.

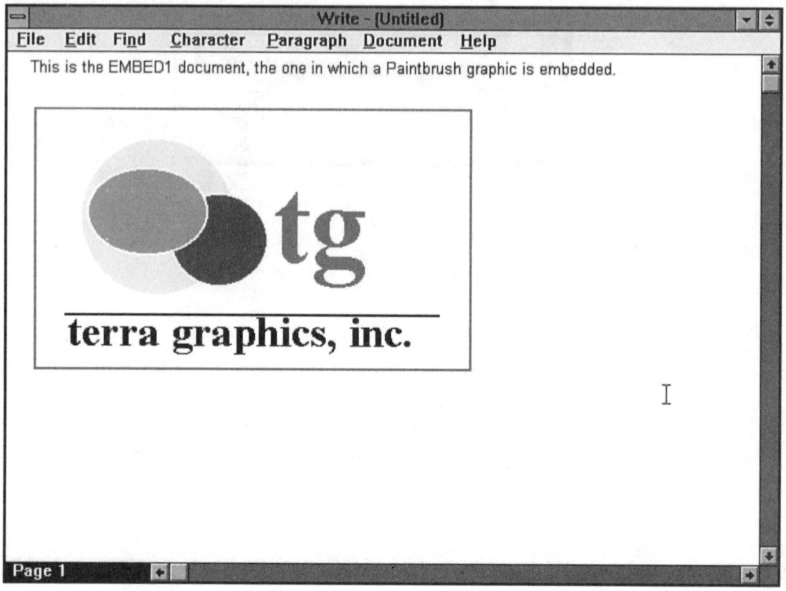

Fig. 7.7.

The Write document with the graphic embedded.

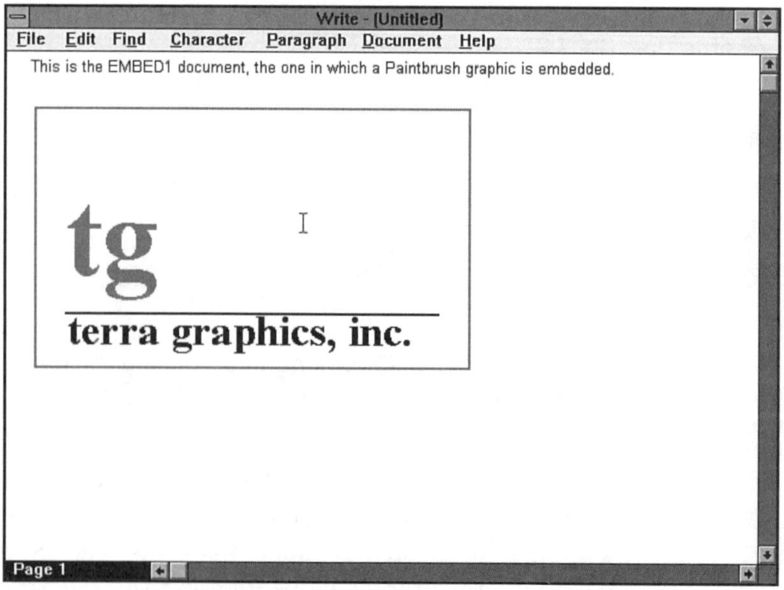

Fig. 7.8.

The changed embedded graphic.

- When you update a linked object, the changes affect all the documents to which you have linked this object.

- When you update an embedded object in a document, your changes don't affect any other copies of the object.

NOTE In the destination document, linked and embedded objects look the same. If you have forgotten whether an object was linked or embedded, select the object and choose Link from the Edit menu. If you see information about the link, it is a linked object. If you don't see such information, it is an embedded object.

Creating Links and Embedding Objects

You have learned the basic concepts and tried linking and embedding with Windows applications. This section summarizes the procedures you use to perform these actions with the Windows accessories (Write, Paintbrush, Cardfile, and Sound Recorder). Bearing in mind that other applications may name these commands differently, you can also use these instructions to try linking and embedding with other OLE-capable applications.

NOTE To link or embed objects, you must use OLE-compatible applications. Specifically, the application you use to create the source must be capable of performing the role of the server application, and the destination application must be capable of performing the role of the client application.

TIP You can tell quickly whether a given application is capable of serving as a client application. Just see whether the application has a Paste Link command in the Edit menu (indicating that the application is capable of dynamic linking) and an Insert Object command in the Edit menu or some other menu (indicating that the application is capable of embedding. If the application doesn't have these or equivalent commands, it still might be capable of functioning as a server application (without client capabilities). In some applications, such as Excel, you might need to choose the command that displays all the menu options (such as Full Menus) before these commands become visible on the menus.

Linking Objects

When you link objects, you place copies of all or part of a server application's document into one or more client application files. You can quickly update the original just by double-clicking any copy, and the changes you make are reflected in all the copies. As explained in the section "Managing Objects" later in this chapter, you can specify update frequencies, control the link format, break the link, repair broken links, and delete the linked object.

To create the link, follow these steps:

1. In the source document, select the portion you want to export as a dynamically linked object. You can select the whole document if you want.
2. From the Edit menu, choose Copy.
3. Switch to the client application, and display the document you want to paste the object into.
4. Choose Paste Link.

If the application has no Paste Link command, this application isn't capable of serving as a server application. If the Paste Link command is dimmed, you might have forgotten to choose Copy after selecting the object. If you're sure that you copied the object correctly, the source application isn't capable of serving as a server for OLE purposes.

NOTE In some applications, you see a dialog box asking you to specify whether you want the link to update automatically whenever the source document changes or whether you want to update manually. Normally, you should choose automatic updating.

Editing a Linked Object

After you have inserted a linked object into the destination document, you can easily edit the object. **Important:** The changes you make affect the object, the source document, and any additional linked copies you have made of the object. In other words, editing the linked object is the same as editing the source document. If you don't want to affect the source document, you can sever the link (see the section "Managing Objects" later in this chapter) before making the changes.

To edit a linked object, follow these steps:

1. Position the cursor within the object, and choose Edit Object. Alternatively, double-click the object.

   Windows starts the server application and displays the source document.

2. Make the changes you want.
3. From the File menu, choose Save.
4. If necessary, choose Exit from the File menu.

Windows updates the object in all destination files.

Embedding Objects

When you embed an object, you place a copy of the source file in the destination file. You can quickly update the object in the destination file by double-clicking the object. Windows starts the server application. The changes you make affect only the embedded object.

You can embed an object in two ways: starting from the destination document or starting from the source document.

- *Starting from the destination document.* This way is the best choice if you need to create the object from scratch. For example, suppose that you want to add an Excel chart to your Write or Word document. The chart doesn't exist; you must create it. To do so, you position the cursor where you want the object to appear, and choose Insert Object from the File menu. Windows starts Excel, and you create your chart.
- *Starting from the source document.* This way is the best choice if the object already exists. In the source document, you select just the portion that you want to serve as an object and copy the object through the Clipboard. In the destination document, you use Paste Special to embed the object without creating a dynamic link. In many OLE-capable applications, such as Write, you can just choose Paste if you're embedding a graphic; embedding is automatic.

To embed an object (starting from the destination document), follow these steps:

1. In the destination document, position the cursor where you want the embedded object to appear.
2. From the Edit menu, choose Insert Object.

You see the Insert Object dialog box.

If the application has no Insert Object command, this application isn't capable of functioning as a client application for OLE purposes.

3. Choose the server application and object type (such as Paintbrush Picture or Excel Chart or Excel Worksheet) from the Insert Object list box.

   Windows starts the server application and displays a blank document.

4. Create the object.

   Alternatively, open the file that contains the information you want to embed and copy it to the file that Windows automatically created in the server application. This file has a complex name, such as *WINWRITE%(Untitled)295b7553#003*. The name includes the name of the client application.

5. From the File menu, choose Update.

6. If necessary, choose Exit from the File menu.

Windows embeds the object in the client application's document. Figure 7.9 shows an Excel worksheet embedded in a Write document.

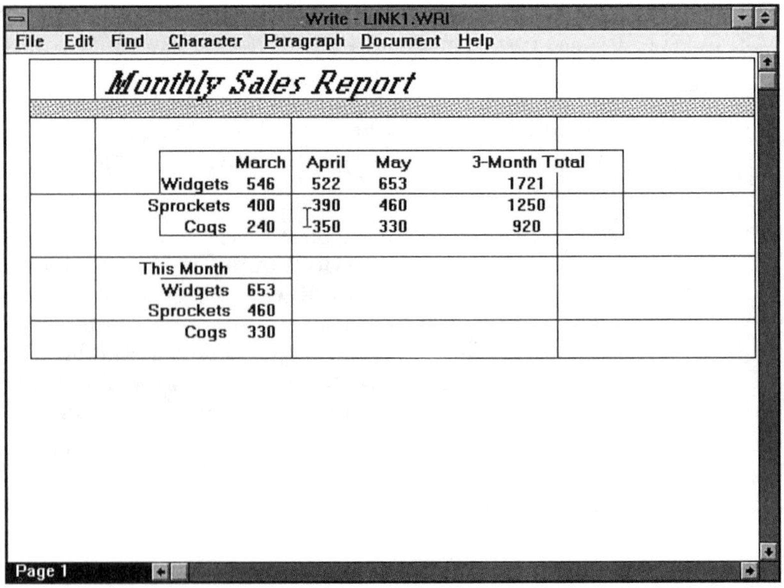

Fig. 7.9.

A Excel worksheet embedded in a Write document.

To embed an object (starting from the source document), follow these steps:

1. In the source document, select the object and choose Copy.

   Windows places a copy of the object on the Clipboard.

2. Open the document you want to embed the information into.
3. If you're embedding an object in a Cardfile document, be sure to choose Picture from the Edit menu.
4. From the Edit menu, choose Paste Special.

   If you're embedding a graphic with Write, you can just choose Paste to embed the graphic; skip the remaining steps.

   You see the Paste Special dialog box (figure 7.10).

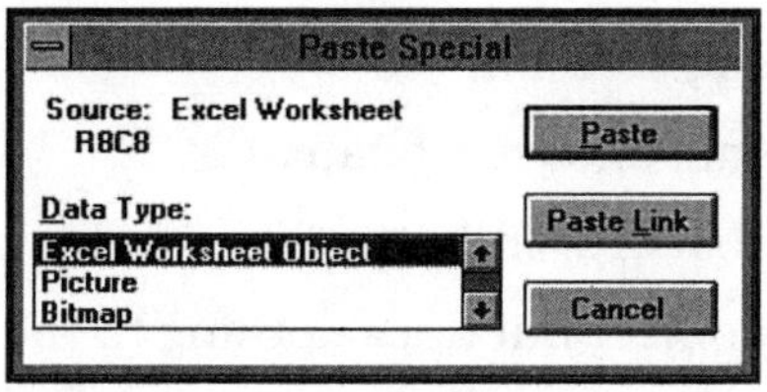

Fig. 7.10.

The Paste Special dialog box.

5. In the Data Type list box, make sure that the server application's object data type is chosen. For example, if you're embedding an Excel worksheet object, the correct data type is Excel Worksheet Object. If you're embedding an Excel chart, the correct data type is Excel Chart Object. If you're embedding a Paintbrush picture, the correct data type is Paintbrush Object.
6. Choose Paste (not Paste Link). This step is very important.

CAUTION: Be sure to choose Paste, and not Paste Link, when you're embedding an object starting from the source document. If you choose Paste Link, Windows creates a dynamic link between the object and the source document. If you later make changes to the embedded object, thinking that the changes would affect only the embedded object (and not the source document), the changes affect the source document, too.

Editing an Embedded Object

An embedded object isn't linked dynamically to any source document; the object contains all the information that the server application needs to let you edit and update the object. The changes you make to the object don't affect the source document (if there was one); these changes affect only the embedded object.

To edit an embedded object, follow these steps:

1. Position the cursor within the object, and choose Edit Object. Alternatively, double-click the object.

   Windows starts the server application and displays the object in a new file. Note that this file is *not* the source document from which the object was drawn; this file is a totally separate file, ensuring that your changes will not affect the source document.

2. Make the changes you want.
3. From the File menu, choose Update.
4. If necessary, choose Exit from the File menu.

Windows updates the object but does nothing to the source document.

Managing Objects

Linking and embedding are easy and automatic. You can exert more control over these processes, however. When linking or embedding, you can choose the data type Windows uses to create the object. When linking, you can specify manual updating. And after you have inserted linked objects into your document, you can copy the linked object, break the link, delete the linked object, or restore a broken link. Here's a quick overview of these object-management procedures; the sections to follow discuss these procedures in detail.

- *Controlling the data type (linking and embedding).* By using Paste Special instead of Paste Link, you can choose alternative data types when linking or embedding. For example, when you're pasting a Paintbrush picture, the default format is Paintbrush Picture Object. If you want, you can import the picture as a bit map or a Write-format picture. If you're importing an Excel spreadsheet, you can import the spreadsheet as an Excel spreadsheet object, a picture, a bit map, or text. With some applications and printers, you might be able to improve print quality by controlling the data type manually; most users will be better off letting Windows choose the data type.

- *Choosing manual updating (linking).* When you choose Paste Link, Windows creates the dynamic link with automatic updating. If the destination file is open when you make changes to the source document, the update occurs instantaneously. If the destination file is closed when you make changes to the source document, you are prompted to update the destination document the next time you open it. You can also choose manual updating. With manual updating, updating does not occur automatically. You must choose the Link command from the Edit menu to perform the update.
- *Copying links.* After you establish a link, you can copy the linked object and place it in other documents. This procedure enables you to make multiple copies of the linked document quickly and easily.
- *Breaking a link.* You can sever the dynamic link between the object and the source document so that the object isn't updated when you make changes to the source document. You still see the object in the source document.
- *Deleting a linked object.* When you delete a linked object, you break the link and erase the object, all in one step.
- *Restoring a broken link.* If you change the file name of the source document, you might inadvertently break the link. You can restore the link, however.

As in the preceding section, the instructions given here work with the OLE-capable Windows accessories (Write, Paintbrush, Cardfile, and Sound Recorder). These procedures work much the same way with many other OLE-capable applications, however. With some adaptation, you should be able to use these instructions to perform these tasks with such applications as Microsoft Word for Windows, Excel 3.0, and AmiPro.

Controlling the Data Type

If you create the link with Paste Special instead of Paste Link, you have an opportunity to choose the data type Windows uses when it places the object in the destination document. Normally, you get excellent results if you choose Paste Link and let Windows choose the data type automatically. Some applications, however, scroll some object data types faster than others. For example, Write can scroll an Excel worksheet copied as a bit map more quickly than the same worksheet copied as an Excel object. In addition, objects take up much more room in your file than linked objects, which don't contain all the information the server application needs to let you update the object. If you aren't happy with the way your destination application scrolls, or if file sizes are too large after you import objects with Paste Link, experiment with alternative data types.

NOTE Not all OLE-capable applications have a Paste Special command, which enables you to specify the data type when you create dynamic links. If the application you're using has a Paste Link command but no Paste Special command or a Paste Special command that performs different functions, you can create a dynamic link, but you must let Windows choose the data type. In Excel 3.0, for example, you can create dynamic links with Paste Link, but Paste Special is used for purposes that have nothing to do with dynamic linking.

To choose the data type when creating the link, follow these steps:

1. In the source document, select the object and choose Copy.

   Windows places a copy of the object on the Clipboard.

2. Open the document into which you want to link the information.
3. Position the cursor where you want the object to appear.
4. If you're linking to Cardfile from Paintbrush or another graphics application, choose Picture from the Edit menu.
5. From the Edit menu, choose Paste Special.

   You see the Paste Special dialog box (again see fig. 7.10).

6. In the Data Type list box, choose the data type you want to use.
7. Choose Paste Link to link the object.

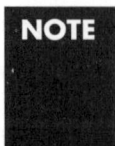

NOTE If the Paste Link button is dimmed, you might have forgotten to save the source document. Choose Cancel, switch to the source document, save it, and try this procedure again. If the Paste Link button is still dimmed, the client application you're using isn't OLE-capable.

Choosing Manual Updating

When you choose Paste Link, Windows specifies automatic updating automatically. If the destination document is open when you make changes to the source document, the update occurs instantaneously. If the destination document is closed when you make changes to the source document, you will see a dialog box prompting you to update the destination document when you open it.

If you prefer, you can choose manual updating. With manual updating, updates occur only when you choose Links from the Edit menu and activate the Update Now button in the Links dialog box. Normally, you have little reason to choose manual updating. This option negates the chief advantage of dynamic linking, automatic updating after you make changes to the source document. If you want to protect the object from the changes you make to the source document, you might want to embed the object instead of linking it.

In some situations, however, you can use manual updating. Suppose that you have created an Excel worksheet and placed linked copies of it in three Word documents. You decide you want to perform some "what if" experiments on the source spreadsheet, but you don't want these experiments to alter the objects in the three Word documents. To prevent alteration of these objects, you select each object and choose manual updating. Later, after you have finished experimenting, you can choose automatic updating again.

To choose manual updating, follow these steps:

1. Open the destination document that contains the linked object and select the subject.
2. From the Edit menu, choose Links.

   You see the Links dialog box (see fig. 7.11). Note that for each link in this document, the program lists the data type (Excel Worksheet), the source document (TOTALS.XLS), the portion of the source document from which the object was drawn (the range R1C1:R17C12), and the update frequency (Automatic).

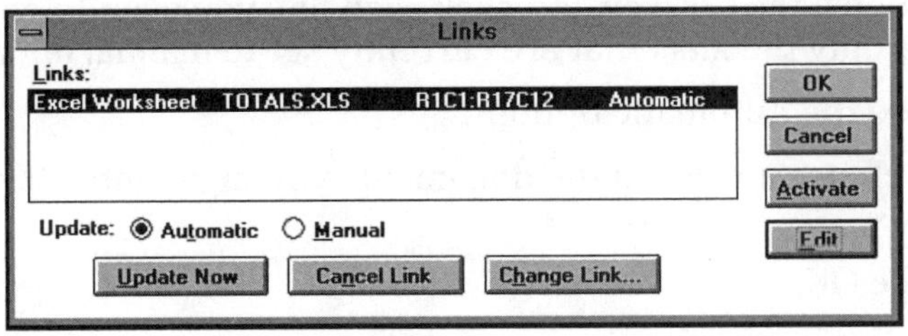

Fig. 7.11.

The Links dialog box.

3. In the Links list box, select the link or links whose update option you want to change. If you're using a mouse, you can select more than one link by holding down the Ctrl key while you click each link you want to change.
4. Choose the Manual option.

   Your choice affects all the documents you highlighted in the Links list box.
5. Choose OK.

Windows will not update the linked object unless you choose Links and activate the Update Now button, as described in the following procedure.

To perform a manual update of a linked object, follow these steps:

1. Open the document that contains the linked object.
2. From the Edit menu, choose Links.

   You see the Links dialog box (again see fig. 7.11).
3. In the Links list box, highlight the link or links you want to update. To select more than one link, hold down the Ctrl key and click each link you want to update.
4. Choose Update Now.
5. Choose OK.

Windows updates the links you selected.

To restore automatic updating, follow these steps:

1. Open the document that contains the linked object.

   You don't need to select the object.
2. From the Edit menu, choose Links.

   You see the Links dialog box (see again fig. 7.11). The column on the right shows the current update setting (Manual or Automatic).
3. In the Links list box, highlight the link or links you want to convert from manual to automatic updating. To select more than one link, hold down the Ctrl key and click each link you want to change. Select only the links that are currently set to manual updating.
4. Choose the Automatic option.

   Your choice affects all the documents you highlighted in the Links list box.
5. Choose OK.

Copying a Link

In the tutorial in this chapter, you linked a Paintbrush graphic to two Write documents. In each Write document, you went through the whole procedure to copy the object to each Write file (LINK1 and LINK2). In this section, you learn an easier way to make additional copies of a linked object. After you have created the link in one of the destination documents, you can just copy the link to the second destination document. Because Windows copies the link information with the object, the object copied into the second destination document is linked to the source document, too.

To copy a linked object from one destination document to another destination document, follow these steps:

1. Open the document that contains the linked object.
2. Select the object.
3. From the Edit menu, choose Copy.
4. Open the document to which you want to copy the linked object.

   If you are using Cardfile, choose Picture from the Edit menu.

5. Position the cursor where you want the linked object to appear.
6. From the Edit menu, choose Paste. You also can press the Ctrl-V keyboard shortcut.

Windows inserts the linked object into your document. Even though you copied the object from another destination document, Windows creates a link to the source document, not the other destination document.

TIP

After you have created multiple copies of a linked object, you can change all the copies (and the source document) by updating any of them. This technique is a powerful capability that, with a little planning and thought, you should be able to exploit to advantage. For example, suppose that you keep a single authoritative source document in which you place crucial contract clauses. Each clause is an object you have copied to the many contracts you're working on. When in the course of working on one of the destination documents, you see that you need to make a change to the source document, you just update the object in the document you're working on. Windows automatically makes the same change to all the copies and to the source document.

Breaking the Link

You can sever the link between a linked object and the source document and all other copies of the object. Breaking the link doesn't remove the object from the screen or the destination file; breaking the link just severs the link between the object and the source document.

NOTE Embedding an object is better than linking an object and then severing the link. When you embed an object, you can still update it easily. If you link an object and then break the link, you cannot update the object easily. If you double-click the object, you see an alert box informing you that Windows cannot activate a static object. To update the object, you must copy it to the server application, make the change, and copy the object back to the destination document.

To break the link between a linked object and the source document, follow these steps:

1. Open the document that contains the linked object.

   You don't need to select the object.

2. From the Edit menu, choose Links.

   You see the Links dialog box (again see fig. 7.11).

3. In the Links list box, highlight the link or links you want to update. To select more than one link, hold down the Ctrl key and click each link you want to update.
4. Choose Cancel Link.
5. Choose OK.

Windows cancels the links you highlighted in the Links list box.

Deleting a Linked Object

When you delete a linked object, you break the link as well as remove the object from the destination document.

To delete a link, follow these steps:

1. Open the file containing the linked object you want to delete.
2. Select the linked object.
3. Choose Cut from the Edit menu, press the Ctrl-X keyboard shortcut, or press the Del key.

Windows removes the link and the object simultaneously.

Repairing a Broken Link

After you have created dynamic links, exercise caution when renaming files. If you change the name of a source document, you break the links between this document and the destination documents that contain linked objects.

You will know that you have somehow broken a link when you try to update an object only to see a dialog box informing you that the linked document is unavailable. Use the procedure described in this section to restore the link.

To repair a broken link, follow these steps:

1. From the document that contains the object you want to link again, choose Links.

   You see the Links dialog box (again see fig. 7.11).

2. Highlight the link with the notation `Unavailable` in the right column of the Links list box.
3. Choose Change Link.

   You see the Change Link dialog box (see fig. 7.12).

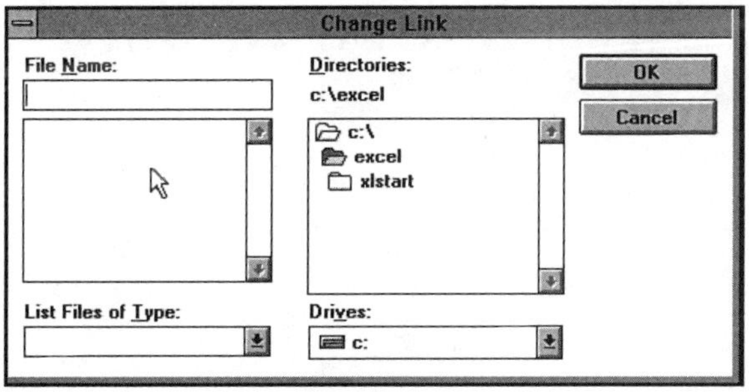

Fig. 7.12.

The Change Link dialog box.

4. In the File Name text box, use the Directories, Drive, and Type boxes to display the name of the document that contains the source of the object in the selections file.
5. Choose OK.

   Windows renews the link, places the new source document name in the Links list box, and updates the link automatically.

6. Choose OK to exit the Links dialog box.

Using Object Packager

When you embed or link an object, you see the object in the destination document. You can, however, insert a package instead of an object when you embed or link. A *package* is an icon that represents an object, and the package contains the embedded or linked object. All you see in the destination document is the icon. To see what's in the package, you double-click the icon.

Why package an embedded or linked object? A package gives you a way to create an *interactive document*, which you can give to a colleague, correspondent, or coworker. In an interactive document created with Object Packager, text is kept to a minimum. If the readers want more information on a subject, they double-click an Object Packager icon, which displays the contents of the packaged object. If necessary, Windows automatically starts the server application. Figure 7.13 shows an interactive letter that contains a package. If the recipient double-clicks the icon, Excel starts and displays the object.

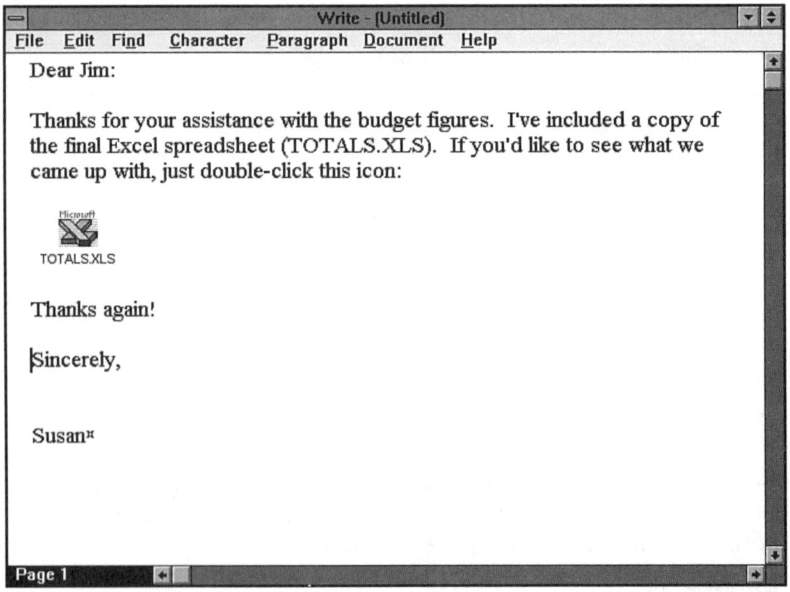

Fig. 7.13.

An interactive letter containing a package icon.

When you create a package, you can package all or part of a document, and you can embed or link the package. You can also customize the icon that represents the packaged object, and you can change the icon's label. All these procedures are described in detail in the sections to follow.

NOTE Object Packager has certain limitations. In order for you to insert a package into a document, the application that created the destination document must be capable of serving as a client application for OLE purposes. To activate the package, the computer on which the document is read must be equipped with Windows 3.1 and the server application.

Packaging an Entire Document as an Embedded Object

In this section, you learn how to package an entire document as an embedded object. (For information on packaging an entire document as a *linked* object, see the next section.) To create a package that you embed in a destination document, you use Object Packager to identify the source document and create the icon; then you paste the icon into the destination document.

NOTE If you're creating a package you're planning to give to someone who uses a different computer, you should package an embedded object, not a linked object. Here's why. If you package a linked object, Windows tries to find the source document when the recipient double-clicks the package icon. But the source document isn't on the recipient's computer system. If you package an embedded object, the recipient needs only the server application in order to view the object's contents.

NOTE This procedure works even if the source document was created by an application that's *not* capable of functioning as a server application for OLE purposes. The application you use to create the interactive document must be capable of functioning as a client application, however.

To use Object Packager to package an entire document as an embedded object, follow these steps:

1. From the Accessories program group, choose Object Packager.

   You see the Object Packager - Package window (see fig. 7.14). This window gives you the tools needed to create a package. The Object Packager window is split into two smaller windows. The left window (the Appearance window) displays the package's icon. The right window (the Content window) contains the name of the document that provides the object's source.

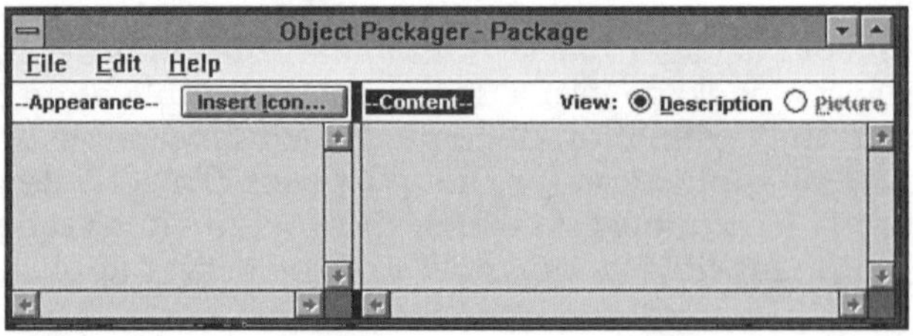

Fig. 7.14.

The Object Packager - Package window.

2. Activate the Content window by clicking within it or pressing Tab.
3. From the File menu, choose Import.

   You see the Import dialog box (see fig. 7.15). This dialog box provides the tools you need to identify the source document.

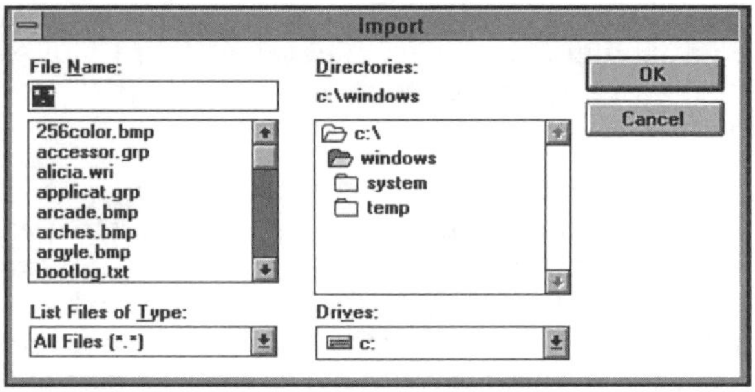

Fig. 7.15.

The Import dialog box.

4. Type the name of the source document in the File Name text box. Alternatively, use the Drives and Directories list box to choose the correct directory, and highlight the file's name in the File Name list box.
5. Choose OK.

   Object Packager creates the icon and returns you to the Object Packager window. You see the icon in the Appearance window and the file name in the Content window (see fig. 7.16).

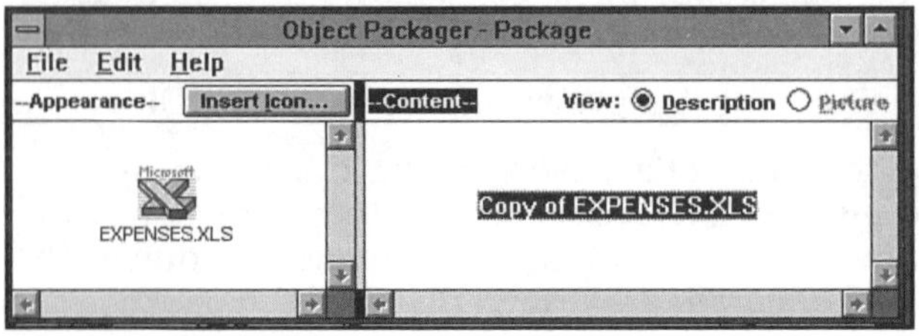

Fig. 7.16.

The icon and file name in the Object Packager window.

6. If you want to change the icon, click the Insert Icon button and choose a new icon from the Insert Icon dialog box. Choose OK to confirm your choice.

> **TIP** To see more icons, type MORICONS.DLL in the File Name list box of the Insert Icons dialog box, and then choose OK.

7. If you want to change the label that Object Packager will insert under the icon after the package is placed in the destination document, choose Label from the Edit menu. Type a new label in the Label text box, and choose OK.
8. From the Edit menu, choose Copy Package.
9. Switch to the document into which you want to insert the package.
10. Position the cursor where you want the package to appear.
11. From the Edit menu, choose Paste.

Windows places the icon in the document (see fig. 7.17).

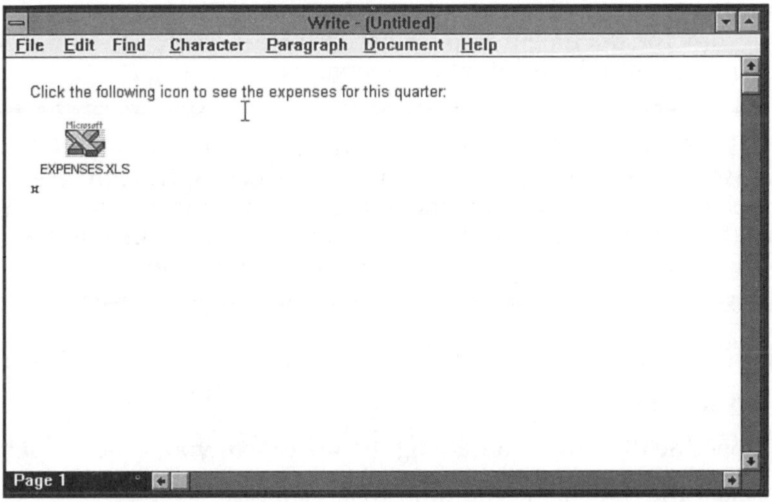

Fig. 7.17.

The icon inserted into a document.

Viewing the Packaged Object

After packaging an object, you can view it easily.

To view the contents of a package, follow these steps:

1. In the destination document, highlight the package icon.
2. From the Edit menu, choose Package Object. When the submenu appears, choose Activate Contents. Alternatively, double-click the icon.

   Windows starts the server application and displays the object in the server application's native format.
3. Choose Exit from the File menu to return to the destination document and repackage the object.

Packaging an Entire Document as a Linked Object

When you package a document with Object Packager, as described in the preceding section, Windows creates the package so that it contains an embedded object. As explained in the introduction to this section, this procedure is normally the best. If you want to create a package that contains a linked object, however, you can. To begin, you use the File Manager to copy the document to the Clipboard. Then you use Paste Link to copy the document into Object Manager, create the icon, and paste the icon into the destination document.

> **CAUTION:** Bear in mind that when you follow the procedure described in this section, anyone who double-clicks the icon sees, and can change, the source document, the document from which the object was copied. If you don't want other people changing the source document, create the package as an embedded object.

To package an entire document as a linked object, follow these steps:

1. Open File Manager.
2. Open the directory containing the document you want to package.
3. Select the document you want to package.
4. From the File menu, choose Copy. You also can press the F8 keyboard shortcut.

   You see the Copy dialog box (see fig. 7.18).
5. Activate the Copy to Clipboard option.

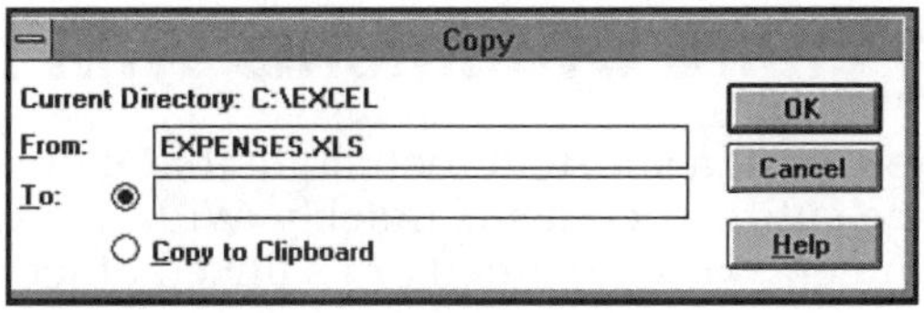

Fig. 7.18.

The Copy dialog box.

6. Choose OK.

   Windows places a copy of the document on the Clipboard.

7. Switch to Object Packager.
8. Select the Content window by clicking it or pressing Tab.
9. From the Edit menu, choose Paste Link.

   You see the package icon in the Appearance window and the file name in the Content window. Note that the file name is preceded by `Link to`, indicating that you have established a dynamic link.

10. If you want to change the icon, click the Insert Icon button and choose a new icon from the Insert Icon dialog box. To see more icons, type MORICONs.DLL in the File Name list box and choose OK.
11. If you want to change the label that Object Packager inserts under the icon after the package is placed in the destination document, choose Label from the Edit menu. Type a new label in the Label text box, and then choose OK.
12. From the Edit menu, choose Copy Package.
13. Open the document you want to insert the package into.
14. Position the cursor where you want the package to appear.
15. From the Edit menu, choose Paste. You also can press the Ctrl-V keyboard shortcut.

The package appears in the document.

NOTE

When you insert a linked package by following the procedure just described, you see the source document when you double-click the package icon or choose Object Package from the Edit menu.

Packaging Entire Documents with the Mouse

In this section, you learn a shortcut technique that mouse users can employ to package entire documents quickly. With this technique, you can package documents as embedded or as linked objects.

To package an entire document with the mouse, follow these steps:

1. Open File Manager, and size the File Manager window so that it occupies the top half of the screen.
2. In the File Manager, choose the directory that contains the source document.
3. Open the destination document, and size the destination document window so that it occupies the bottom half of the screen.

   Your screen should look like the one in figure 7.19.

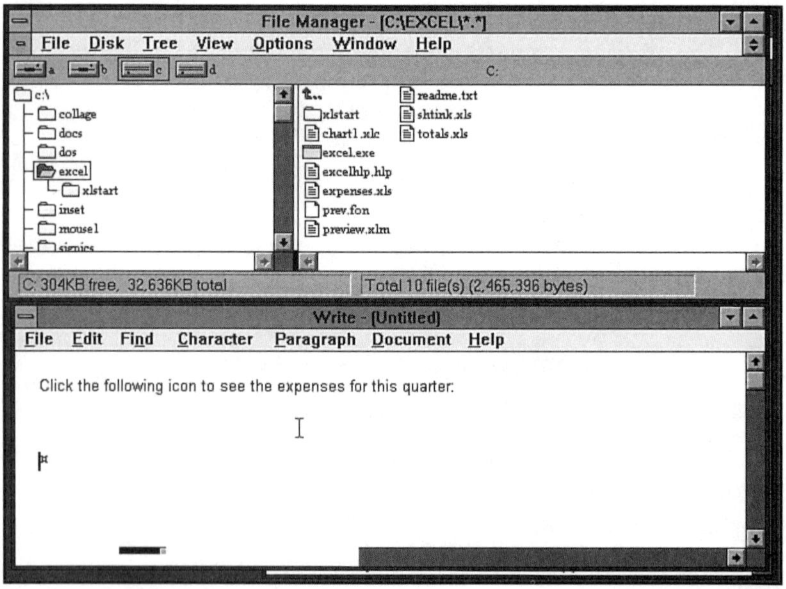

Fig. 7.19.

The File Manager and document windows on-screen.

4. In the destination document, position the cursor where you want the package to appear.
5. Do one of the following:

   To create a package with an embedded object, drag the source document from the File Manager's files list window to the destination document and release the mouse button.

To create a package with a linked object, hold down the Ctrl and Shift keys as you drag the source document to the destination document window.

Windows places the package at the cursor's location.

Packaging Part of a Document

To package part of a document, you begin by selecting the portion of the document you want to package and copying this portion to the Clipboard. In Object Packager, you paste the Clipboard's contents into a package, and then you copy the package to the destination document. You can create an embedded or linked package this way.

NOTE You can package part of a file only if the document you want to package was created by an application that is capable of functioning as a server application for OLE purposes. Among the Windows accessories, only Paintbrush and Sound Recorder are capable of functioning as server applications; Write and Cardfile cannot. In addition, the application that created the source document must be capable of functioning as a client application for OLE purposes.

To package part of a document, follow these steps:

1. Open the document that contains the information you want to package.
2. Select the information.
3. From the Edit menu, choose Copy.
4. Switch to Object Packager.
5. Activate the Contents window.
6. From the Edit menu, choose Paste to create an embedded object package.

   Alternatively, choose Paste Link from the Edit menu to create a linked object package.
7. If you want to change the icon, click the Insert Icon button and choose a new icon from the Insert Icon dialog box. Choose OK to confirm your choice.
8. If you want to change the label that Object Packager will insert under the icon after the package is placed in the destination document, choose Label from the Edit menu. Type a new label in the Label text box, and then choose OK.

9. From the Edit menu, choose Copy Package.
10. Open the document into which you want to insert the package.
11. Position the cursor where you want the package to appear.
12. From the Edit menu, choose Paste. You also can press the Ctrl-V keyboard shortcut.

Changing the Icon or Label after Creating the Package

When you create a package with Object Packager, you have an opportunity to change the icon and the label that Object Packager would otherwise choose automatically. You can also change the label and icon after inserting the package into your destination document.

To change the label or icon after inserting the package, follow these steps:

1. In the destination document, highlight the package.
2. From the Edit menu, choose Package Object. When the submenu appears, choose Edit Package.

   Windows starts Object Packager, and you see the icon and label in the Appearance and Content windows, respectively.
3. Do one or both of the following:

   To change the icon, click the Insert Icon button and choose a new icon from the Insert Icon dialog box. Choose OK to confirm your choice.

   To change the label, choose Label from the Edit menu. Type a new label in the Label text box, and then choose OK.
4. From the File menu, choose Update.

Windows updates the package.

Packaging a DOS Command

An unusual feature of Object Packager is its capability to package a DOS command line. You can use this feature to create even more interesting interactive documents. For example, you can include a DOS command line that, when you double-click the icon, automatically starts another application or launches a batch file.

> **CAUTION:** Don't package commands that perform destructive acts, such as formatting disks or erasing files.

To package a DOS command, follow these steps:

1. Start Object Packager and activate the Content window.
2. From the Edit menu, choose Command Line.

   You see the Command Line dialog box (see fig. 7.20).

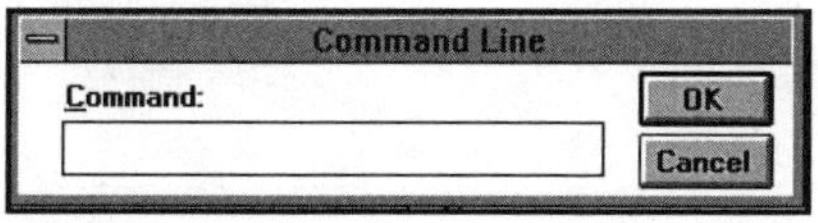

Fig. 7.20.

The Command Line dialog box.

3. In the Command text box, type the DOS command you want to package.

   If you're typing the name of a program or file, be sure to include the full path name (such as D:\WP51\LETTER1.DOC).

4. Choose OK.

   Object Packager shows the command in the Content window (see fig. 7.21).

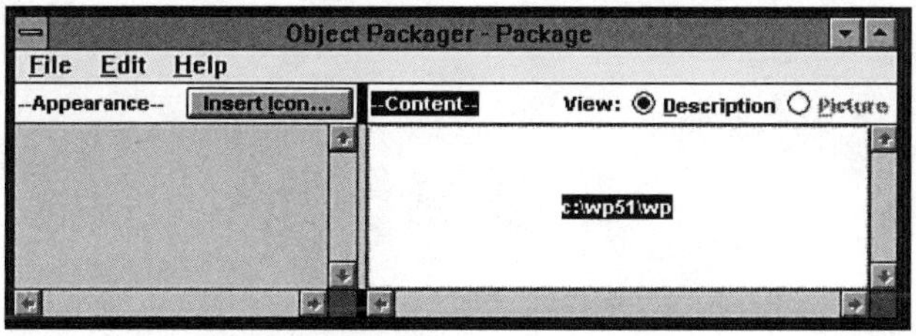

Fig. 7.21.

A DOS command in the Content window.

5. Choose the Insert Icon button.

   You see the Insert Icon dialog box (see fig. 7.22). In the Current Icon box, you see many nifty icons.

6. Click the right scroll arrow to display additional icons. When you see the icon you want, click the icon to highlight it.
7. Choose OK.

   Object Packager shows the selected icon in the Appearance window (see fig. 7.23).

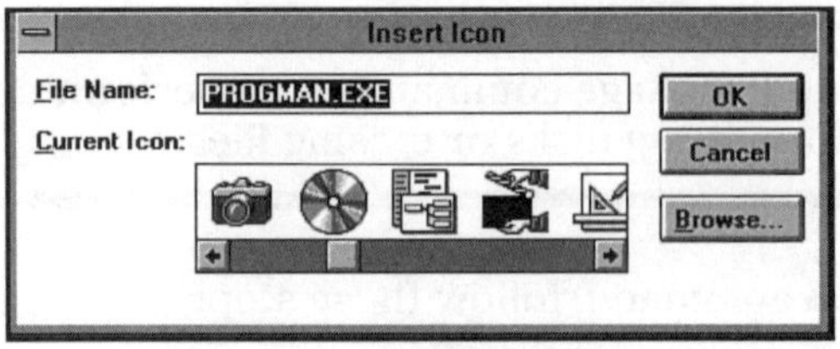

Fig. 7.22.

The Insert Icon dialog box.

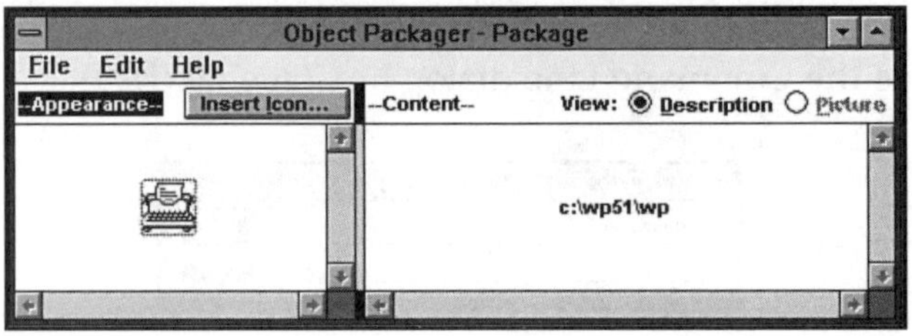

Fig. 7.23.

The selected icon in the Appearance window.

8. From the Edit menu, choose Copy Package.
9. Open the destination document.
10. From the Edit menu, choose Paste. You also can press the Ctrl-V keyboard shortcut.

You see the package's icon in the destination document (see fig. 7.24).

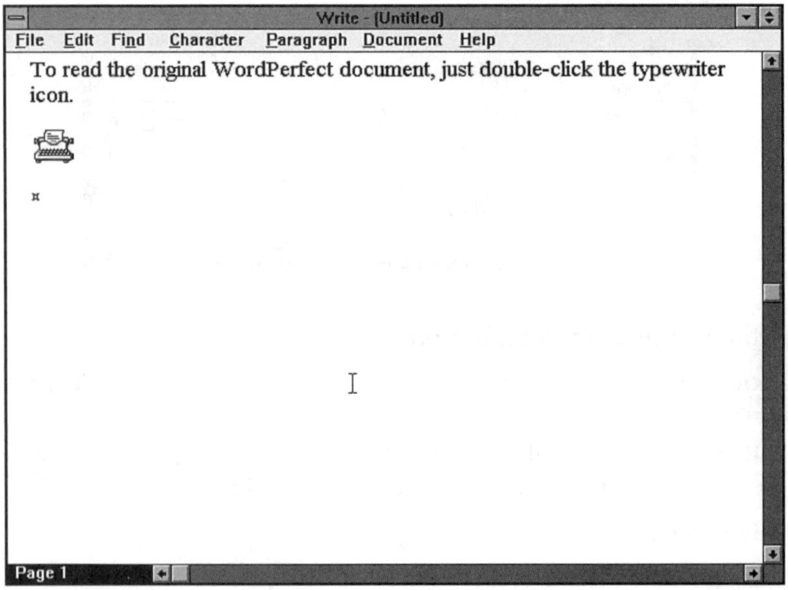

Fig. 7.24.

The package icon in a document.

Putting It All Together: Creating Interactive Documents

To create exciting and useful interactive documents, you can tie together several strands of Windows 3.1's new capabilities: multimedia (see Chapter 8), object embedding, and object packaging. In figure 7.25, you see these three capabilities combined in a useful way. This Write document contains an embedded sound (created with Sound Recorder) and four embedded objects stored in packages: a Write document, an Excel spreadsheet, an Excel chart, and a Paintbrush graphic. Just by double-clicking the icons, new team members get a quick introduction to the project—complete with an inspiring, audible message from the Project Director!

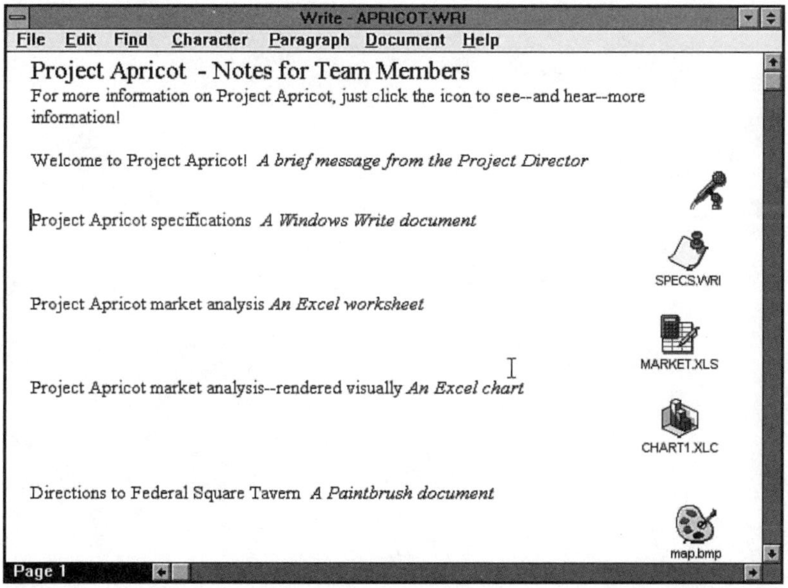

Fig. 7.25.

An interactive document combining several capabilities.

Summary

As this chapter suggests, Windows' enhanced OLE capabilities aren't just for advanced users of the Windows system. Remember to use OLE features whenever you are copying information that you might otherwise find yourself updating manually.

8

CHAPTER

Using Non-Window Applications

The use of Windows in the MS-DOS world is growing by leaps and bounds. The Windows graphical environment is easy to use and helpful to both new and experienced computer users. Windows applications designed specifically for this environment embody this ease of use. Non-Windows applications, however, do not take advantage of the graphical interface and tools offered by the Windows environment.

So if Windows applications are so wonderful, why would anyone run non-Windows applications? In fact, there are a variety of reasons why you might want to continue running non-Windows applications. Perhaps your company's accounting package has not been converted to Windows. Maybe your favorite shareware program will never be converted. In some cases, you simply might be more comfortable with the character-based version of a program. As with previous versions of Windows, Windows 3.1 enables you to run DOS applications from the Windows environment.

This latest version of Windows adds several features to enhance the processing of non-Windows applications. In this chapter, you will learn about these changes and enhancements.

How Windows Runs Non-Windows Applications

Windows is designed primarily to run Windows applications. These applications adhere to certain Windows standards. They work well together, and Windows can handle their needs for resources (such as processing time and memory), devices (such as modems and printers), and multitasking.

Non-Windows applications, as the term implies, are not designed to run under Windows. They normally run directly under the MS-DOS operating system are not programmed to consider multitasking or graphical environments like Windows.

Windows creates an environment where each of these programs can run as if it were on its own machine and not running under Windows. It tailors the look of the "machine" by using Program Information Files (PIFs). These special files contain settings to communicate information to Windows that the non-Windows program cannot—such as how much memory to allocate, whether to share the processor with other applications, and how the applications should be displayed on-screen.

If a PIF is not available in either the directory of the application's program file or in the Windows directory, Windows uses a default PIF to run the non-Windows application using some basic assumptions and allocations. This default PIF works well for most non-Windows applications. If problems occur, creating a custom PIF for an application often resolves the problems. Custom PIFs also enable you to reserve certain Windows shortcut keys for a non-Windows application's use. Shortcut keys in Windows let you use two keystrokes to perform a Windows function that would otherwise take more time and user input to perform. Sometimes, however, non-Windows applications reserve these same keystroke combinations for a different function. By creating a custom PIF, you can specify that the keystrokes should perform the non-Windows application's function rather than the Windows function.

Windows does more than run non-Windows applications as they would run under DOS. On a computer with a 286 processor, Windows runs in Standard mode. While running non-Windows applications in Standard mode you can

- Only run DOS applications in full-screen display mode.
- Start multiple applications and switch between them. While you are running a non-Windows application, however, Windows suspends other applications, and when the non-Windows application is in the background, it is suspended.

- Assign expanded memory to an application only if your computer has an expanded memory card.

On computers with 386 or better processors, Windows enables you to

- Multitask to process information in several applications simultaneously.
- Run multiple copies of an application.
- Run non-Windows applications in a window (also called *windowed applications*) so that you can use the Windows Clipboard to move information easily between non-Windows or Windows applications.
- Use the mouse in windowed applications if the application supports mouse action.
- Change the display font size for windowed applications.
- Instruct Windows to use your computer's extended memory to emulate expanded memory. Applications that run better with more memory and support expanded memory then can use this emulated expanded memory.

What Is New, Improved, or Changed in Windows

Windows 3.1 offers improved support for running non-Windows applications. These improvements include

- Changes to the order and placement of fields in the PIF Editor 386 Enhanced mode screens
- The new No Save Screen field in the PIF Editor in Standard mode
- The ability to identify a specific non-Windows application to set up instead of scanning the entire path or drive for applications
- More application PIF files and a new collection of application icons for setting up existing non-Windows applications or new non-Windows applications easily
- An improved method of choosing different icons for non-Windows applications
- The Ctrl-Alt-Del key combination, which enables you to reboot a single window within Windows rather than reboot the computer
- Improved virtual memory management so that you can run more non-Windows applications in the background and switch between them

- Improved handling of non-Windows applications running in Graphics mode, which allows them to run in a window
- The ability to specify different fonts and font sizes for non-Windows applications running in a window
- Mouse support for non-Windows applications running in a window, provided that the applications support a mouse
- DOS environment variables, which let you pass information to Windows through PIFs and the Program Manager's Program Item Properties dialog box
- The ability to start non-Windows applications automatically by placing them in the Program Manager StartUp group

Setting Up a Non-Windows Application

Non-Windows applications can be set up under Windows 3.1 using the following methods:

- During installation, allow the Windows Setup program to scan your disks and look for applications. (This step occurs automatically with the Express Setup option.) If Windows finds a non-Windows application whose name is in its database of applications, it creates a PIF and selects an icon for the application. The program item icon for the application is placed in the Applications program group. (For more information on installing Windows 3.1, see Chapter 2.)
- After installation, use the Windows Setup program to add an individual application or scan your disks to find all applications.
- From the File menu, choose New, and then choose Program Item. You can manually set up a new non-Windows application. Choosing Properties from the File menu enables you to change the Program Item information for an existing non-Windows application.
- Use the Windows File Manager to choose an application program or PIF file. Then drag the file to a group in Program Manager and drop the file. You then can change the application's information by selecting it and, in Program Manager, choosing Properties from the File menu.

After you set up an application to run from Program Manager, or if you intend to run the application from File Manager, you might want to change the information Windows uses to run the program (such as the amount of memory allocated to the program). Either an application-specific PIF or the Windows default PIF contains this information. You use the PIF editor to change the information. See the section "PIF Files and the PIF Editor" later in this chapter for a description of the process.

Using the Windows Setup Program

When you install Windows with the Express Setup option, Windows scans your disks and, for each non-Windows application it finds and recognizes, creates a PIF and places an entry in the Applications program group. The Custom Setup option, if chosen, asks you whether you want Windows to set up applications automatically. (For more information on the process, see Chapter 2.)

If Windows does not set up these applications during installation, you can instruct it later to set up all or selected applications automatically. When you use the Windows Setup program to set up applications automatically, Windows checks to see whether it recognizes each non-Windows application. If Windows finds a non-Windows application it recognizes, it creates a PIF file for the application and places a program item icon for the application in the Applications program group. Windows Setup places the PIF file in the directory where you installed Windows.

To have Windows Setup automatically set up applications, follow these steps:

1. Open the Main program group.
2. Double-click the Windows Setup program icon. The Windows Setup dialog box appears (see fig. 8.1).

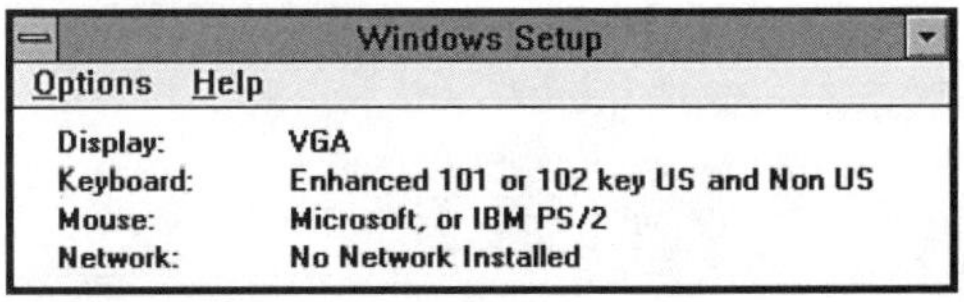

Fig. 8.1.

The Windows Setup dialog box.

3. From the Options menu, choose Set Up Applications. The Setup Applications dialog box appears.
4. Choose the Search for Applications button, and then choose OK. The Setup Applications appears, requesting you to select where to search for applications (see fig. 8.2).

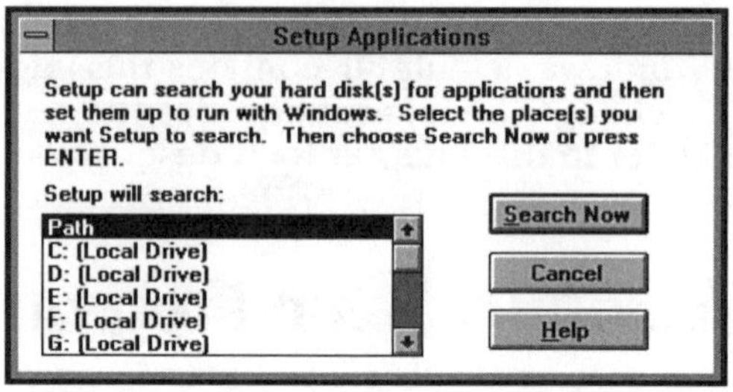

Fig. 8.2.

The Setup Applications dialog box requesting where to search.

5. Select as many search areas as you want. Selecting Path tells Windows to search the directories specified in your current Path command. Selecting a fixed disk drive letter tells Windows to search that entire drive for applications.

   After making your selections, choose Search Now.

   If Setup encounters an executable file name (or a batch file that calls an executable file) for which its APPS.INF data file (which it uses to build the PIFs and select the icons from PROGMAN.EXE and MORICONS.DLL) contains more than one entry, it will ask you which of the candidate programs is installed on your system. It then places the choice you indicated in the Applications Found window of the Setup Applications dialog box.

6. When Windows finishes searching for applications, the Setup Application dialog box displays the found applications (see fig. 8.3). From the list of found applications (displayed in the left window), select the ones you want to add for Window's use.

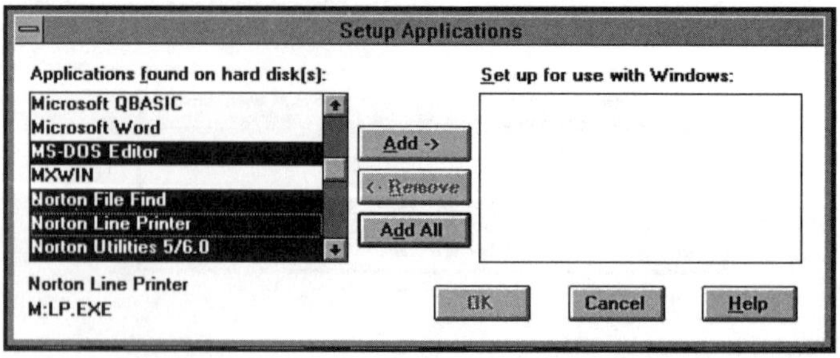

Fig. 8.3.

The Setup Applications dialog box for adding found applications to Program Manager.

After making your selections, choose Add. (If you want to add all found applications, choose Add All.) Windows sets up these applications by adding into the Applications program group a program item icon with the name of the program. For non-Windows applications, Windows also creates a PIF file and places it in the Windows directory.

As you install new non-Windows applications, you might want to use Windows Setup to add the applications to a program group in Program Manager. You then can run the programs from Windows.

To add a single non-Windows application, follow these steps:

1. Follow steps 1-3 in the preceding procedure for instructing Windows Setup to set up applications automatically.

2. Select the option button labeled Ask you to specify an application, and then choose OK. A Setup Applications dialog box appears (see fig. 8.4). The dialog box allows you to select the application you want to set up and the program group you want the application added to. (If you don't remember the exact location or file name of the application, choose Browse).

   If you want to place the application into a new program group, you need to add the program group before using Windows Setup. See Chapter 4 for information on program groups.

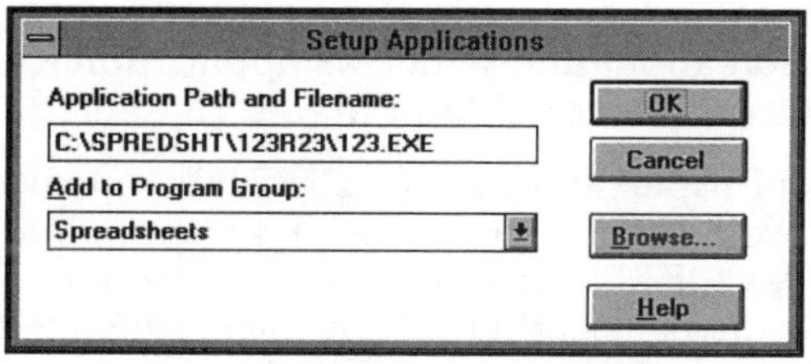

Fig. 8.4.

The Setup Applications dialog box for specifying an application.

3. Type the requested information and choose OK. If Windows recognizes the application and has a custom icon available, it selects the appropriate icon for use in Program Manager. If no custom icon is available, it uses a generic icon. Also, a PIF file for the application is added to the Windows directory. Figure 8.5 shows a program item icon in a selected program group window.

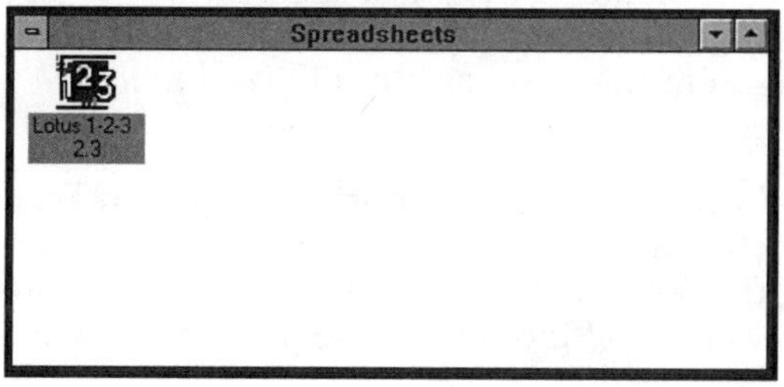

Fig. 8.5.

A program group window with a program item icon.

If Windows Setup does not have information in its database about the application you are setting up, you see the message `Setup cannot find this application`. If you want to run this application from an icon in Program Manager, you must manually set up the application. For more information on manually setting up applications, see the various "Setting Up" sections later in this chapter.)

Using Program Manager

Although using Program Manager to set up applications seems similar to using the Windows Setup Program, the results are different. When you use Program Manager to add a non-Windows application, Windows does not create a PIF file or use a custom program item icon.

With Program Manager, if you want to use an icon other than the plain MS-DOS icon, you must select it. (Windows Setup, in contrast, selects an icon for you.) Windows 3.1 includes a new collection of application icons and an improved process for selecting icons to represent program items. (For more information about non-Windows application icons, see the section "Enhanced Icon Selection" later in this chapter.)

In the Program Item Properties dialog box (which appears when you choose Properties from the File menu within Program Manager), you can type the application's PIF file name in the Command Line: box (for example, 123.PIF). Windows uses that PIF for the settings to run the application. If you don't type a PIF file name, Windows looks for a PIF file in the application's directory or the Windows directory. If it doesn't find a PIF with the same name as the application (for example, 123.PIF for 123.EXE) it uses the Windows default PIF for information about how to run the non-Windows application.

The Program Items Properties dialog box in Windows 3.1 contains three new parameters: Working Directory, which shows the location of files that the application opens or saves; Shortcut Key, which runs the application from Program Manager or, if the applications is already running, brings it to the foreground; and a Run Minimized check box, which enables you to start an application as a minimized icon.

NOTE The Working Directory, Shortcut Key, and Run Minimized properties are new in Version 3.1. If you create program items using these fields and then use the applications with an earlier version of Windows, these properties will not be used.

Many manufacturers of non-Windows applications are now including icon (.ICO) and program information files (.PIF) with applications. If both the manufacturer and Windows provides a PIF, open both with the PIF Editor and use the PIF that contains the setting you want. If you are not sure which settings to use, try the PIF provided with the non-Windows application. This PIF is generally updated with each release of the non-Windows software. If problems occur when trying to run the application, contact the manufacturer for assistance. Lotus 1-2-3, for example, includes the files 123.PIF and 123.ICO.

To install this application into an existing program group called Spreadsheets, follow these steps:

1. From Program Manager, open the Spreadsheet program group window. (This step is necessary because Windows will place the program item into the active program group window.)
2. From the File menu, choose New. Then choose Program Item. The Program Item Properties dialog box appears.
3. Enter the following information, as appropriate:

   In the Description field (optional), type the name you want to appear beneath the program item icon. If you leave this field blank, the program file name in the Command Line field appears.

   In the Command Line field, type the command—with its directory—that starts the program.

   If you are unsure what directory and file name should be entered in the Command Line field, choose Browse. A Browse dialog box appears that enables you to move through your disk drives, directories, and files so that you can make the proper command line entry.

   In the Working Directory field (optional), type the directory from which you want to start the application if you want to start it in a directory different from where the program files are located. You might find this field useful if you place your data files in a directory different from the application's program files. The working directory you specify becomes the current directory where the application stores and retrieves files unless the program overrides the working directory with a specific directory for saving and retrieving files.

   In the Shortcut Key field (optional), type a unique combination of keys that, when pressed while Program Manager is active, will run the application. If the application is running but not in the foreground, pressing the shortcut key displays the application in the foreground.

   Choose Run Minimized if you want the application to start minimized as an icon.

   The dialog box now looks like figure 8.6.

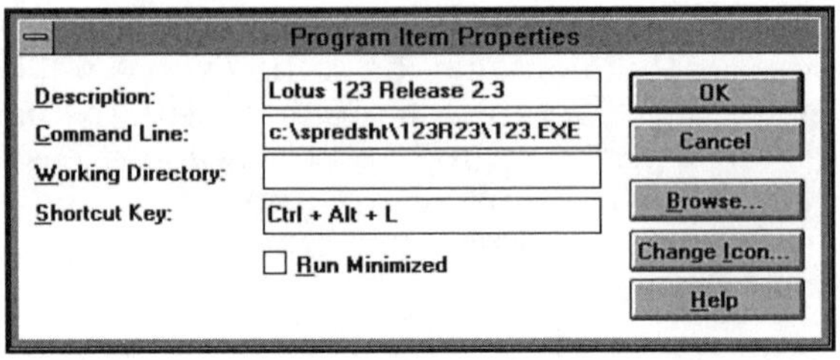

Fig. 8.6.

The Program Item Properties dialog box with Lotus 1-2-3 information.

4. If the manufacturer has provided an icon, choose Change Icon. The Change Icon dialog box appears (see fig. 8.7). Type the path and file name for the icon file or choose Browse. For more information on selecting and changing program item icons, see the section "Enhanced Icon Selection" later in this chapter.

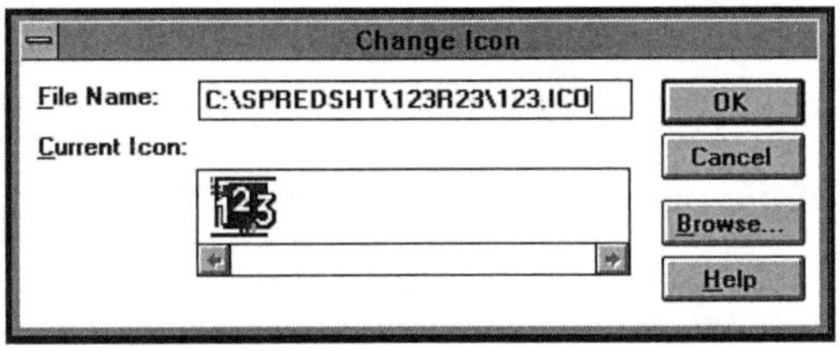

Fig. 8.7.

The Change Icon dialog box.

5. Choose OK twice to return to the Program Group window. The program item icon appears.

For detailed information about Program Manager, see Chapter 4.

Using File Manager

You can also set up a program item for a non-Windows application by dragging its program file (.EXE, .COM, or .BAT) or PIF from the File Manager window into a program group window.

To set up a non-Windows application using File Manager, follow these steps:

1. Start File Manager.
2. Move and resize the File Manager window so that you can see the program group where you will place the new program item icon for the application.
3. Using File Manager, select the directory that contains the program file or PIF of the application you want to set up.

4. Locate the program or batch file (.EXE, .COM, or .BAT) or PIF.
5. Move the mouse pointer to the program file icon, press and hold the mouse button, and drag the icon to the program group icon or window in the Program Manager window. Release the button to create a program item icon for the application.

   Windows uses the standard MS-DOS icon to represent the program item.
6. If you want to change the icon, begin in Program Manager. Choose Properties from the File menu. Then choose Change Icon. Use the menu choices to change the icon. (For more information, see the section "Using Program Manager" earlier in this chapter.)

PIF Files and the PIF Editor

After you set up a non-Windows application, you can run it under Windows. If the application doesn't run properly, you probably need to create or change a PIF for the application. You use the PIF Editor to create or change a PIF.

NOTE Program Manager File Property settings override equivalent entries in the PIF file.

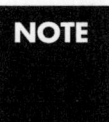

NOTE Most settings for Program Information Files have not changed from Version 3.0 to Version 3.1. For detailed information about all PIF Editor settings, refer to Que's *Using Windows 3.1*, Special Edition, or your Windows manuals.

The Revised PIF Editor

The PIF Editor is revised slightly in Windows 3.1. In 386 Enhanced mode, the order of the fields that the PIF Editor displays has been changed to make them easier to use. The Standard mode PIF Editor screens contain a new field.

In 386 Enhanced mode, three of the more commonly used options have moved from the Windows 3.0 PIF Editor Advanced Options screen to the Windows 3.1 first PIF Editor screen. These options are Video Memory, EMS Memory (expanded memory), and XMS Memory (extended memory).

Figure 8.8 shows the revised 386 Enhanced PIF Editor first screen.

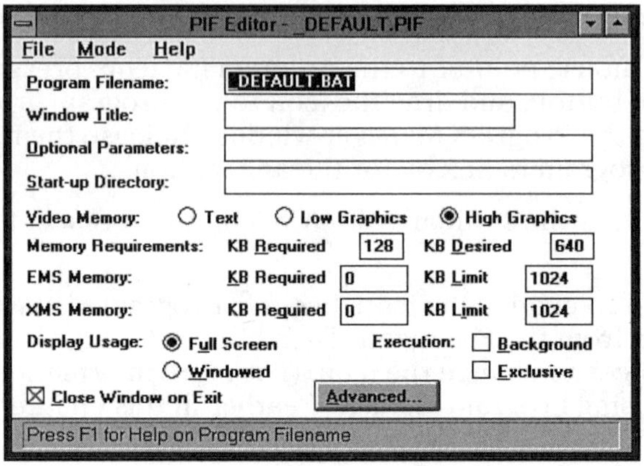

Fig. 8.8.

The Windows 3.1 386 Enhanced mode first screen.

Figure 8.9 shows the revised PIF Editor 386 Enhanced Advanced Options screen.

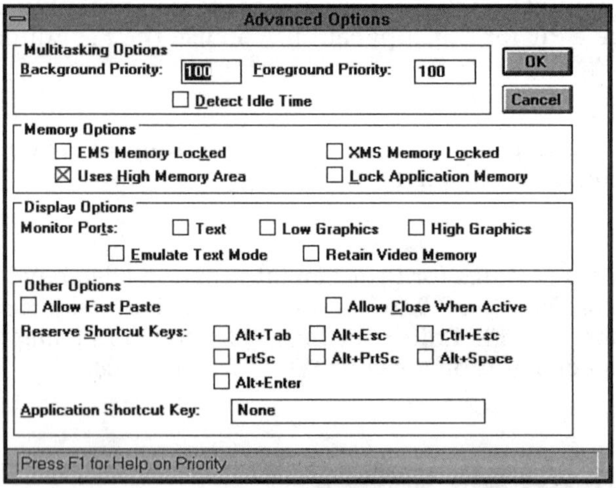

Fig. 8.9.

The Windows 3.1 386 Enhanced Advanced Options screen.

The PIF Editor screen for Standard mode has also been changed. The screen now includes a new field, No Save Screen, which gives you increased flexibility, especially when memory is limited. When you switch between applications in Standard mode, Windows saves the on-screen information in memory. Then when you switch back to the application, Windows can redisplay the screen as it was when you left the application.

When you select the No Save Screen check box, Windows no longer saves the screen information for the application, and the memory becomes available. When you switch back to the application, the screen is not redisplayed correctly unless the application can store its own screen information. Use this option only when an application can store its own screen information and has a command enabling it to redraw the screen. To determine whether an application stores screen information and can redraw the screen, check the index of the applications' user manual or call the vendor's technical support staff.

Using a PIF Provided with a Non-Windows Application

More and more companies are providing PIF files for running non-Windows application under Windows. These PIF files are normally copied into the directory where the application is installed. When Windows runs a a non-Windows application, it searches for a PIF with the same name as the running application in the directory where it found the application program file. If Windows does not find the PIF, it also searches in the Windows directory.

TIP

By keeping PIF files in the directory of each application, you ensure that when you install a new version of the application, Windows will use the updated PIF when running the application.

Windows 3.1 can pass information to the PIF Editor using DOS environment variables. You can type a variable name in the Program Filename, Window Title, Optional Parameters, and Start-up Directory PIF Editor fields. When you use the PIF, Windows replaces the variable name with the value you assigned to the variable before running Windows. When you type the variable name, enclose it in percent signs (%). You might, for example, assign the value C:\SPREDSHT\123R23\123.EXE to the environment variable LOTUSDIR. In the PIF Editor, you would type

```
%LOTUSDIR%
```

in the Program Filename field. (For more information about using environment variables, see the section "Using DOS Environment Variables To Pass Information to Windows" later in this chapter.)

Using the Default PIF

If Windows does not find a PIF in the application program file directory file or the Windows directory, it uses a PIF named _DEFAULT.PIF.

In Windows 3.0, this PIF was located in the main Windows directory. In Windows 3.1, however, it is located in the SYSTEM subdirectory under the directory where you installed Windows.

The 386 Enhanced _DEFAULT.PIF file has changed from Version 3.0 to Version 3.1: the Multitasking Background Priority has been changed from 50 to 100. This change slightly increases the processing time given to a non-Windows application using the default PIF and running in the background. No changes were made in the Standard mode _DEFAULT.PIF.

The default PIF options should work for most non-Windows applications. Microsoft determined the settings based on much experience working with common non-Windows applications. In most cases, you should not change the default PIF options.

If you change _DEFAULT.PIF, the new options are used for all non-Windows applications that do not have their own PIF. Therefore, if the PIF default options do not work with a specific application, do not change _DEFAULT.PIF to work with that application. Instead, create a new PIF.

To create a new PIF for a specific non-Windows application, follow these steps:

1. Run the PIF Editor.
2. In the various fields, type the values necessary to run your non-Windows application properly.

   (For a detailed description of the PIF Editor settings, see Que's *Using Windows 3.1*, Special Edition, or your Windows documentation.)
3. From the File menu, choose Save As. The Save As dialog box appears (see fig. 8.10).

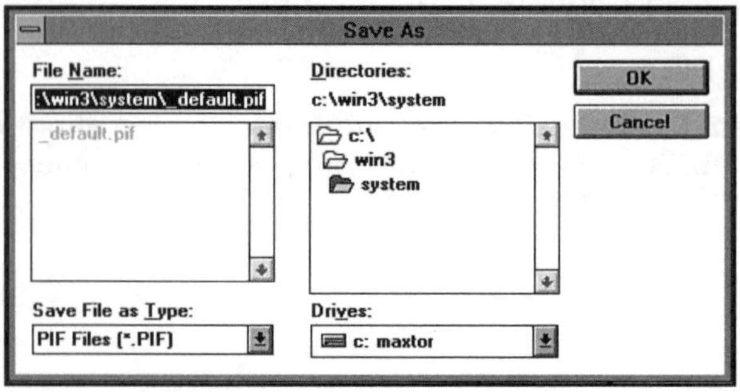

Fig. 8.10.

The file Save As dialog box.

4. In the File Name field, type the name of your non-Windows application program or batch file (for example, 123.PIF for the file 123.EXE). To make sure that the new PIF file is used, in the Drives list box, select the drive that contains the application program file or the Windows directory. In the Directories box, select folders as necessary until the path of the non-Windows application or Windows is displayed above the Directories box.

Running Non-Windows Applications

After you set up a non-Windows application, you can run it. If you have placed a PIF file in the directory of the application's program file or in the Windows directory, the file will provide information to Windows about running the application.

If Windows cannot find the PIF file, it uses the parameters in the default PIF to run your non-Windows application.

> **TIP**
> If your non-Windows application does not run properly when you double-click its icon, you might need to use the PIF Editor to change the application's PIF or create a PIF. For more information on PIFs, see "PIF Files and the PIF Editor" earlier in this chapter.

In Windows 3.0, some non-Windows applications that ran in Graphics mode could not be run in a window. They could be displayed in a window but were suspended (not processing) until returned to full screen. In Windows 3.1, non-Windows graphics applications can run in a Window as well as full screen.

You can run non-Windows applications several ways. The following sections describe the various methods.

From Program Manager

Running a non-Windows application from Program Manager is as easy as opening the appropriate program group window and double-clicking the program item icon of the application. If you have identified a shortcut keystroke, you can press those keys and the application will run.

Using the MS-DOS Prompt

Another method for running a non-Windows application from Program Manager is to double-click the MS DOS Prompt icon in the Main program group. A window appears that displays the traditional DOS prompt (for example, `C:>`). From this prompt, you can change drives and directories using standard DOS commands and run the application by typing its file name. You can also use various DOS menuing and shell programs to run the application.

TIP When you run a program or batch file using the DOS Prompt icon, you are using the memory, multitasking, and other options specified in the DOS Prompt PIF (DOSPRMPT.PIF). Specific programs might have different needs than the DOS Prompt PIF allows. For example, some programs might require more memory than is allocated, while others might be able to run on less memory. To make the PIF specification match the requirements of each application, you might want to create a program item specific to each application with the appropriate memory and multitasking options specified in the PIF.

Using the Run Command

You can also start an application using the Run command. From Program Manager, choose Run from the File menu. The Run dialog box appears (see fig. 8.11). Choose Browse, type the path and program or batch file name, or type the path and PIF name.

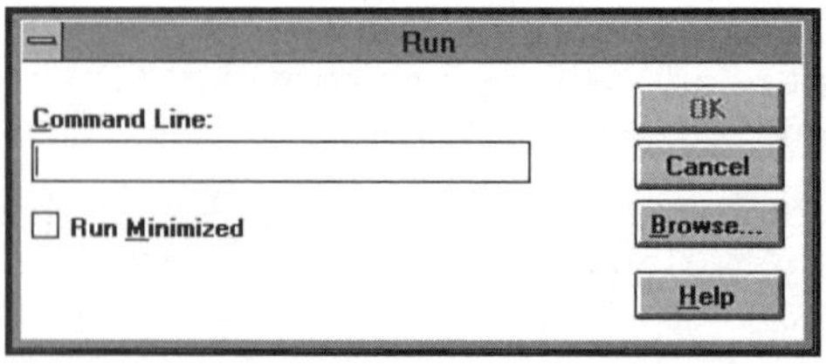

Fig. 8.11.

The Program Manager Run dialog box.

Using Automatic Application Startup

With Windows 3.0, the only way to load or run an application automatically was to use a word processing application to add an entry in the WIN.INI file. With Version 3.1, Program Manager includes a new program group called StartUp. If you want an application to load automatically each time you start up Windows, simply place its program item icon into the StartUp group.

To move an icon into the StartUp group, drag the icon from its current location and drop it into the StartUp group. To copy a program icon to the StartUp group, press and hold the Ctrl key while dragging and dropping the icon.

From File Manager

You also can run Non-Windows applications from File Manager. If a PIF is not found for the application either in the directory of the program file or the Windows directory, the Windows default PIF (_DEFAULT.PIF) will control running the application.

To run non-Windows applications from File Manager, follow these steps:

1. Run File Manager.
2. Change drives and directories until the one containing the non-Windows application is displayed.
3. Locate and double-click the application program file or PIF. The program will load and begin running.

Working with a Non-Windows Application

After an application is running, you can change certain parameters and perform Windows Edit functions. In Standard mode, you can only perform functions such as pasting information from the Windows Clipboard or closing the application. In 386 Enhanced mode, you can do the following:

- Change settings, including screen display options, multitasking options, and processor resource use.
- Change the display fonts for an application running in a window (new in Windows 3.1).
- Use Edit functions to move information to and from the Windows Clipboard.

For detailed information about each of these options, see Que's *Using Windows 3.1*, Special Edition.

Because Windows 3.1 does not contain significant changes from Version 3.0 for non-Windows applications in Standard mode, this section only discusses non-Windows applications running in 386 Enhanced mode.

To change the settings of a non-Windows application while it is running in 386 Enhanced mode, follow these steps:

1. If the application is currently displayed and running in a window, click the Control-menu box in the top left corner of the window. If the application is running in full-screen mode, press Alt-Tab to switch to Program Manager. Click the application's icon located at the bottom of the screen on the desktop.

   The Control menu appears (see fig. 8.12).

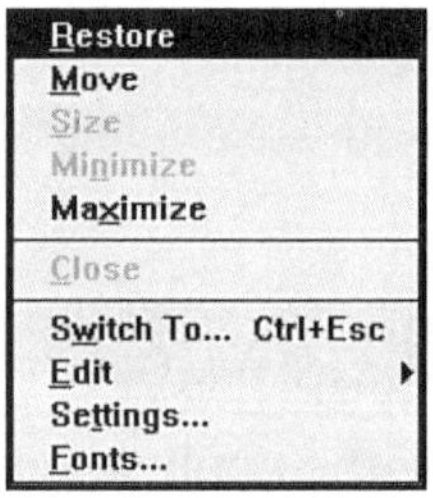

Fig. 8.12.

The 386 Enhanced non-Windows application Control menu.

2. Choose Settings. The Settings dialog box appears (see fig. 8.13).

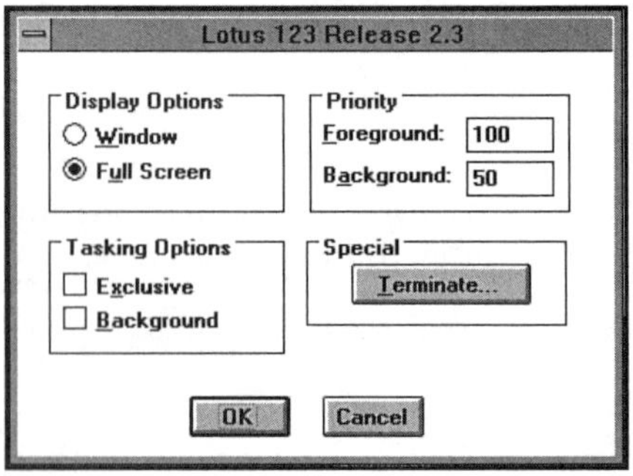

Fig. 8.13.

The Settings dialog box for Lotus 1-2-3.

3. Change the settings as desired. The settings for running non-Windows application are the following:

   Display Options:

   Choose Window to display the application in a window. You then can resize the window, use the Windows Edit function to move information to and from the Windows Clipboard and, in text applications, set the display font to a different size.

Choose Full Screen to display the application on the full computer screen as if you are not running Windows. The features that are available when you choose Window are not available when you choose Full Screen.

You can quickly switch between display options by pressing Alt-Enter. **TIP**

Tasking Options:

Choose Exclusive to stop all other applications from processing while this application is active.

Choose Background so that the non-Windows application will continue to process, even when it is not active and displayed on-screen.

If neither Exclusive nor Background are chosen, the non-Windows application only runs when it is active and displayed in the foreground.

NOTE If a non-Windows application is in the foreground and has been checked to run exclusively, all other applications stop processing, even if their tasking option is checked to run in the background.

Priority:

Normally, you will want an application to have its full share of the processor when it is running in the foreground. If, however, you want another background task to run more quickly while you are working on this task in the foreground, type a number less than 100 in the Foreground box.

Running an application in the background will take processor time, and performance of the application in the foreground will generally decrease. Normally, Windows gives the current application more processor time than the applications running in the background. If you want an application to run its background tasks more quickly, type a number greater than the default of 50 in the Background box.

NOTE Windows ignores the background number if another non-Windows application is running in the foreground and has been set to run exclusively.

Special:

The Terminate Command button in this option lets you terminate a non-Windows application without using the application's exit command. You should only use this option as a last resort and if you understand the consequence of what you are doing. If you choose this option, you will lose any unsaved modified or new files.

4. When you have made the desired selections, choose OK to apply the changes and continue. The changes are immediate and affect the application for the current session. Permanent changes must be made to the application's PIF; these changes affect the application each time it is run. Figure 8.14 shows a non-Windows application (Lotus 1-2-3) running in a window.

Fig. 8.14.

Lotus 1-2-3 running in a window.

Changing the Display Font Size

When you are in 386 Enhanced mode in Windows 3.1, you can change the display font of a windowed application. This capability enables you to resize the window and adjust how much text will be displayed in the window so that you can ensure that all the text from your application appears in the window. In essence, Windows lets you scale the font to fit the size you want the window to be.

NOTE

Changing the display font of an application running in Graphics mode (such as Lotus 1-2-3 WYSIWYG mode or WordPerfect 5.1 View Document) has no effect while the application is displaying text as a graphic.

To change the display font for a non-Windows application running in a window, follow these steps:

1. If the application is running in full-screen mode, press Alt-Enter to run it in a window. Then click the Control-menu box in the top left corner of the window.

   The 386 Enhanced mode Control menu appears.

2. Choose Fonts. The Font Selection dialog box appears (see fig. 8.15).

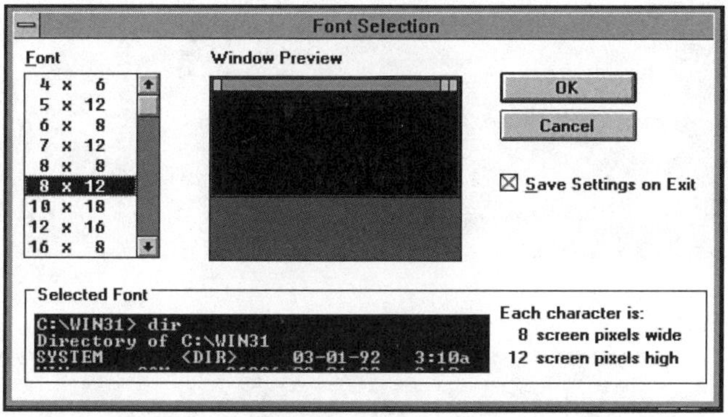

Fig. 8.15

The Font Selection dialog box.

3. Choose Font to select a different font size. The default font size for a VGA monitor is 8 by 12. You can change the size of characters from a very small size of 4 screen pixels wide by 12 screen pixels high to a very large size of 16 wide by 8 high.

   As you change the size of the font, Windows shows you in the Selected Font area how the font will appear. The Window Preview area shows the approximate size the window would be if you use the new font size.

   Figure 8.16 shows an example of WordPerfect 5.1 being run in a window with a very large Windows display font. Figure 8.17 shows the same text with a very small Windows display font.

4. If you want to use the new font size whenever you display this application in a window, choose Save Settings on Exit.

Using the Windows Edit Function

You can use the Windows Edit function to copy information between applications—either non-Windows applications running in a window or Windows applications.

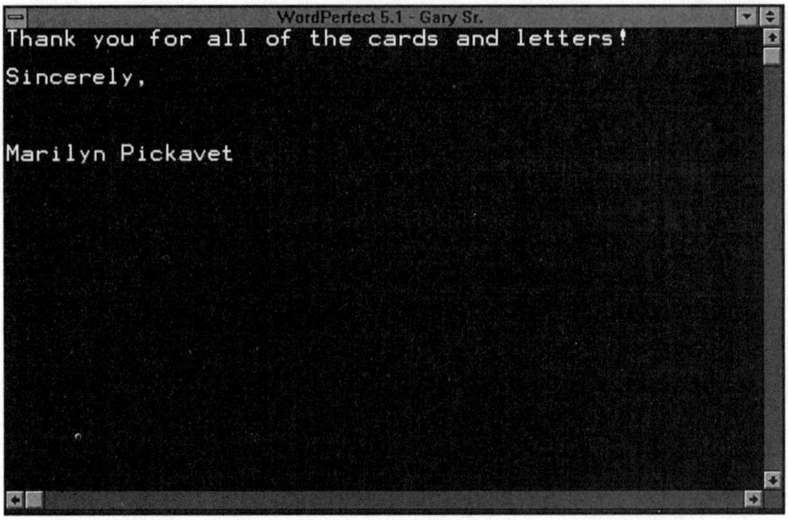

Fig. 8.16.

WordPerfect in a window with a large display font.

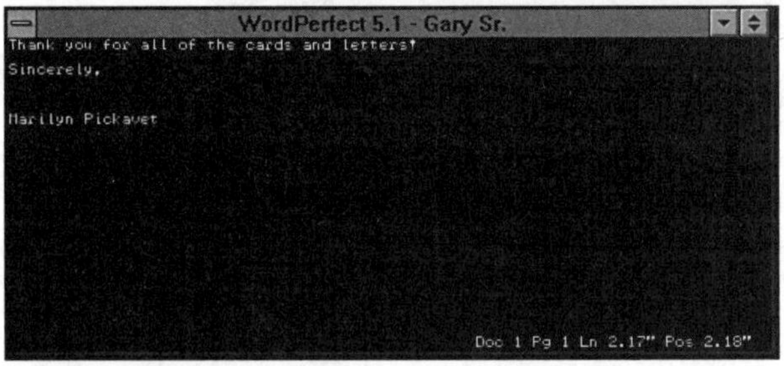

Fig. 8.17.

The same WordPerfect text in a window with a small display font.

Because mouse support is now provided for windowed applications, using the mouse in a window no longer automatically activates the Windows Mark Text mode. If it did, there would be confusion about whether the mouse was to be used for an application function or a Windows function. Windows 3.1 requires that you specify that you want to use the mouse with the Windows Edit function.

To copy text from a non-Windows application to the Windows Clipboard to paste into another application, follow these steps:

1. Make the non-Windows application active in a window in the foreground. (Press Alt-Enter to switch between running in a full screen and running in a window.)
2. Click the Control-menu box to open the Control menu for the application.

3. Choose Edit. The Windows Edit menu appears.
4. Choose Mark. You return to the application and the mouse now functions in the Windows Edit mode. A flashing box appears in the top left corner of the window

   To select text, drag the mouse.
5. Press Enter to copy the marked text to the Windows Clipboard. You can now choose Paste to paste the text to another application.

Using DOS Environment Variables To Pass Information to Windows

Windows 3.1 lets you pass information to Windows using DOS environment variables. Windows replaces the variable name with the value you assigned it in DOS.

You create a DOS environment variable and assign it a value by using the SET command at the DOS prompt. Environment variables normally are set in the AUTOEXEC.BAT file because that file is read each time you start the computer.

The following Windows fields affect non-Windows applications and can use environment variables to pass information.

In Program Manager's Program Item Properties:

Command Line

Working Directory

In the PIF Editor:

Program Filename

Window Title

Optional Parameters

Start-up Directory

To create a variable with the Lotus 1-2-3 path and program name, for example, you could type the following command at the DOS prompt:

```
SET LOTUS123=C:\SPREDSHT\123\123.EXE
```

After this variable is set, Windows can reference it. To use this path and file name as the program file name in the PIF Editor, enter the environment variable name enclosed between percent (%) signs, such as

```
%LOTUS123%
```

Because the variable name does not have an extension when you save the PIF file, you see the error message `Invalid extension in program name.`

Click OK to ignore the error. When Windows uses the PIF to run the program, it replaces the variable name with the command line you have set, which does have a valid program file extension.

Likewise, if the variable name (including the %) is greater than eight characters long, you see the error message `Invalid program filename.`

Simply click OK to ignore this error.

NOTE You must set DOS environment variables before running Windows. If you want to set a new variable, you must exit Windows, set the variable, and run Windows again. Other than for testing purposes, you generally will want to set the environment variable in the AUTOEXEC.BAT file.

Enhanced Icon Selection

When you add a program item to a program group, Program Manager selects an icon for that item. In Windows 3.0, unless you acquired your own icons or the manufacturer of a non-Windows application provided one, you could only choose from a limited selection of icons provided in the PROGMAN.EXE file. These standard icons were not very imaginative, and the limited variety made using icons to differentiate applications difficult.

Windows 3.1 greatly increases the number of icons provided for non-Windows applications. In addition to the new generic icons in the file PROGMAN.EXE, the MORICONS.DLL file contains many new generic icons, as well as icons created specifically for a variety of non-Windows applications.

Selecting icons in Windows 3.1 is much easier than in Version 3.0. When you choose Change Icon from the Program Item Properties dialog box, the Change Icon dialog box shown appears (see fig. 8.18). In this dialog box, you can choose to Browse to find files or, after you have selected a file, you can use the displayed scroll bar to view and select an icon quickly when several are contained in a file.

For more information about Program Manager and program item icons, see Chapter 4.

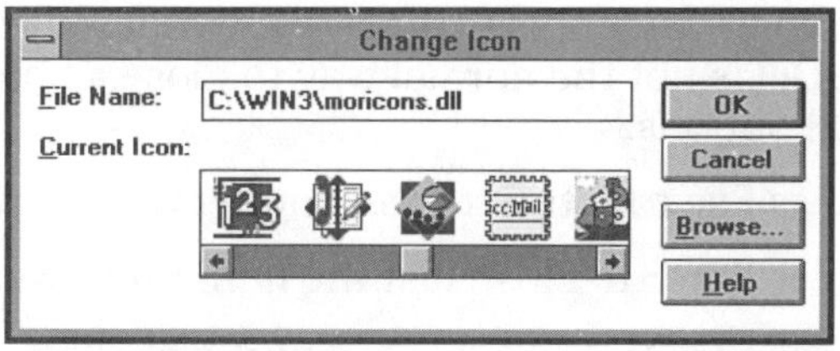

Fig. 8.18.

The Change Icon dialog box displaying several icons.

Using a Mouse with Non-Windows Applications

In Windows 3.0, when you ran a non-Windows application that supported a mouse in a window, you could not use the mouse for any of that program's functions. The mouse was only available for Windows Edit functions (such as copying and pasting text to and from the Windows Clipboard). Mouse support in a non-Windows application was only available when running in a full screen.

With Windows 3.1, you can use the mouse with a non-Windows application running in a window and perform functions as if you were running the application in a full screen. You still can use the mouse for Windows Edit functions. You can, for example, choose the Windows Edit function Mark from the application's Control menu. You then could use the mouse to perform the Window's mark text function and press Enter to copy the marked text to the Clipboard or Esc to cancel the operation. When you complete the Windows Edit function, the mouse again works with the application.

To use a mouse with a non-Windows application running in a window, you must use the MOUSE.SYS or MOUSE.COM files included with Windows 3.1. MOUSE.SYS is a driver that is placed in the CONFIG.SYS file. MOUSE.COM is placed in the AUTOEXEC.BAT file. Normally, the Window's Setup procedure places the appropriate mouse driver in the AUTOEXEC.BAT file during installation.

Rebooting a Non-Windows Application

With Windows 3.0, when a non-Windows application locked up your computer, your only choice was to press Ctrl-Alt-Del to reboot the machine.

In Windows 3.1, when you press Ctrl-Alt-Del, Windows reminds you that pressing Ctrl-Alt-Del is not the normal way to close an application. You then have several options:

- You can press Esc to return to the non-Windows application.
- You can press Enter to close just the non-Windows application.
- You can press Ctrl-Alt-Del again to abort everything and restart the computer system.

You should only use the latter two options as a last resort and if you understand the consequence of what you are doing. Any unsaved changes to an existing file or new files that have not been saved will be lost. When possible, you should quit an application by displaying it in the foreground and exiting using its normal exit procedure.

Handling Device Contention

Occasionally, two non-Windows applications running in 386 Enhanced mode want to use the same device (such as a modem or printer) at the same time. Windows 3.0 and 3.1 handle this situation the same way.

You can specify how Windows handles contention for a device using the 386 Enhanced option from Control Panel in the Main group. For detailed information about these settings for handling Device Contention, see Que's *Using Windows 3.1*, Special Edition, or your Windows 3.1 reference manual.

Summary

Although Window 3.0 greatly improved the ability to run non-Windows applications under Windows, Windows 3.1 builds on that tradition and offers improvements. This chapter demonstrated that although non-Windows applications are not designed to run under Windows, Windows attempts to provide the ability to run them under Windows efficiently and with the fewest possible problems. You learned that Windows 3.1 improves this ability over Version 3.0 through the addition of various features.

9

CHAPTER

Using Multimedia and Sound

As computer technology becomes more powerful and affordable, multimedia is predicted to become the biggest PC growth market in the 90s. *Multimedia* is the integration of computer text, graphics, sound, video, compact discs, and just about every other computer device into a single, interactive product. Windows 3.1 supports the trend toward multimedia and includes multimedia extensions for users and developers.

Until now, there have been very few multimedia hardware and software products on the market. The primary reason for the lack of products has been a lack of standards. The market is expanding considerably now, and Microsoft decided to help promote that expansion by adding multimedia extensions to Windows 3.1.

This chapter will introduce you to the capabilities and possibilities of multimedia. You will see how multimedia technology interacts with users and helps them in virtually every aspect of computing. Multimedia adds a dimension to computers that was formerly unavailable (or too expensive for general use). Thanks to Windows 3.1, multimedia now has a platform of extensions that developers can rely on and use to bring standards into the multimedia arena.

What is Multimedia?

In its purest definition, multimedia means "multiple media." The word *media* refers to a method of communication. Telephones, televisions, paper, monitors, and satellites are all examples of media. Multimedia implies that you can get information from a wide variety of sources. PCs actually have been multimedia computers since their inception; you have been able to view text on the screen as well as on the printer. You could give keyboard input, or modem input.

Today's multimedia goes much farther than its literal definition. The computer adds an interactive dimension to multimedia. As you are reading about a famous composer, for example, you can hear his music in the background, see his picture on-screen, and print a score of his music (see fig. 9.1). As you are learning about the great cats of the jungle, you can see a movie of one on-screen (see fig. 9.2). This capability opens up an exciting and new method of learning, working, teaching, and playing.

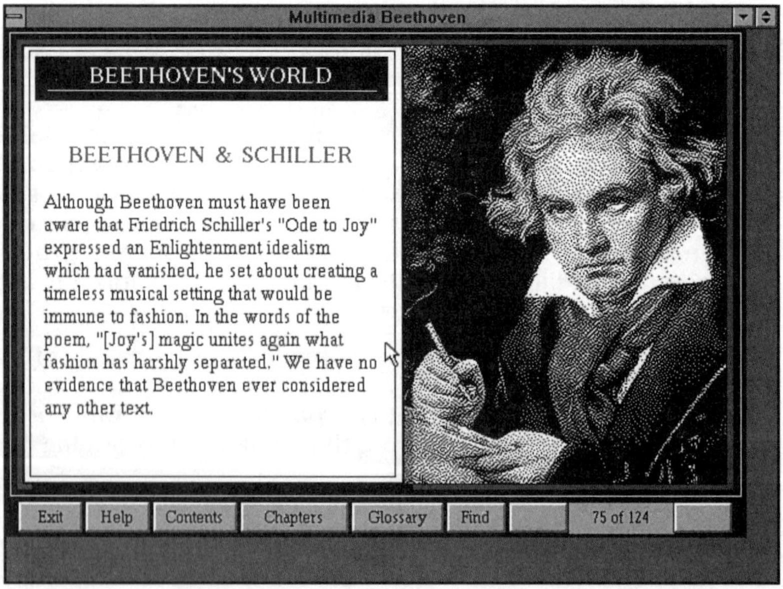

Fig. 9.1.

With multimedia, you can learn by interacting with text, graphics, and music.

Actually, we can now see only a glimpse of the future of multimedia. Hardware and software improvements are advancing rapidly. With those advances, the uses of multimedia become more apparent. Many people believe that tomorrow's schools, workplaces, entertainment, and customer relations will include some means of multimedia that was never before possible—or even considered.

Fig. 9.2.

Multimedia lets you see full-motion video on-screen.

Defining *multimedia* is difficult because the term means different things to different people. Despite the various definitions, most people agree that multimedia combines text, graphics, and sound. At the heart of most multimedia systems is usually a computerized compact disc system, typically referred to as a *CD-ROM* (for Compact Disc Read-Only Memory). One compact disc can hold a tremendous amount of storage—much more than many of today's hard disks. A typical CD-ROM drive can access over 600M of information (600 million characters) from a single disc.

Because there were no multimedia standards, Microsoft decided to develop some. You can spend thousands of dollars purchasing a multimedia computer, but Microsoft saw the need for establishing an affordable multimedia standard that was within the reach of most computer users. The company joined ten other companies and pioneered the MPC standard so that developers could use existing hardware and software tools to produce a multimedia system.

MPC: The Multimedia Personal Computer

The struggle for multimedia standards was silenced when Microsoft and ten computer hardware makers, shown in table 9.1, met in October of 1991. They formed a multimedia consortium and developed an affordable multimedia standard. They called the new standard *MPC*, meaning Multimedia Personal Computer.

Table 9.1 Companies Comprising the MPC Consortium

AT&T Computer Systems
CompuAdd Corporation
Creative Labs, Inc.
Media Vision
Microsoft
NEC Technologies
Olivetti
Phillips Consumer Electronics Co.
Tandy Corporation
Video Seven
Zenith Data Systems

The MPC symbol means that you now can buy multimedia hardware and software that work together. When purchasing a multimedia CD-ROM or an additional device that adds another multimedia dimension to your computer, look for the MPC label (see fig. 9.3). Companies that use this label must pay to license it, and they must follow the standards written by the MPC committee.

Fig. 9.3.

The new MPC symbol ensures compatibility between multimedia products.

When buying a new CD-ROM drive for your computer, look for the MPC label on the box to guarantee that it follows the MPC standard. Vendors who deviate from the MPC standard will not be able to use the label. This requirement should cause a tremendous boom in the multimedia industry. (Think of what the standardized cassette tape did for the music industry!) As a user, you will benefit from more compatibility and lower prices due to the larger number of vendors.

NOTE Many hardware and software products do not carry the MPC symbol but still meet or exceed the MPC specifications. The MPC label is primarily a guide for you when buying multimedia products.

As a Windows 3.1 user, you already have the foundation of the MPC requirements: the set of multimedia extensions provided with Windows 3.1. Table 9.2 shows the full set of MPC specifications. These specifications are the *minimum* requirements that hardware and software must meet to conform with MPC and carry the MPC symbol. You do not need to have the entire MPC-compatible system to enjoy many of the MPC-compatible software products.

Table 9.2 The MPC Minimum Specifications

80386-SX 20MHz PC *
2M of RAM
VGA graphics adapter and monitor
3 1/2-inch, high-density disk drive
30M hard disk
One serial and one parallel port
Joystick
CD-ROM drive with CD-digital audio output and a minimum sustained data transfer rate of 150 kbits per second.
101-key keyboard
Two-button Microsoft-compatible mouse
MS-DOS 3.3, 3.31, 4.01, or 5.0 or compatible
Windows 3.0 with multimedia extensions (3.1 includes the extensions)
MIDI-in/MIDI-out (Musical Instrument Digital Interface)
8- or 16-bit DAC (Digital-to-Analog Converter), DMA, and interrupt
8- or 16-bit linear ADC (Analog-to-Digital Converter)
Music synthesizer
Digitally controlled analog audio mixer
* Changed in December, 1991, from an 80286 10 MHz PC

Microsoft actually offered multimedia extensions to owners and developers of hardware and software products for Windows 3.0. These extensions were not generally available to users, but developers used them to begin producing multimedia products. Because the software multimedia extensions are now part of Windows 3.1, you can use MPC multimedia hardware and software immediately.

TIP Many companies offer complete MPC upgrade kits that include an MPC-compliant CD-ROM, an audio card, and speakers to convert your existing nonmultimedia 386 or 486 PC into an MPC multimedia PC.

Multimedia Software

Multimedia is seeing its first uses in education and entertainment. The interactive searching power of a computer makes it a fantastic research tool. With multimedia, using the computer for study is easier than ever. Multimedia software replaces yesterday's cryptic programming commands with find-and-point data lookups.

Vast amounts of information can be at your fingertips using a CD-ROM drive. You can find encyclopedias, history books, great fictional and nonfictional writings, and even translations of the Bible, including original Hebrew and Greek texts, on CD-ROM. This list, however, is only a sampling of the types of information that you can obtain on CD-ROM.

All this information on CD-ROM is convenient for students. Rather than carting book after book from the library, students can simply carry a few CD-ROMs containing all needed information. Instead of perusing page after page, the student can choose a few commands and let the computer compile the necessary information.

Multimedia, however, takes all this information one step further. Rather than only providing you with necessary text, graphics and sound are added for a total educational experience. Suppose, for example, that you are looking for information on a chimpanzee. Simply start a search for *chimpanzee*. Not only will you see information about the chimpanzee, you will hear the pronunciation for the word *chimpanzee* and see a motion picture showing the chimpanzee in its natural habitat. Multimedia truly brings information to life.

Multimedia Hardware

Now that you have Microsoft Windows 3.1 and want to upgrade your computer to take advantage of its multimedia extensions, you need to consider the hardware you purchase. The MPC standard is new and is still evolving. If you can find hardware with the MPC symbol, you can be sure that it will work with the Windows extensions. However, not all MPC-compatible hardware contains the MPC symbol yet. Some companies, trying to save costs that they would eventually have to pass along to you, will never license the MPC symbol, even though their products comply fully with the specifications.

Even when using the MPC symbol as a guide, choosing the right hardware can be confusing and expensive. Not all CD-ROMs are created equally. Some are fast, some are slow. Some are expensive, others are cheap. Some come bundled with hundreds of dollars of multimedia CD-ROM titles, others do not even have cables you need to connect the device to your computer.

There is no way to cover all the specifics you need to consider when purchasing multimedia equipment; vendor and product information changes very rapidly. Before you purchase multimedia equipment, however, the following sections might help guide you in your decision. They concentrate on the "big three" of multimedia: CD-ROM, video, and sound.

Multimedia CD-ROM Drives

Because the MPC standard requires a CD-ROM, it should be your first consideration when upgrading to multimedia equipment. The tremendous storage required for interactive multimedia text, graphics, and sound would quickly overflow most users' hard disks. A CD-ROM's storage capabilities, as well as the relatively inexpensive CD-ROM software, make the CD-ROM a must-have for multimedia users.

When purchasing a CD-ROM, make sure that it has the following features:

- Capability to play CDs that store up to 600M of data
- Sustained data-transfer rate of at least 150 kbits per second
- Access time between 320 and 400 milliseconds
- Headphone jacks, external speaker jacks, or both, and a volume control

You can expect to pay anywhere from $375 to $2000 for a CD-ROM drive. The price is affected by the speed of the drive and whether it is external or internal. Some manufacturers sell a limited number of CD-ROM drives, so their prices remain high.

NOTE Vendors are now making portable CD-ROM drives for laptop computer users who need the easy access to information that CD-ROMs provide.

Multimedia Video Hardware

Most current computer users have VGA (Video Graphics Array) graphics adapters. The VGA offers both high-resolution graphics and high-quality text resolution. Because the MPC standard requires nothing more than a VGA graphics adapter and monitor, you are probably set up in this area already.

Some industry-accepted video adapters, such as Super-VGA, improve on the VGA standard by offering more colors and a high-resolution output. IBM now offers the XGA (for extended graphics adapter), which is fully VGA-compatible, but also offers extended resolution and colors over the regular VGA adapter.

Because the MPC specifications require at least a color VGA, you must upgrade to color VGA if you have not already. Anything less than VGA is generally unacceptable for color pictures and motion video.

Multimedia Sound Hardware

The rich sound provided by multimedia is one of the most appealing aspects of multimedia computing. The Windows 3.1 extensions integrate sound directly into the Windows environment. (For more information, see the section “Multimedia Extensions” later in this chapter.)

Although multimedia supports sound, the sound cards available for your PC vary widely in quality and compatibility. You need more than an internal speaker to meet the requirements of the MPC sound specifications. Deciding how you will produce sound can be confusing; several methods are available, most of which vary in price and compatibility. Currently, some sound hardware vendors support the full MPC sound spectrum, and most probably will soon.

The sound issue is complicated further because although the CD-ROM drive plays beautiful stereo sound, you also need an additional sound card or device. Some multimedia software programs use the CD-ROM speakers for sound, others use your sound-generating cards, and others use both. If you have speakers (as opposed to headphones) attached to your CD-ROM drive, you need at least one additional speaker (preferably two for stereo) for the sound card. You can purchase an audio mixer to run the CD-ROM and the sound card into the same set of speakers. As you can imagine, you have some speaker placement and cabling issues to solve.

TIP Keep all speakers away from your disks and CRT. The magnets in the speakers can destroy data on the disks and throw your screen out of alignment.

If you want to use multimedia software that plays voices through your sound cards, you need a sound card that can reproduce 11 Kilohertz sound. Table 9.3 is a list of the more popular sound cards that reproduce voices as well as the full music spectrum. More vendors will offer the voice frequency in the future.

Table 9.3 Sound Cards that Reproduce 11-Khz Voice

Adlib Gold Card
Disney Sound Source
Pro Audio Spectrum
Soundblaster
Soundblaster Pro
Thunderboard

NOTE Microsoft has plans to develop its own MPC-compatible sound card. This sound card would be one of a scant number of hardware products sold by Microsoft.

Windows 3.1 supports three types of sound resources. Table 9.4 lists the three sound resources, along with an explanation of each.

To learn more about how Windows 3.1 supports these sound modes, read the following section, which describes the inner workings of the multimedia extensions and how you can control sound from within Windows 3.1.

Table 9.4 Sound Resources Supported by Windows 3.1

Sound Resource	Description
CD Audio	Specification used by audio CD players to play, but not record, stereo sound. Also called *red book* specification.
Waveform	Specification to record and play back sounds. Waveform is not as good reproduction quality as CD audio, but it takes less storage space. This resource requires an 8- or 16-bit digital-to-analog converter, DMA and interrupt, and an 8- or 16-bit linear analog-to-digital converter for MPC specification.
MIDI	Specification for Musical Instrument Digital Interface. Enables you to connect MIDI compatible keyboards and synthesizers to your PC.

Multimedia Extensions

Ever since Microsoft developed the multimedia extensions for Windows, users seemed confused as to how they were affected by these extensions. If you never use multimedia, you might notice a few menu options on Control Panel, but you will never really notice that Windows 3.1 supplies multimedia extensions. As a user of Windows 3.1 and multimedia, you enjoy the benefits of the multimedia extensions without having to worry about how they manipulate your multimedia system.

If you are writing multimedia software and device drivers, you would need to know the details of the multimedia extensions. Even if you never plan to develop multimedia hardware and software, however, a little understanding of these extensions will help you comprehend how your sound and graphics come together in a Windows multimedia product.

The multimedia extensions are actually APIs (Application Program Interfaces) that sit between your programs and the computer's hardware. Microsoft includes over 120 APIs. These APIs allow software manufacturers more freedom in how they implement their software. The APIs also ensure that sound-generating programs and CD-ROM interfacing programs work with any MPC hardware you connect to your system.

In an API system, the hardware is independent of the software. When you buy a CD-ROM drive or a new sound card, the makers of the hardware supply a disk of device drivers for that hardware. These device drivers tell Windows how to integrate with the hardware, not how to integrate with each program on your computer. As long as the program uses the multimedia extensions, it will not write directly to hardware. Instead, it will write to the Windows extensions. Programs then can ignore the specifics of the hardware and write to the multimedia APIs supplied with the Windows extensions.

TIP

If you want to pursue the programming details of multimedia device-independent APIs, you might want to contact Microsoft for a copy of the Windows Software Development Kit (SDK). The Windows SDK provides the API to C programmers who want to control multimedia devices from their programs without worrying about the hardware specifics of each manufacturer's device.

Installing Devices

For the average user, the most obvious multimedia extensions in Windows 3.1 are the new sound features. Several additions to Windows 3.1 make it more than just a visual environment. Windows is now closer to becoming a multimedia environment, especially in the area of sound.

Before using the new sound extensions to Windows 3.1, you must install appropriate sound drivers that match your hardware. To install your sound driver, choose Main from the Program Manager and then choose Control Panel.

Windows cannot recognize hardware on your system until you install the hardware driver. From the Control Panel window, open Drivers. A list of one or more installed sound drivers appears. Many sound drivers are bundled with Windows 3.1 (see table 9.5). If your sound board is not listed in the table, your hardware dealer must supply a software driver with the sound card in order for the sound card to work with the Windows multimedia extensions.

Table 9.5 Sound Drivers Bundled with Windows 3.1

Ad Lib
Creative Labs Sound Blaster 1.0
Creative Labs Sound Blaster 1.5
Media Vision Thunder Board
MIDI Mapper

continues

Table 9.5 Continued

Roland LAPC1
Roland MPU401
Timer (for MIDI)
MIDI sequencer
MIDI sound device

Suppose, for example, that you have the Ad Lib sound card installed on your system. Because multimedia software will not talk directly to Ad Lib but will talk to the Windows multimedia extensions, you must install the Ad Lib driver so that Windows will recognize the card.

From the Drives window, choose Add. Windows 3.1 displays a list of drivers for your system, similar to those in table 9.5. To add the Ad Lib driver, highlight the Ad Lib line in the list and choose OK. Windows 3.1 prompts you for one of the installation disks. Insert that disk into drive A: (or B:, depending on the size of your Window's disks) and press Enter. Windows reads the Ad Lib driver from the disk and installs it on your system.

After you install the driver, Windows displays the new Drivers window; your newly added driver appears in the list. You can add another driver or close the Drivers window to perform another function.

Assigning Sounds to Events

You can map various sounds to Windows 3.1 events, such as errors. This feature might seem like a strange use of multimedia, but it fits nicely with the goals of the MPC committee: giving the user a fully interactive environment with sensory input for the ears as well as the eyes.

If you do nothing, Windows 3.1 defaults to the PC's internal speaker for error beeps. You can assign other musical happenings to Windows events. You can choose a chime or song that plays when you start or exit Windows. You can assign any song stored in a waveform audio format (with the .WAV extension) to a Windows event.

Not all Windows applications will play the .WAV file, however, even if it produces one of the events in this dialog box. Each application must be programmed to play the associated .WAV file. As more people begin using Windows 3.1, more software vendors will add the sound to their Windows events.

To experiment with event sounds, choose the Sound icon from the Control Panel window. A selection box of sounds and events appears. Notice that the left side of the box is labeled Events and the right side is labeled Files. You see only those files with the .WAV extension. Choose the event to which you want to assign a sound. If you want to hear a sound before assigning it to an event, choose the sound file and click Test. The sound plays.

Figure 9.4 shows the chord.wav file being assigned to the asterisk event. (An *asterisk event* is a message window of information that sometimes appears as you use Windows 3.1.) Notice that you also can assign sounds to play when you start Windows, exit Windows, or receive a Window's question box or warning box.

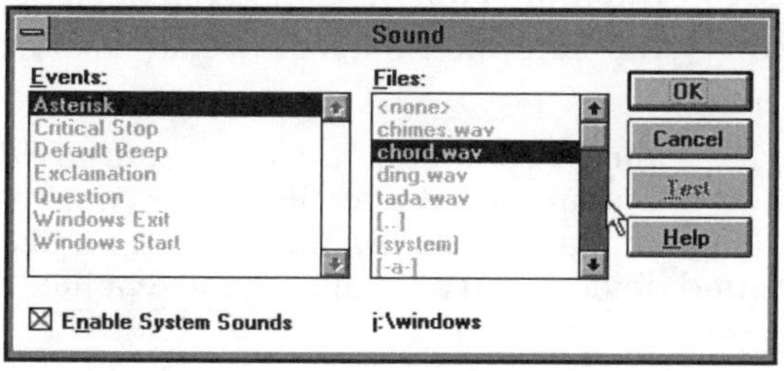

Fig. 9.4.

Assigning a sound to an event.

One of the most important options in the Sound box is the Enable System Sounds check box. Clicking this box turns on the event sounds. When one of the events occurs, you hear the waveform file play on your sound card. If you turn off Enable System Sounds, you will not hear any sounds—including the PC's speaker—until you turn on the sounds again.

NOTE

For practice, assign the CHIME.WAV to the Windows Start event. Exit and then restart Windows. You will hear a chiming sound while you wait for Windows to begin (assuming you installed your sound card's driver in the previous section).

Using the Media Player

With the Media Player supplied with Windows 3.1, you can play a CD audio disc, a laser disc, animated sequences from the CD-ROM, or just about any other MPC equipment.

Choose Media Player from the Accessories window. The Media Player appears on-screen, as in figure 9.5; this window is the control center for your multimedia devices. Notice that it resembles the controls on a cassette deck or compact disk player.

Fig. 9.5.

The Media Player control center.

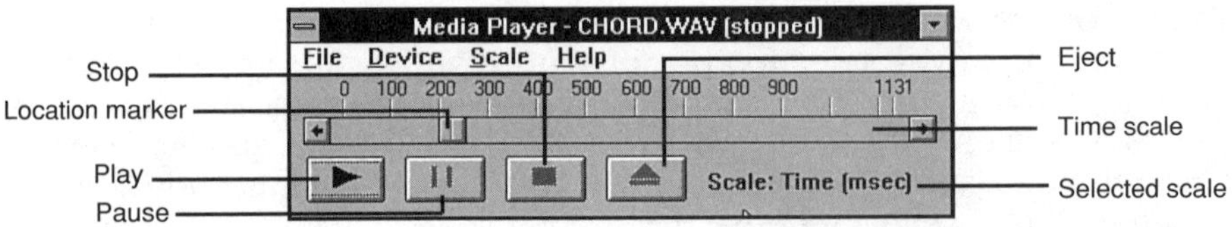

You first must open a device to play sounds. Probably the most commonly played media device will be the CD-ROM or MIDI player device, although you can opt for a MIDI synthesizer, keyboard, or sound board. From the Device menu, select the device you want to play. If the message `<None>` appears, you must go to Control Panel and configure your hardware for Windows. (Generally, this step is completed for you when you install Windows 3.1. You only have to change the devices on Control Panel if you change your computer's hardware after you install Windows.)

One type of device, called a *compound device*, requires data files in order to play. A CD-ROM and sound card play files from your disk and CD, for example. A MIDI instrument plays MIDI files stored on disk. When you choose a compound device, you also must choose a file to play on the devices.

You choose another type of device, called a *simple device*, to control an item, such as a laser disc player, that does not depend on files from the computer. Such a device only requires a computer-controlled interface. Although Windows 3.1 supports simple devices, the hardware interfaces of these devices are not yet standardized and are difficult to connect to your computer. Some very expensive video-based training systems use simple devices. Notice that the name is a little misleading. *Simple* devices are much more difficult to connect than compound devices, and they must be self-contained so that they do not need any files from your computer.

Because you probably will choose a compound device, such as the CD-ROM or MIDI device, you also must choose the file to play. (If you choose a simple device, you do not need to select a file to play.) To choose a device, follow these steps:

1. From the File menu, choose Open. A list of files appears.
2. Choose a file that matches the type of device you want to play. If you are playing a MIDI device, for example, choose a MIDI file (typically ending with the extension .MID). Windows 3.1 supplies two MIDI files: CANYON.MID and PASSPORT.MID.

   You can now play the device.

NOTE Be sure to turn on any amplified speakers attached to your system before playing the device. Otherwise you will not hear the sound.

3. Using the mouse, choose the Play, Pause, Stop, or Eject button. The chosen operation begins. As you play, the scroll bar travels across the control, showing you the relative position in the file you are playing.

   If you like, you can change the scale display of the file being played. The Scale menu supplies the scale-playing options. You can scale the playing for either Time or Tracks. These options determine how the scroll bar increments. If you choose Tracks, the CD tracks being played display across the scroll bar. The time option displays the time, in minutes and fractions of minutes, as the CD plays. You can move to a different track or time location by dragging the scroll box to another part of the song and clicking the Play button.

NOTE If you start playing a CD audio disc, it will continue to play after you leave the Media Player window.

4. To stop playing the device, press the Stop button. If the device is ejectable, such as the CD-ROM drive, press the on-screen Eject button to eject the media from the device. (You can, of course, also press the Eject button on the CD-ROM.)
5. Choose Exit from the File menu to exit the Media Player.

Using the Sound Recorder

The multimedia Sound Recorder lets you record and play back sounds that you record. To operate the Sound Recorder, you must have an MPC-compatible sound card with recording capabilities. The Sound Recorder is your computerized tape recorder; all voice, music, and sounds that you record are stored electronically on your disk drive.

The Sound Recorder opens the door for myriad multimedia possibilities. It is more than just a computerized recorder; with it, networking electronic mail can include voice mail in addition to text. You can leave your secretary or boss verbal instructions for using a program, for example, or you can attach voice commands for teaching software for your children.

Of course, the software you use must recognize the sound recording files. The purpose of the Windows 3.1 Sound Recorder is to get the sound information into a file. Various software makers will have to write their programs to work with the sound recorded files, but with the multimedia extensions, this task is relatively easy.

The sound files are called *waveform* files. These files end with the .WAV extension. You can store up to one minute of sound in each file. Windows 3.1 comes with four waveform audio sound files. You can blend the created waveform files with those that come with Windows. The four sound files are

- CHIMES.WAV
- CHORD.WAV
- DING.WAV
- TADA.WAV

You can probably guess what each sound is from its descriptive name. The CHIMES.WAV file rings chimes similar to a wind chime or a melodic doorbell. The CHORD.WAV file plays a chord (three or four notes played together in harmony). The DING.WAV file plays a *ding-dong* sound. The TADA.WAV file produces a big *tadaaa!* sound. Your sound card might come with several other waveform files. Many electronic bulletin boards, such as CompuServe, also have many waveform audio files available that you can download.

If you are just upgrading to Windows 3.1, take the time to familiarize yourself with the Sound Recorder (assuming that you have an MPC-compatible sound card with a microphone for input). To start the sound recorder, choose the Sound Recorder icon from the Accessories window. The Sound Recorder window appears (see fig. 9.6).

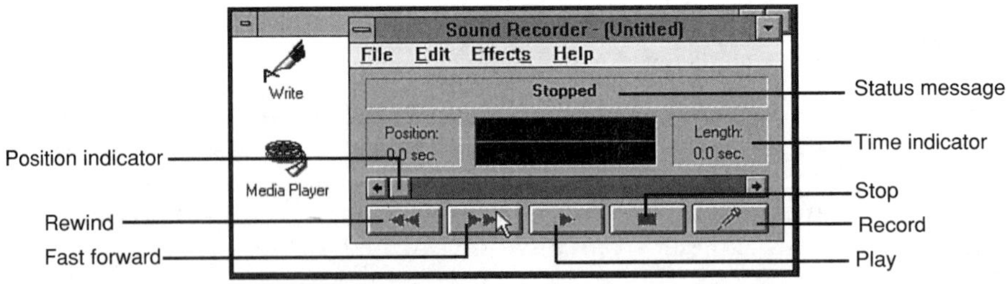

Fig. 9.6.

The Sound Recorder window.

If you get the following message

```
No recording or playback devices are present
```

you must install your sound card through the Drivers icon on Control Panel, as explained earlier. This message also will appear if you have a sound card that does not have recording capabilities.

You can record sounds by recording directly, inserting one sound file into another sound file, or mixing sound files. As you build your collection of sounds, you might want to store them so that you can incorporate them into other sound files. If you record and store people laughing, for example, you can use that laughing sound file in other sound files without recording it again.

Recording a New Sound File

You can record a completely new sound using the Sound Recorder. To record your own sound file, follow these steps:

1. From the File menu, choose New.
2. Click the Microphone button on the Sound Recorder control panel. Clicking this button has the same effect as pressing the Record button on a tape recorder.
3. Speak into the microphone to record your voice. To record music from another source, cable the outside source directly into the microphone jack on your sound card. If you record sources other than a voice with the microphone, you will lose some sound quality.
4. When you finish recording the sound, click the Stop button.

   Click the Play button to hear the sound. If you want to rerecord the sound, drag the sound cursor to the beginning and press Record.

   When you record a sound that you like, save it to a file. From the File menu, choose Save; then type the file name. (Windows assigns the .WAV extension if you do not specify an extension.)

As you play the sound, the Position indicator updates to show you how many seconds you are into the file, and the Sound Recorder graphically depicts the waveform as you listen to the sound. You can determine the length of the total sound from the Length indicator at the right of the sound recorder window.

Modifying the Sound Playback

Recording a sound file is only the beginning of creating spectacular sounds in Windows. The Effects menu on the Sound Recorder enables you to modify the way a recorded sound file plays. Table 9.6 explains the menu options you can choose.

Table 9.6 Options on the Effects Menu

Option	Purpose
Increase Volume	Increases the volume of a sound by 25 percent.
Decrease Volume	Decreases the volume of a sound by 25 percent.
Increase speed	Increases the speed of a sound by 50 percent.
Decrease speed	Decreases the speed of a sound by 50 percent.
Reverse	Reverses a sound file so that it plays backward. Choose Reverse again to restore the original direction of the file.
Add Echo	Adds an echo to the file.

After adding a lot of sound effects, you might want to restore a sound file to its original state. From the File menu, choose Revert. The sound reverts to its original recorded (or last saved) state, wiping out any added effects.

TIP As you create a sound, save several copies of the sound file at various stages under different names. For example, you might keep a file with an echo and one without. You then can go back to any of the renditions of the sound.

Inserting Sounds into Sound Files

Because you are storing sounds digitally instead of on tape, you can insert sounds directly into another sound file. You also may record into the middle of an existing file. To insert sounds into sound files, follow these steps:

1. Choose Open from the File menu to open the sound file that you will insert a sound into.
2. Play the sound file until you reach the point where you want to insert the new sound.
3. Click the Stop button to stop the file from playing.
4. Click the Record button and record the sound you want to insert.

> Using the sound insert technique lets you append sounds to the end of a sound file. Play the original sound file through to its conclusion, and then record your new sound. The Sound Recorder places the new sound at the end of the original one.
>
> **TIP**

After you insert a sound into the file, be sure to save the new sound. From the File menu, choose Save to overwrite the original file with its expanded version, or choose Save As to create a new file with the combined sounds.

You also can remove the beginning or end of a sound. To delete the beginning of a sound, follow these steps:

1. Using the Sound Recorder, play through the sound until you get to the start of the portion you want to keep.
2. Click Stop to stop the file from playing.
3. From the Edit menu, choose Delete Before Current Position. The sound from the beginning of the file to the current position is deleted.

   To delete the end of a sound, follow these same steps but choose Delete After Current Position from the Edit menu. The portion of the sound from the current position to the end of the file is deleted.

You also can send sounds to the Windows Clipboard. You can only send an entire sound to the Clipboard, however, not a portion of a sound. When you have the sound loaded that you want to copy to the Clipboard, choose Copy from the Edit menu (or press Ctrl-C). Windows overwrites the original contents of the Clipboard and replaces it with your sound.

To use a Clipboard sound file, you must have an application that reads waveform audio directly. Many of the newer Windows-based sequencing programs include this feature. If you want to view the contents of the Clipboard after you paste a sound into the Clipboard, you can do so. From the Main Program Manager's window, choose Clipboard Viewer. A large microphone appears in the middle of the Clipboard (see fig. 9.7). To hear the sound, choose Wave Audio from the Display menu in the Clipboard viewer. You also may embed or paste link sounds into documents. See Chapter 7 for more information.

> To copy a portion of a sound file to the Clipboard, first remove those parts of the sound that you do not want copied. Then save the partial sound under a different file name. Load the file and copy it to the Clipboard.
>
> **TIP**

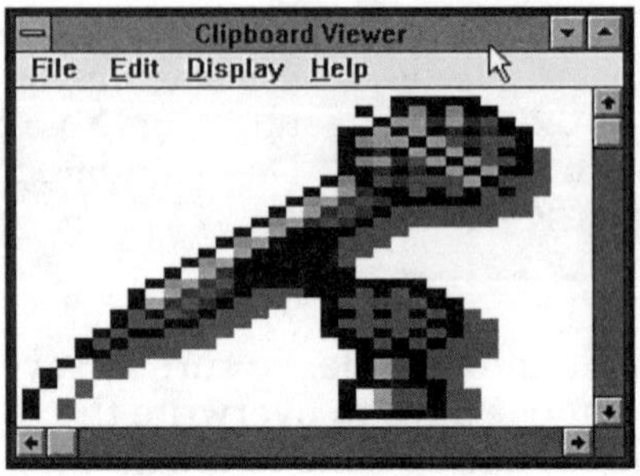

Figure 9.7.

"Viewing" a sound file in the Windows Clipboard.

Combining Sounds

You do not need a microphone to insert and combine sounds. You can merge sound files or mix one on top of the other, making the Sound Recorder your own electronic sound mixer!

Suppose, for example, that you want to produce a new sound from the supplied chime and tada waveform files. You might want to play the chime, then the tada sound, and then the chime again. You do not need a microphone to create this type of sound. Follow these steps:

1. From the File menu, choose New to create a new sound waveform file.
2. From the Edit menu, choose Insert File. The Sound Recorder displays a list of waveform files.
3. Choose the CHIME.WAV file to place the chime sound at the beginning of the new sound file. Notice that the Length value changes from 0.0 to 0.7.
4. From the Edit menu, choose Insert File and insert the TADA.WAV file. The Length indicator again increases, this time by the length of the tada sound.
5. From the Edit menu, choose Insert File and insert the CHIME.WAV file again.

When you play the new sound, you hear the three combined sounds play back-to-back: first the chime, then the tada, and then the chime again. If you like the results, save the file under a new name.

TIP Do not overwrite the original waveform files that came with Windows 3.1. They are good building-block files for other sounds.

Instead of combining two files sequentially, you might want to mix sounds together to produce an interesting blended effect. The sounds do not have to be the same length. At the point where you mix them, both sounds will play simultaneously until the shorter of the two sounds stops. The longer sound will continue playing to its conclusion.

To mix files, follow these steps:

1. Load and play the first sound until you reach the point where you want to blend another sound with it. (If you want to mix two sounds from the start, load—but do not play—the first sound.)
2. From the Edit menu, choose Mix with File.

   A list of waveform files appears.
3. Select a file that you want to mix with the currently loaded file.
4. Choose OK. You now can play the newly combined sound.

Summary

This chapter gave you an overview of how Windows 3.1 supports the new MPC multimedia standard. MPC makes multimedia available to almost everyone who owns a PC. Just the beginnings of multimedia are emerging in education, entertainment, and business. Multimedia brings users a world of audio and visual interactive computing.

A

APPENDIX

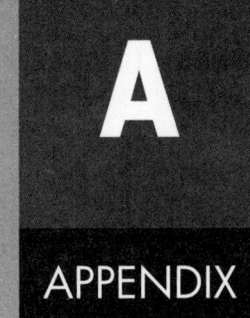

Optimizing DOS for Windows

This appendix covers squeezing the maximum performance from Windows 3.1 by optimizing your system to use system resources better. Some of the more important decisions you can make concerning the operation of Windows 3.1 involve the configuration of DOS and the DOS utilities used with Windows. You also must determine how to use your system memory and hard drive space effectively.

Windows enables you to use system RAM beyond the DOS 640K conventional memory barrier. You also can run multiple programs simultaneously in a simple, easy-to-learn icon- and menu-based graphical user interface. But in optimizing your computer system, Windows also demands much from your system. The performance of Windows 3.1—whether it does the job for you correctly—depends largely on configuring your system to run as quickly and efficiently as possible. This appendix covers several important configuration issues.

Maximizing Conventional Memory

One of Windows' greatest strengths is that it takes advantage of the hardware capabilities of computers, based on the 80286 and 80386 processor chip. You then can access your system's extended memory, or the memory beyond the DOS 640K conventional memory barrier, and run multiple programs. Windows does require between 400K and 450K of conventional system RAM, however, and the more conventional memory you have available, the better Windows runs.

To check how much conventional memory is available, run the DOS CHKDSK command when you start your system. This command provides details about your system memory and hard drive. To run CHKDSK, you must quit Windows, and then reboot your computer. At the DOS prompt, type *CHKDSK* and press Enter. The screen displays installed conventional memory, available conventional memory, total hard drive space, and available hard drive space (see fig. A.1).

```
C:\>CHKDSK
Volume DRIVE_C     created 08-15-1991 3:19a
Volume Serial Number is 2F6F-1BF4

 114282496 bytes total disk space
   8763392 bytes in 202 hidden files
    112640 bytes in 39 directories
  73691136 bytes in 1878 user files
      2048 bytes in bad sectors
  31713280 bytes available on disk

      2048 bytes in each allocation unit
     55802 total allocation units on disk
     15485 available allocation units on disk

    655360 total bytes memory
    633472 bytes free

C:\>
C:\>
C:\>
C:\>
C:\>
C:\>
```

Fig. A.1.

The CHKDSK display.

CAUTION: Do not run CHKDSK while in Windows. Windows creates files on your hard drive that can be corrupted by running CHKDSK with the /F parameter. *Always* exit Windows before running CHKDSK.

Check the `bytes free` line of the CHKDSK display. To optimize conventional memory, you want to increase the bytes free amount by deleting TSRs and device drivers from CONFIG.SYS and AUTOEXEC.BAT.

If you are running MS-DOS or PC DOS 4.0, 4.01, or 5.0, you can avoid using CHKDSK to check available memory by using the MEM command. Typing this command at the DOS prompt displays the amount of free conventional memory, as well as the amount of free extended and expanded memory, if they are available on your system. You can run this command from within Windows without danger. Open the Main group, double-click the DOS Prompt icon, type *MEM* at the prompt, and press Enter. When you finish with the MEM command, type *EXIT* and press Enter to return to Windows.

AUTOEXEC.BAT and CONFIG.SYS are text files located in the root directory of your boot drive (normally C:\). DOS uses these files to determine your startup system configuration. CONFIG.SYS loads device drivers (such as ANSI.SYS), loads extended memory managers, and creates environment space, which is the amount of memory DOS allocates for its own use. AUTOEXEC.BAT defines the system's path and other environment variables, and it launches programs you want started every time you start up.

In editing these files, you must balance the importance of a particular driver or TSR against the need for Windows to have as much conventional memory as possible. When the best environment for Windows outweighs the benefit from a device driver or TSR, remove the line from CONFIG.SYS or AUTOEXEC.BAT that loads these programs. Before editing CONFIG.SYS and AUTOEXEC.BAT, be sure to make backup copies. Consider eliminating the following types of programs:

- Device drivers, such as ANSI.SYS
- TSR programs, such as DOSSHELL, Sidekick, or DOS menus
- Memory resident DOS commands, such as APPEND and FASTOPEN

Figures A.2 and A.3 provide examples of CONFIG.SYS and AUTOEXEC.BAT files that have been edited to give Windows maximum conventional memory while preserving necessary device drivers. You might not be able to eliminate your device drivers and TSRs to this degree, or you might be able to free up even more memory by eliminating device drivers such as ANSI.SYS. Every byte of conventional memory you save here helps Windows run more quickly and efficiently and determines, to some degree, whether you have enough memory to run a particular program in Windows.

The following sections explain what needs to be in CONFIG.SYS and AUTOEXEC.BAT to make Windows run optimally.

```
C:\QUE\APENDIXA>TYPE CONFIG.SYS
DEVICE=C:\DOS\SETVER.EXE
SHELL=C:\DOS\COMMAND.COM /E:512 /P
FILES=30
BUFFERS=25
STACKS=0,0
DEVICE=C:\DOS\ANSI.SYS
INSTALL=C:\DOS\SHARE.EXE

C:\QUE\APENDIXA>
```

Fig. A.2.

A sample CONFIG.SYS file.

```
C:\QUE\APENDIXA>TYPE AUTOEXEC.BAT
@ECHO OFF
PROMPT $P$G
PATH C:\WINDOWS;C:\DOS;C:\QEMM;D:\NU;D:\UTILITY;D:\SHEZ;C:\BAT;
set mouse=C:\windows
C:\WINDOWS\mouse.COM /Y
C:\WINDOWS\SMARTDRV.EXE
SET TEMP=C:\windows\TEMP

C:\QUE\APENDIXA>
```

Fig. A.3.

A sample AUTOEXEC.BAT file.

The CONFIG.SYS File

A typical CONFIG.SYS defines device drivers, such as ANSI.SYS. It also specifies the location of COMMAND.COM, the number of files that can be open simultaneously in an application, and how many buffers and stacks your system will have available each time you boot your computer. For Windows to run at its best, CONFIG.SYS should contain these entries:

- **BUFFERS=10 (or 20).** Buffers enable MS-DOS to improve hard drive access. Of course, the more buffers you create, the more additional memory is used. If you are using MS-DOS 5.0 or later, however, you can specify *BUFFERS=30* without using additional memory.
- **FILES=30.** This setting specifies the number of files a program may open. Allocating more than 30 might use conventional memory unnecessarily.
- **STACKS=0,0.** This setting sets hardware stacks and is applicable for DOS 3.3 or later. If you are using an earlier version of DOS, consult your DOS manual for the required stacks setting.
- **SHELL=C:\COMMAND.COM /p /e:1024.** This command specifies environment space, which is the space allocated to DOS for completing certain tasks. Environment space should always be at least 1024 bytes.
- **DEVICE=HIMEM.SYS.** This entry loads Windows' HIMEM.SYS extended memory driver. You also can include the path where HIMEM.SYS is located if it is not in your root directory.
- A line that installs SHARE.EXE (or a line in AUTOEXEC.BAT that installs Share).
- A line that specifies LASTDRIVE. Lastdrive is used to prepare DOS for the number of drives on your system. An example of using the LASTDRIVE command in CONFIG.SYS is

  LASTDRIVE=F.

  (Check your DOS manual to determine whether this line is needed on your system.)

The AUTOEXEC.BAT File

AUTOEXEC.BAT defines the system's path and contains other information about your configuration, including the programs (such as a mouse driver) that you want loaded automatically each time your system is booted. For Windows to run at its best, your AUTOEXEC.BAT should contain the following entries:

- **PROMPT.** Usually PG (for a prompt that reads, `C:\>` in the root directory and `C:\WINDOWS>` in the Windows subdirectory).
- **PATH=.** Usually includes the root drive, C:\, as well as C:\WINDOWS, C:\DOS, and other subdirectories that contain files DOS needs to find quickly.
- **SMARTDRV.EXE.** Loads SMARTDrive, the Windows 3.1 disk cache. (For more information on SMARTDrive, see the section "Speeding Up Your System with SMARTDrive" later in this chapter.)
- **SET TEMP = C:\WINDOWS\TEMP.** Specifies where Windows stores temporary files.

Hard Drive Optimization

The amount of available hard disk space, and the way the files are structured on your hard drive, can greatly affect your system's speed and efficiency. As mentioned in Chapter 3, Windows uses a virtual memory scheme to free up memory for applications by using hard drive space as if it were system RAM. This function enables you to run more programs simultaneously under Windows than the physical RAM of your computer alone allows. In addition, some Windows programs use temporary swapfiles to store files.

The amount of available hard drive space is only one factor that determines your system's performance, however. The information taking up space on your disk must be structured as efficiently as possible. The following tasks will improve your hard disk's efficiency:

- Deleting unneeded files
- Running CHKDSK with the /F parameter to recover lost disk space
- Running a disk-compaction utility

The following sections cover each of these tasks in more detail.

Deleting Unneeded Files

In order to offer Windows and Windows programs as much temporary space as possible for swapping, you should frequently remove files that you don't need or don't use. These files can include programs, documents, temporary files, and programs installed with Windows that you do not use. Before you delete any program files or documents, make sure that you have backups, in case you find you do need them later. Temporary files that might be on your hard drive include Windows files with the characters ~WOA and TMP. These files usually are deleted when Windows finishes using them, but they sometimes remain on your drive if you press Ctrl-Alt-Del to restart a locked-up computer. You can delete the following Windows files:

- Files with the extension .TMP.
- Files with the extension .BMP, which are used as Windows wallpaper. (Setup copies several wallpaper files to your Windows directory when you install Windows, but they might be deleted to save space.)
- SOL.EXE and SOL.HLP, which are the Solitaire game and its help file.
- WINMINE.EXE and WINMINE.HLP, which are the Minesweeper game and its help file.
- PBRUSH.EXE, PBRUSH.HLP, and PBRUSH.DLL, which are Paintbrush, its help file, and its dynamic-link library.
- WRITE.EXE and WRITE.HLP, which are the Write word processor and its help file.
- CALENDAR.EXE and CALENDAR.HLP, which are the Calendar and its help file.
- CALC.EXE and CALC.HLP, which are the Windows calculator and its help file.
- CARDFILE.EXE and CARDFILE.HLP, which are Cardfile and its help file.
- TERMINAL.EXE and TERMINAL.HLP, which are Terminal and its help file.
- RECORDER.EXE, RECORDER.HLP, and RECORDER.DLL, which are Recorder, its help file, and its dynamic-link library.
- CLOCK.EXE, which is the Windows clock.

You also can delete unnecessary files by running Setup. For more information, see Chapter 2.

Run CHKDSK /F Parameter To Recover Lost Disk Space

Running CHKDSK with the /F parameter diagnoses your hard drive to ensure that its directory and file structure is sound. Any existing problems, such as data files that DOS has lost track of due to a system lockup, might be taking up disk space that you need. Running CHKDSK /F finds those lost clusters and lets you save their data to files with names such as FILE0000.CHK and FILE0001.CHK. You can examine these files and determine whether they contain data you want to keep. If the files do not contain necessary data, you can delete them. You should run CHKDSK regularly. Many people, in fact, use it daily.

Remember that you should never run CHKDSK from within Windows or you will risk damaging files and directories on your hard drive. To run CHKDSK /F and save any lost clusters to a file (if CHKDSK finds lost clusters), follow these steps:

1. From the DOS prompt, type *CHKDSK /F.*
2. Press Enter.
3. If CHKDSK finds lost clusters, it asks you whether to save the clusters to files. (You then can examine the data in the files to determine whether you want to keep them.) Press Y and examine the files created by CHKDSK immediately.
4. Use the DOS DEL command to delete any files you do not want to keep. Rename the files you do want to keep.

Running a Hard Drive Optimization Utility

When your hard drive is new and relatively empty, DOS writes new information to disk in a logical manner, which is in adjacent clusters. A data file that needs six data storage units on your hard drive might use clusters 3-9. The next file, which needs nine clusters, would get 10-19. After you delete data, however, DOS is not so efficient.

If you delete a six-sector file, and then save a nine-sector file to disk, DOS might write the first six sectors to the space made available by deleting the six-sector file, and the last three sectors to a completely different area of the hard drive. The result is called *fragmentation*. Over time, fragmentation can result in your files being scattered across the hard drive in tiny pieces—none of them contiguous. Fragmentation greatly decreases the performance of your system, and the negative effects will be even greater under Windows because Windows uses the hard drive for virtual memory and swapping, which requires large amounts of unfragmented disk space.

You can use a disk-compaction utility to examine your file structure and rearrange files so that their pieces are adjacent (contiguous). Such a utility can significantly speed up the time needed for Windows and applications to start; it will also make Windows' virtual memory capabilities work more efficiently.

Various disk-compaction utilities that defragment the disk are available. Do not run such a utility from within Windows; you might damage your hard drive's directory structure, program files, and data files.

> **CAUTION:** If you are using the Windows disk cache, SMARTDrive, with write caching enabled, type the command *SMARTDRV C-* (substituting the drive letter for your hard drive) before you run a disk-compaction utility. This command disables write caching. Allowing SMARTDrive's write caching to remain active while you run a disk-compaction utility can severely damage your hard drive's directory structure, program files, and data files.

Speeding Up Your System with SMARTDrive

SMARTDrive, a disk-caching program provided with Windows, helps speed up the performance of Windows by removing the bottleneck that most often slows system performance: hard disk reads and writes.

SMARTDrive uses two strategies for making Windows speedier. Like the version of SMARTDrive included with Windows 3.0, the new SMARTDrive reads information from disk, before an active program actually needs it, and holds it in your system's RAM. When a program tries to access the information from your hard drive, SMARTDrive instead supplies the information from the RAM, which is faster. SMARTDrive increases performance even more by caching writes, which means that SMARTDrive temporarily holds in memory data to be written to the hard drive. SMARTDrive writes this data to the drive when system resources are less in demand.

Installing SMARTDrive on Your System

Windows Setup normally copies the SMARTDrive file to your Windows directory and adds the SMARTDrive command line to your AUTOEXEC.BAT file during installation. If your system has at least 2M of RAM, you should use SMARTDrive. How you set up SMARTDrive depends on your system memory configuration. After installing SMARTDrive, you might want to experiment with the settings to find the best ones for your system. (For more information on the available settings, see the section "The SMARTDrive Command Line.") If Setup failed to install SMARTDrive, or you removed it, you can install it by following these steps:

1. Make a backup copy of your AUTOEXEC.BAT file.
2. Open AUTOEXEC.BAT within a plain ASCII text editor such as Notepad. (A word processor adds formatting symbols to AUTOEXEC.BAT, which will prevent it from working properly.)
3. Add the command line for SMARTDrive to your AUTOEXEC.BAT file. (For more information about the SMARTDrive command line and setup parameters, see the section "The SMARTDrive Command Line.")
4. Disable or remove any other command lines for disk-caching software. You even need to remove the line in CONFIG.SYS that loads the SMARTDrive included with an older version of Windows (SMARTDRV.SYS).
5. Save the changes to AUTOEXEC.BAT.
6. Quit Windows, and then restart your computer.

The SMARTDrive Command Line

If your system has at least 2M of RAM, you can load SMARTDrive by simply typing *SMARTDRV* at the DOS prompt and pressing Enter. SMARTDrive will load, using its defaults. SMARTDrive recognizes two parameters, or sets of numbers, on the command line that determine the size of the cache. These parameters set the initial cache size and the Windows cache size. Because you will have more extended memory available when Windows is not running, you can configure SMARTDrive to create a large cache before you load Windows, and then shrink the cache when Windows is loaded and more of your extended memory is needed for programs. The SMARTDrive command line might, for example, look like the following:

```
SMARTDRV 1024 512
```

The following table shows SMARTDrive's default values for initial cache size and Windows cache size based on the amount of Extended memory on your computer.

Extended Memory	Initial Cache Size	Windows Cache Size
Up to 1M	All extended memory	Zero (no caching)
Up to 2M	1M	256K
Up to 4M	1M	512K
Up to 6M	2M	1M
6M or greater	2M	2M

Besides the initial cache size and the Windows cache size, SMARTDrive understands other command line parameters. Use the following format for these parameters:

*d:path***SMARTDRV.EXE** *drive + /E:elementsize initcachesize wincachesize /B:buffersize /C /R /L /Q /S /?*

Table A.1 defines each parameter in this syntax line.

Table A.1 SMARTDrive Command Line Parameters

Parameter	Meaning
d:path	The drive and path where SMARTDRV.EXE is located, usually C:\WINDOWS.
SMARTDRV.EXE	SMARTDrive's executable file name.
drive	The drives you want to cache (usually only hard drives C:, D:, E:, and so on).
+	Follows the drive letter and is used to turn on caching for the selected drive. You also can use the minus symbol to turn off caching for one or more drives. If you do not specify a drive, SMARTDrive caches all drives on your system, although it caches writes only for the hard drives.
/E:elementsize	The amount of the cache (in bytes) that SMARTDrive reads from or writes to the disk at one time. This number must be greater than or equal to 1, and be a power of 2 (such as 1, 2, 4, 8, 16, 32, 64, and so on). The default value is 8K.
initcachesize	The cache size in kilobytes while Windows is not running.
wincachesize	The cache size in kilobytes while Windows is running.

continues

Table A.1 Continued

Parameter	Meaning
/B:buffersize	The size of the read-ahead buffer that SMARTDrive uses to read and hold information in memory until a program calls for it. If a program reads 512K of information from a file, SMARTDrive then reads the amount of information specified in Buffersize and saves it in memory. The default size of the read-ahead buffer is 16K, but a larger value greatly increases SMARTDrive's efficiency. Its value can be any multiple of *elementsize*.
/C	Writes all write-cached information to disk. Normally, SMARTDrive writes information from memory to the hard disk at times when other disk activity has slowed. You might use this option if you turn off your computer and want to ensure that all cached information has been written to the hard disk.
/R	Clears the contents of the existing cache and restarts SMARTDrive.
/L	Prevents SMARTDrive from loading into DOS 5.0 upper memory blocks (UMBs), even if UMBs are available.
/Q	Prevents SMARTDrive information from appearing on-screen when it is first loaded, usually in AUTOEXEC.BAT.
/S	Displays detailed information about the status of SMARTDrive.
/?	Displays on-line Help for SMARTDrive options.

The following sample SMARTDrive command line caches drive C (but not drive D) with a 2M cache before Windows loads and a 1M cache while Windows runs, specifies an element size of 32K and a buffer size of 32K, and suppresses the screen display when SMARTDrive is loaded from AUTOEXEC.BAT:

```
C:\WINDOWS\SMARTDRV C+ D- /E:32 2048 1024 /B:32 /Q
```

CAUTION: Before you turn off your computer, you must ensure that all cached information has been written to the hard disk. Were you to turn off your computer's power before SMARTDrive writes this information to disk, you will lose data. Type *SMARTDRV /C* at the DOS prompt to force SMARTDrive to write all data to disk. After the drive light on your hard drive goes off, you can turn off your computer safely.

SMARTDrive Double Buffering

If your computer's BIOS is more than three years old, you probably need to use the double-buffering feature of SMARTDrive. Double buffering provides compatibility for computers that cannot work with virtual memory.

Windows Setup places a SMARTDrive command line in CONFIG.SYS. If your computer requires double buffering, this line is required. If your computer does not require double buffering, you can remove the command line. This line reads

```
DEVICE=SMARTDRV.EXE /DOUBLE_BUFFER
```

To determine whether you can remove the SMARTDrive command from CONFIG.SYS, follow these steps while Windows is running:

1. Shell to DOS by double-clicking the DOS Prompt icon in the Main group. (You also can open the Main group, select the DOS prompt icon, and press Enter.)
2. From the DOS prompt, type *SMARTDRV* and press Enter. SMARTDrive displays a screen similar to the one in figure A.4.
3. Look at the Buffering column. If every line in this column reads `no`, you can remove the SMARTDrive double buffer command line from your CONFIG.SYS file.

Using the DOS Utility Share

You should install the device Share in your CONFIG.SYS file (or optionally the AUTOEXEC.BAT file). Share is used when two or more programs running on the same computer will need to share certain files. All programs that use Share must check to see whether a file is in use by another program before modifying data in that file. Two programs trying to modify the same data file at the same time can result in data damage or loss. If another program has exclusive use of a data file, a second program is denied access.

```
C:\>smartdrv
Microsoft SMARTDrive Disk Cache version 4.0.091
Copyright 1991,1992 Microsoft Corp.

Cache size: 2,097,152 bytes
Cache size while running Windows: 2,097,152 bytes

            Disk Caching Status
drive   read cache   write cache   buffering
--------------------------------------------
  A:       yes           no            no
  B:       yes           no            no
  C:       yes           yes           no
  D:       yes           yes           no

For help, type "Smartdrv /?".

C:\>
```

Fig. A.4.

The SMARTDrive screen.

Because Windows is a multitasking environment, in which several programs often run simultaneously, there is some chance two or more of these programs might try to access the same data file at the same time. Although many Windows programs (and to an extent Windows itself) provide protection from two programs trying to change data simultaneously, you still should load Share as an extra precautionary measure. Share protects your data files from being modified by programs that do not have a protection scheme. Certain Windows programs, such as Word for Windows 2.0, require the use of Share. Word for Windows' Setup program installs Share in your AUTOEXEC.BAT file if it is not already loaded.

To install Share in your CONFIG.SYS file, assuming Share is located in your C:\DOS subdirectory, add the following line:

    INSTALL=C:\DOS\SHARE.EXE

Install Share in your AUTOEXEC.BAT file only if you prefer not to add it to your CONFIG.SYS file. Assuming that Share is located in your C:\DOS subdirectory, install Share in AUTOEXEC.BAT by adding the following line:

SHARE.EXE

Share should be loaded in AUTOEXEC.BAT before any other program that modifies data files; for example, if you automatically boot Windows and Lotus 1-2-3 for Windows each time you turn on your system, add the line that loads Share before the line that loads Windows. The simplest way to ensure that Share is loaded correctly is to place the line that loads it first in your AUTOEXEC.BAT, before any other lines.

Using the HIMEM.SYS Extended Memory Manager

HIMEM.SYS is like the traffic cop of Extended Memory Manager. It monitors extended memory to ensure that no two applications use the same memory at the same time. Generally, Setup installs HIMEM.SYS by adding it to CONFIG.SYS. If HIMEN.SYS is not in CONFIG.SYS, reinstall it by adding the following line to CONFIG.SYS:

DEVICE=HIMEM.SYS

NOTE Windows 3.1 comes with a new version of HIMEM.SYS. Do not run Windows 3.1 with the version that came with Windows 3.0 or MS-DOS 5.0. These versions will conflict with Windows 3.1.

The HIMEM.SYS command line must come before the command line for an application or device driver that uses extended memory. In most cases, you will not need to specify command-line options; the default values are designed to work with most hardware. To load HIMEM.SYS using default values, add the following line to CONFIG.SYS:

DEVICE=HIMEM.SYS

The HIMEM.SYS command line uses the following syntax:

DEVICE=*d:path***\HIMEM.SYS** */HMAMIN=m /NUMHANDLES=n /INIT15=xxxx /SHADOWRAM=on ¦ off /MACHINE:name /A20CONTROL:on ¦ off /CPULOCK: on ¦ off*

The command line syntax for HIMEM.SYS can look complex. Table A.2 defines each parameter and includes a sample command line.

Table A.2 HIMEM.SYS Command Line Parameters

Parameter	Meaning
DEVICE=	The command for loading any device driver in CONFIG.SYS.
d:path	The drive letter and path where HIMEM.SYS is located; usually C:\WINDOWS.
HIMEM.SYS	The full file name of HIMEM.SYS.
/HMAMIN=m	Kilobytes of high memory an application must require for HIMEM.SYS to let that application use the High Memory Area (HMA). Only one application can use the HMA at a time. HIMEM.SYS allocates the HMA to the first application that meets this memory-use requirement. The default is zero. If you omit this option, HIMEM.SYS allocates the HMA to the first application that requests it, regardless of how much HMA the application will use. You can set a value from 0 to 63, based on the amount of memory required by the application that uses the most HMA.This option has no effect when Windows is running in 386 Enhanced mode.
/NUMHANDLES=n	The maximum number of Extended Memory Block (EMB) handles that can be used simultaneously. You can specify a value from 1 to 128; the default value is 32. Each additional handle requires an additional six bytes of memory. This option has no effect when Windows is in 386 Enhanced mode.
/INIT15=xxxx	An amount of extended memory (in kilobytes) to be reserved for the Interrupt 15h interface. Some older applications use the Interrupt 15h interface to allocate extended memory rather than the XMS method provided by HIMEM.SYS. If you use these applications, you can ensure that enough memory is available to them by setting *xxxx* to 64K larger than the amount the application requires. You can specify a value from 64 to 65535, up to the amount of memory on your system. If you specify a value less than 64, the value reverts to the default of zero.
/SHADOWRAM:on ¦ off	Specifies whether to disable shadow RAM. Some computers make ROM code run faster by copying ROM code into faster RAM memory at startup (called *shadowing*). This procedure does use some Extended memory. On computers that use shadow RAM and have less than 2M of RAM, HIMEM.SYS attempts to disable shadow RAM to recover

Parameter	Meaning
	additional extended memory for Windows; your computer then runs slightly slower. HIMEM.SYS can disable shadow RAM only on certain types of systems. To leave the ROM code running from RAM, even on systems with less than 2M of RAM, type */SHADOWRAM:on*. To have HIMEM.SYS disable shadow RAM, type */SHADOWRAM:off*.
/MACHINE:name	Specifies the type of computer you are using in case HIMEM.SYS fails to detect your system type correctly. There are a few computers that HIMEM cannot detect. On such systems, HIMEM uses the default system type (IBM AT or compatible). You might need to include the /machine option if your computer is a type that HIMEM cannot detect and if HIMEM does not work properly on your system by using the default system type. Currently, systems that require this option include Acer 1100, Wyse, and IBM 7552. The value for *name* can be any of the codes or their equivalent numbers listed in the table A.3.
/A20CONTROL:on ¦ off	Specifies whether HIMEM.SYS takes control of the A20 line regardless of whether A20 was on when HIMEM.SYS was loaded. The A20 handler lets your computer access the HMA. If you specify */a20control:off*, HIMEM.SYS takes control of the A20 line only if A20 was off when HIMEM.SYS was loaded. The default setting is /a20control:on.
/CPUCLOCK:on ¦ off	Specifies whether HIMEM.SYS is to lock the clock speed of your computer. If your computer's clock speed changes when you install HIMEM.SYS, specifying */cpuclock:on* might correct the problem. Enabling this option does slow down HIMEM, however. The default setting is /cpuclock:off.

Table A.3 lists values you can use with the *MACHINE:name* parameter.

Table A.3 Values To Use with the MACHINE:name Parameter

Code	Number	Computer Type
at	1	IBM AT or 100 compatible
ps2	2	IBM PS/2

continues

Table A.3 Continued

Code	Number	Computer Type
ptlcascade	3	Phoenix Cascade BIOS
hpvectra	4	HP Vectra (A & A+)
att6300plus	5	AT&T 6300 Plus
acer1100	6	Acer 1100
toshiba	7	Toshiba 1600 & 1200XE
wyse	8	Wyse 12.5 Mhz 286
tulip	9	Tulip SX
zenith	10	Zenith ZBIOS
at1	11	IBM PC/AT
at2	12	IBM PC/AT (alternative delay)
css	12	CSS Labs
at3	13	IBM PC/AT (alternative delay)
philips	13	Philips
fasthp	14	HP Vectra
ibm7552	15	IBM 7552 Industrial Computer
bullmicral	16	Bull Micral 60

The following sample command line loads HIMEM.SYS and specifies that an application can access the HMA only if that application uses at least 40K of memory. Because no other options are specified, HIMEM uses default values for the remaining parameters. In this example, HIMEM.SYS is located in the Windows subdirectory:

```
DEVICE=C:\WINDOWS\HIMEM.SYS /HMAMIN=40
```

B

APPENDIX

Handling Windows 3.1 Errors

One of the most frequent complaints about Windows 3.0 was the Unrecoverable Application Error, also called the UAE. Generally, when a UAE occurred, Windows locked up. That meant that you not only would lose the data you were working with in the current program, but that any background programs would also lose data.

The Windows 3.0 Unrecoverable Application Error has been replaced in Windows 3.1 with two separate error messages. These new error messages are more informational, and they might even enable you to recover your application from the error.

This appendix describes the new error messages, explains what each means, and clarifies why Windows generates the error. The appendix also instructs you about actions to take when you receive one of these messages.

The Replacement of the UAE

The replacements for the UAE can take one of two forms. First is the Application Error, which does not let you recover your application. The error might give you information, however, so that you, or the manufacturer of the application, might be able to find the cause of the error and perhaps prevent it from recurring.

The second error that replaces the UAE is the Recoverable Application Error, which gives you the option of continuing with your application, therefore letting you save your data files.

Several situations can cause these errors to occur, including

- One program overwriting the data or code of another program
- Insufficient memory to perform an operation
- An incompatible TSR or device driver
- An application designed for a version of Windows prior to Version 3.0
- Improper configuration of Windows for your hardware
- Data files cross-linked with other files
- An incorrect version of DOS

The most likely cause is that one application overwrote another application's data or code. If the offended application was either DOS or Windows, the system is left in an unstable state. You might be tempted to continue working without closing Windows, rebooting your computer, and restarting Windows. Don't. Continuing to use the system without rebooting could result in the complete loss of your data.

The Application Error

The Application Error in Windows 3.1 bears a close resemblance to the UAE in Windows 3.0. This error tells you which module in your application caused the error, which error occurred, and which address was affected (see fig. B.1) When this error occurs, close all open applications, exit Windows, and reboot your computer. These steps help minimize the risk of any further data loss.

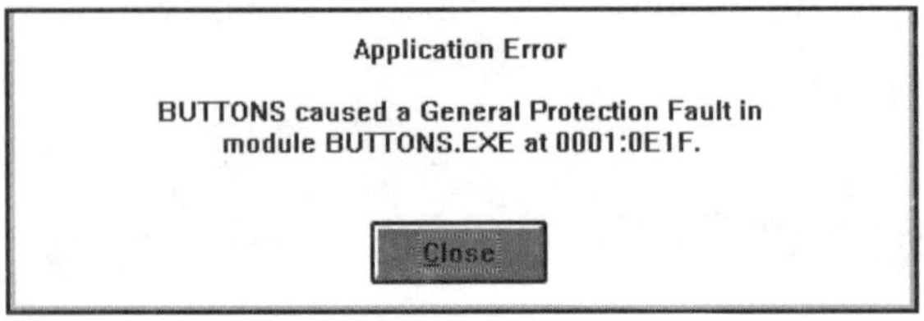

Fig. B.1.

The Application Error.

When the application terminates, you only lose any unsaved data in that application. You do not lose data in any other programs. Remember, however, that continuing to use the system without rebooting might cause other programs to crash, as well.

The Application Error occurs because Windows could not stop the offending application from executing an instruction that in some way jeopardized the system's stability. Rebooting forces the system to reload all data and program code from the hard disk, which ensures that the data or code is not corrupted.

If the program code affected is in a Windows module, Windows tells you which module is involved. The most common error that causes this message is the General Protection Fault.

A General Protection Fault occurs for one of two reasons. First, it might occur when a program attempts to execute program code that is not available to its authorization level. In the protected modes of the Intel 80286, 80386, and 80486 families of microprocessors, the CPU instructions are divided into four authorization levels. The operating system—or in this case, Windows—controls the highest authorization level. Windows can assign the lower levels to programs. This capability allows Windows to control how much individual programs can access the system. If an application attempts to execute an instruction with an authorization level higher than its own, a General Protection Fault occurs.

The second reason for a General Protection Fault is that a program attempts to write to or read from an area of memory that it is not allowed to access. Windows can designate areas of memory to specific programs that should not be accessed by other programs. When another program attempts to access that memory, the processor generates a General Protection Fault.

The Recoverable Application Error

The second replacement for the UAE is the Recoverable Application Error. This error provides less information than the Application Error, but it allows you to recover your application. Figure B.2 shows a common Recoverable Application Error.

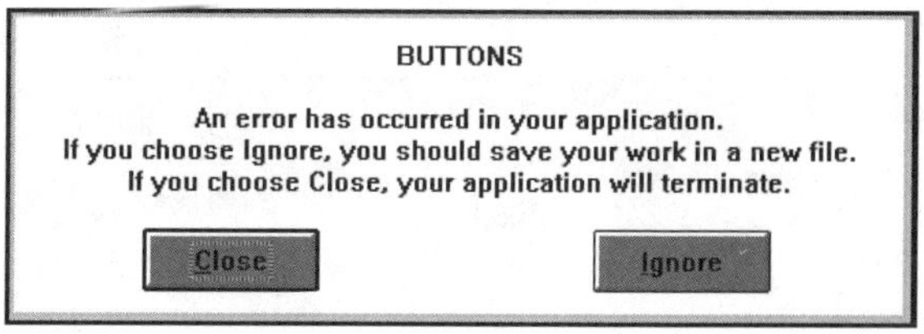
BUTTONS
An error has occurred in your application.
If you choose Ignore, you should save your work in a new file.
If you choose Close, your application will terminate.
Close
Ignore

Fig. B.2.

The Recoverable Application Error.

A Recoverable Application Error occurs when an application attempts to execute an instruction that would jeopardize the stability of the system, and Windows has the capability to stop the application from executing the bad instruction.

When this type of error occurs, you have two choices: close the application or ignore the error. If you select the Close button, the application simply terminates. If you select Ignore, the application continues to run and you might be able to save your data files.

> **CAUTION:** If you choose Ignore so that you can continue the application and save your data files, do not overwrite the data files on the disk. You might be saving bad files. Use the Save As option from the File menu, if your application contains this option, to save the data to a new file. If you save over your current data files on disk, you might destroy your data.

Application Execution Errors

Windows displays Application Execution Errors when it has a problem executing a program. These errors are not fatal errors—errors that cause the system to be left in an unstable state—and you will not lose your data. Instead, the application only needs you to correct a condition.

This class of errors includes the following types:

- Insufficient memory
- Insufficient disk space
- Protected mode application error

The first type of Application Execution Error is due to insufficient memory (see fig. B.3). This error indicates one of two situations: too many applications are running or the application requires more memory than is available in your system.

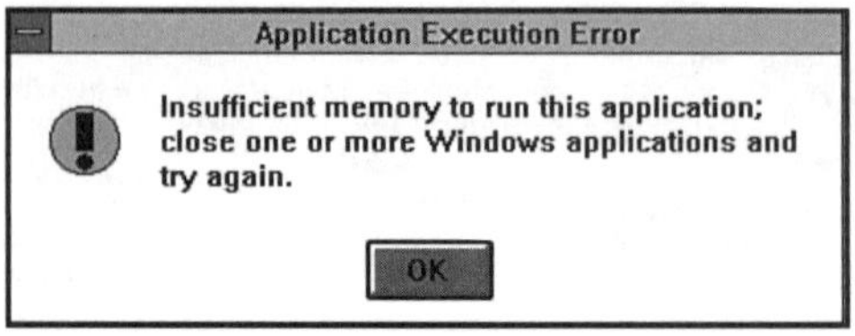

Fig. B.3.

Insufficient memory error.

You can correct an insufficient memory error one of two ways. You can close any applications that you are not using or expand the RAM memory in your computer.

An insufficient disk space error indicates that there is not enough disk space for Windows' use. Unless you have created a permanent swapfile, used in 386 Enhanced mode, Windows creates temporary swapfiles. These swapfiles enable Windows to transfer some of the contents of memory to a disk file, freeing up other memory. When insufficient disk space exists, the temporary file cannot be created, and you see this error.

To correct an insufficient disk space message, you can delete files on your disk that you do not need. You also may transfer to floppy disks data files that you do not currently use, and then delete those files from your hard disk. Finally, you can increase the amount of disk storage on your computer.

Windows uses the CPU in Protected mode. Protected mode enables the CPU to address extended memory and protect areas of memory. If you execute another program that tries to use Protected mode, you get a Protected mode application error. To remedy this error, follow the on-screen instructions.

Application-Specific Errors

The error messages that have been described up to this point are Windows-specific errors. The programs that you use in Windows, however, can generate error messages when something goes wrong with an individual program.

The types of application-specific errors vary from application to application. To learn the cause and remedy for an application-specific error, consult the application's documentation.

Generally, the error results when you try to perform an operation that the application cannot perform. These errors can be compared to an Application Execution Error. Suppose, for example, that you are using a word processor and want to check the spelling of a document. You might get an error if the application cannot find the dictionary that contains the correctly spelled words. This error might be caused because you mistyped the name of the dictionary file that the program was to use. When you receive an application-specific error message, a message also appears that explains the problem so that you can correct it.

General Error Procedures

You should take some basic actions whenever you receive an error. First, write down the exact text of the message you receive so that you can remember the message and determine what further action to take. If you must call the technical support department of the software, you can quote the message verbatim, which will help the support staff assist you in resolving the problem. Also note exactly what you were doing when the error occurred.

Sometimes an error causes your computer to lock up. If this occurs, and you are running in 386 Enhanced mode, press Ctrl-Alt-Del. This key sequence generally reboots your computer. In Windows, however, these keys have a different function.

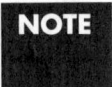

NOTE Do not press Ctrl-Alt-Del when running Windows in Standard mode. Pressing Ctrl-Alt-Del in Standard mode resets the entire computer, and you will lose any unsaved data.

When running in 386 Enhanced mode, Windows protects against one program locking up the entire computer. Also, each DOS program you are running is protected. Each DOS program thinks it is operating on a separate computer because Windows uses the virtual 8086 mode of the 80386 and 80486 families of processors. In Windows, pressing Ctrl-Alt-Del only reboots the program that locked the computer, rather than rebooting the entire computer.

If a Windows application appears to have locked up, press Ctrl-Break to try breaking the program from a possible loop. Wait for a few minutes to see if the Windows application "time outs" and gives you an error message. If the program remains locked, Press Ctrl-Alt-Del. A message appears on-screen that offers you the following three possible routes of action:

- Press Esc to return to Windows, just as if you had not pressed Ctrl-Alt-Del. The program will still be in the locked condition. This option protects you from losing work if you accidentally pressed Ctrl-Alt-Del when nothing was wrong with the program.
- Press Enter to release the offending program and return Windows to the screen. Any unsaved work in the offending program is lost. Close other programs that you have running, exit Windows, and reboot the computer.
- Press Ctrl-Alt-Del again to reboot the system. Use this option only as a last resort in unrecoverable situations, such as if you reboot one application and the next seems to be locked up, or if Windows still will not respond to any entry.

Rebooting a DOS program that you are running in Windows is similar to rebooting a Windows program. When you reboot the DOS program, another screen appears that offers you the same three options for rebooting a DOS program as were available for rebooting a Windows program. Follow the same procedures described for rebooting a Windows program.

INDEX

C

D

J-K

L

M

N

O

P

Q-R

S

T

Que Helps You Get The Most From Windows!

Using MicrosoftWindows 3, 2nd Edition

Ron Person & Karen Rose

With numerous screen shots and illustrations, this book is a power-packed introduction to Windows 3! It combines tutorials, examples, and reference material as well as a **Windows Shopping Catalog** and thorough **Troubleshooting** guide.

Versions 2 & 3

$24.95 USA

0-88022-509-2, 662 pp., 7 3/8 x 9 1/4

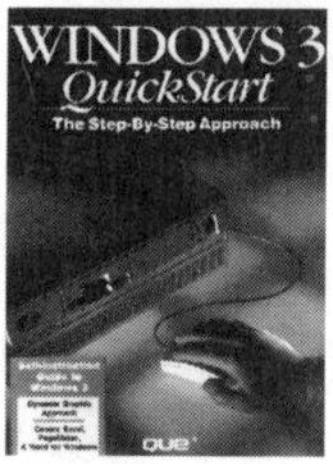

Windows 3 QuickStart

Ron Person & Karen Rose

Version 3

$19.95 USA

0-88022-610-2, 440 pp., 7 3/8 x 9 1/4

Windows 3 Quick Reference

Que Development Group

Version 3

$8.95 USA

0-88022-631-5, 160 pp., 4 3/4 x 8

Windows 3 Beyond the Basics

Rick Hellewell

Windows 3

$29.95 USA

0-88022-678-1, 500 pp., 7 3/8 x 9 1/4

To Order, Call:
(800) 428-5331 OR (317) 573-2500

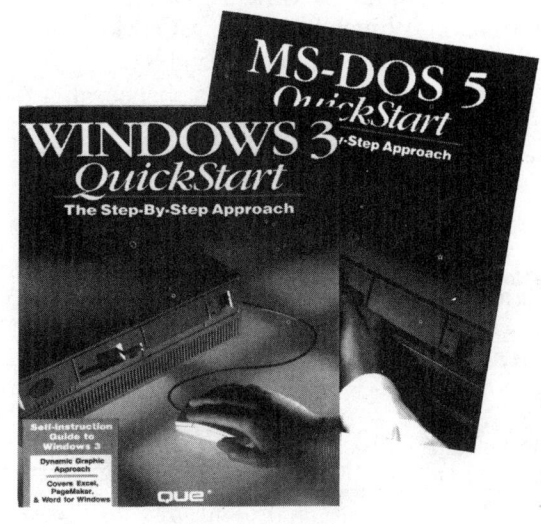

Learning is Easy with Easy Books from Que!

Que's Easy Series offers a revolutionary concept in computer training. The friendly, 4-color interior, easy format, and simple explaniations guarantee success for even the most intimidated computer user!

Easy WordPerfect

Shelley O'Hara

The ideal coverage of WordPerfect for beginners! 4-color illustrations and text as well as before-and-after screen shots illustrate each task. The book also includes a command summary and a glossary.

Version 5.1

$19.95 USA

0-88022-797-4, 200 pp., 8 x 10

Easy Lotus 1-2-3

Shelley O'Hara

Releases 2.01 & 2.2

$19.95 USA

0-88022-799-0, 200 pp., 8 x 10

Easy Quattro Pro

Shelley O'Hara

Versions 3.X, 4.X, & 5

$19.95 USA

0-88022-798-2, 200 pp., 8 x 10

Easy Windows

Shelley O'Hara

Versions 3 & 4

$19.95 USA

0-88022-800-8, 200 pp., 8 x 10

To Order, Call: (800) 428-5331 OR (317) 573-2500